Finance: Markets, Investments and Financial Management

Finance: Markets, Investments and Financial Management

Edited by Daisy Scott

STATES
ACADEMIC PRESS
www.statesacademicpress.com

States Academic Press,
109 South 5th Street,
Brooklyn, NY 11249, USA

ISBN: 978-1-63989-200-6

Cataloging-in-Publication Data

Finance : markets, investments and financial management / edited by Daisy Scott.
p. cm.
Includes bibliographical references and index.
ISBN 978-1-63989-200-6
1. Finance. 2. Capital market. 3. Money market. 4. Investments.
5. Finance--Management. I. Scott, Daisy.
HG173 .F56 2022
332--dc23

For information on all States Academic Press publications
visit our website at www.statesacademicpress.com

STATES
ACADEMIC PRESS

Contents

Preface

This book has been a concerted effort by a group of academicians, researchers and scientists, who have contributed their research works for the realization of the book. This book has materialized in the wake of emerging advancements and innovations in this field. Therefore, the need of the hour was to compile all the required researches and disseminate the knowledge to a broad spectrum of people comprising of students, researchers and specialists of the field.

Finance is a broad term that encompasses activities associated with banking, leverage or debt, credit, capital markets, money and investments. A financial investment is an asset in which money is put into with the aim that it will appreciate into a larger sum of money. The idea is to sell the asset later at a higher price in order to make a profit out of it or make money while owning it. Financial market is any marketplace, where the financial instruments are traded. A few of its examples are the stock market, bond market, foreign exchange market, and derivatives market. Financial management is the practice of strategic planning, organizing, directing, and controlling financial undertakings in an organization. The book is appropriate for students seeking detailed information in this field. It will provide comprehensive knowledge to the readers. The topics covered in this book offer the readers new insights in the field of finance.

At the end of the preface, I would like to thank the authors for their brilliant chapters and the publisher for guiding us all-through the making of the book till its final stage. Also, I would like to thank my family for providing the support and encouragement throughout my academic career and research projects.

Editor

1

Market Structure, Macroeconomic Shocks, and Banking Risk in Kenya

Nderitu Kingori[*♣]

[♣]School of Economics, University of Nairobi

ABSTRACT: This paper investigates the effect of changing market structure and macroeconomic shocks on the borrowing and lending risk exposure of Kenyan commercial banks using a GMM estimation approach. Borrowing risk exposure was found not to be persistent, being mainly affected by the degree of concentration and external economic shocks. Interestingly, the results also suggest that changes in the short-term interest rate do not affect the net interest margin, which may imply that bank deposit and lending rates are rigid and that the interest rate channel may be ineffective. The lending risk exposure was found to be persistent, and it was affected by the degree of concentration, internal economic shocks, and external economic shocks. The positive relationship between degree of concentration as well as borrowing and lending risk exposure supports the concentration-fragility view, as the declining franchise value did not lower incentives for making good loans during the study period where the degree of concentration was on a downward trend. Further analysis of the factors contributing to the persistence of lending risk exposure using a PVAR model found that the banks' loan growth rate and the market interest rate were key determinants. The effect of the loan growth rate was about double the effect of interest rate risk, implying that risk taking by some of the medium-sized and small banks is the key determinant of the persistence of lending risk exposure.

Keywords: market structure, macroeconomic shocks, macro-financial linkages, banking risk, dynamic panel data, Kenyan banks

[*]Corresponding Author. Email: nderitukb@gmail.com

Introduction

Banks are generally in the business of managing financial risk, because they earn their profits mainly by taking on specific forms of risk. Heffernan (2005) explained that risk management is a bank's core business. Banks face a number of financial risks that are atypical to those faced by non-financial firms and inadequate management of these risks can threaten their profitability, solvency, and shareholder value-added.

The first phase of the financial liberalization process in Kenya began in 1989 resulting in the deregulation of various banking activities, the reduction of reserve requirements, and the implementation of various other policy measures aimed at increasing competition in the banking sector (Ngugi and Kabubo, 1998). According to Central Bank of Kenya (2003), the second phase of reforms began in 2003 and was based on the findings of two studies: the Banking Sector Reform Strategy and the IMF's Financial Sector Assessment Program. These studies covered the adequacy of prudential regulation and supervision, interest rate spreads, banking sector risks and vulnerabilities, banking competition and costs, and improving access to financial services.

In addition to managing normal banking risks and the risk-taking opportunities created by financial liberalization, banks operating in developing countries such as Kenya were also exposed to frequent macroeconomic shocks. Agenor and Montiel (2008) explained that these economic shocks arose mainly because most developing economies are characterized by unique internal and external factors that cause instability. Some of these internal factors included political instability, frequent changes in policy regimes, and weak institutions. External factors included trade volatility, exchange rates, and capital flows. However, Hausmann and Gavin (1996) found that though domestic and external economic shocks have contributed to macroeconomic volatility in developing countries, the economy's vulnerability to these changes has depended on its institutional structure and economic policy regimes. Similarly, Acemoglu et al. (2003) found that the main cause of macroeconomic volatility was not "bad" policies (such as excessive government spending, high inflation, and overvalued exchange rates), but rather the underlying institutional weaknesses. They explained that "weak institutions (such as political institutions that do not constrain politicians and political elites, have ineffective enforcement of property rights, widespread corruption, and a high degree of political instability) foster the adoption of distortionary macroeconomic policies, which in turn lead to macroeconomic volatility." In their study, Kilishi et al. (2013) found that with regard to the six governance indicators used to measure institutions, Kenya ranked poorly among Sub-Saharan Africa countries with respect to political stability, rule of law, and control of corruption.

Financial liberalization is therefore expected to influence banking risk exposure by affecting the ability and incentives for risk taking. Deregulation of the various banking activities increases the ability to take risks and the resulting competitive environment creates incentives to take additional risks to grow market share. Similarly, macroeconomic shocks are expected to influence banking risk exposure by affecting the economic performance of banks and their borrowers. Negative shocks reduce their earnings, which in turn affect bank capitalization. Positive shocks reduce risk perceptions, which creates an environment conducive to increased risk taking.

Various cross-country studies (Demirguc-Kunt and Detagiache, 1998; Bohachova, 2008; Allen et al., 2009; Laeven, 2011) that link macroeconomic shocks to banking risks have provided valuable insights on the specific macroeconomic shocks associated with banking vulnerabilities. Additionally, various other cross-country studies (Demirguc-Kunt and Detragiache, 2001; Weller, 2001; Goodhart et al., 2004; Agosin and Huaita, 2011) have also linked banking crises in developing economies to financial liberalization. The Kenyan financial system is predominantly bank-based; therefore, analyzing the effect of changes in market structure and macroeconomic shocks on the banking sector is important because of their potential to adversely affect the real economy by causing credit restrictions and costly liquidations that result in output losses and high unemployment.

According to Government of Kenya (2007), the financial services sector is expected to play a critical role in the mobilization of funds to implement Vision 2030 projects.[1] However, this will be contingent on addressing some of the identified constraints such as the high interest rate spread, inadequate provisioning against losses from bad loans, and weak internal controls. One of the factors contributing to the high interest rate spread is the risk premium charged by banks to compensate for the uncertainty of macroeconomic variables and for the resulting effect of rising problem loans on bank capitalization. Therefore, a better understanding of the factors contributing to risk exposure may contribute to a reduction in the risk premium by improving bank risk management. This study may also generate policy implications by identifying the significant factors that affect banking risk. Finally, this research study will contribute to the empirical literature on the effect of financial liberalization and macroeconomic shocks on banking risk in Kenya.

The main objective of this study will be to analyze factors influencing the risk exposure of commercial banks in Kenya by focusing on two primary hypotheses. First, the changing market structure in the wake of financial liberalization increases banking fragility by increasing the ability and incentives for risk taking. Second, positive and negative macroeconomic shocks influence banking risk exposure by affecting the economic performance of banks and their borrowers.

The remainder of the paper is organized in four sections. Section 1 reviews some of

[1]Vision 2030 projects refers to development projects identified in the government's development plan as critical for the achievement of long-term development goals by the year 2030.

the relevant literature, section 2 explains the research methodology, section 3 reports the empirical results, and section 4 summarizes and concludes the paper.

1 Literature Review

1.1 Market Structure and Banking Risk

Degryse and Ongena (2005) explained that there are conflicting predictions about the relationship between bank rents and banking fragility in economic theory. According to the concentration-stability view there is a positive link between bank concentration and financial stability. The concentration-fragility view on the other hand, states that there is a positive link between bank concentration and financial fragility. Bank concentration affects financial stability because one of the key sources of bank rents is market structure, which consists of the number of banks in the market and the existence of alternative providers of finance.

The concentration-stability view is mainly based on the argument by Hellman et al. (2000), which stated that financial liberalization increases competition, and this resulting competition reduces profit margins. The lower profit margins result in lower franchise values (the value of expected future profits that act as intangible capital), and lower franchise values in turn lower incentives for making good loans. Therefore, the higher franchise values associated with concentration increase stability by lowering the incentives for risk-taking. The concentration-stability view is also based on the study by Allen and Gale (2004), who modeled how bank competition, as a result of financial liberalization, can induce banks to bid up deposit rates and reduce franchise value. Hellwig (1995) explained that the problem of "excessive risk taking" results from the disappearance of oligopoly rents due to the intensification of competition following deregulation, banks are tempted to replace oligopoly rents with *premia* on risk taking.

In contrast, the concentration-fragility view is based on the study by Boyd and De Nicolo (2005) who argued that the model used by Allen and Gale (2004) focused on banks' strategic interactions in deposit markets but ignored bank competition in loan markets. Instead, they claimed that market concentration could affect bank stability in different ways, depending on the net effect across the deposit and loan markets. Specifically, they pointed out that "concentration in the loan market can lead to increased lending rates that raise the borrowers' debt loads and default probabilities, as well as their incentive to engage in riskier projects."

A study by Mwega (2011) found that the Kenyan banking sector experienced reduced concentration during the period of 1998 to 2008, following the various financial reforms that were implemented. His analysis of bank peer groups found that small banks were the least competitive, followed by large banks and then medium-sized banks. However, the degree of competitiveness indicated that the Kenyan banking sector is still characterized by monopolistic competition, and this was also confirmed by the persistence-of-profit measure.

1.2 Macroeconomic Factors and Banking Risk

Bohachova (2008) pointed out that because banks perform intermediary functions for the real sector, they are exposed to the business cycle conditions that affect the real sector. Generally, the risks of intermediation rise as economic conditions worsen since banks become more vulnerable to adverse selection and moral hazard behaviour during periods of economic stagnation or recession. The main source of output fluctuations in developing countries, as explained by Agenor and Montiel (2008), is the supply shock that accounts for over half of the volatility in aggregate output, partly because a significant proportion of exports consist of a narrow range of primary commodities. In addition, shocks to the relative prices of imported goods and intermediate inputs also contribute to output volatility.

According to Stiglitz and Weiss (1981), high bank interest rates will affect the "riskiness" of a bank's loan portfolio by either discouraging safer potential borrowers (the adverse selection effect) or by inducing borrowers to invest in riskier projects (the incentive effect). Demirguc-Kunt and Detagiache (1998) argued that banks are also exposed to interest rate risk through their maturity transformation functions; therefore, a large increase in short-term interest rates is likely to be a major source of systemic banking problems. Greuning and Bratanovic (2003) explained that when interest rates change, a bank's earnings and expenses change along with the value of its assets, liabilities, and off-balance-sheet positions. Changing interest rates affect a bank's bond portfolio holdings by increasing the risk of reinvestment and the risk of realization (Esch et al., 2005), while high interest rates increase credit risk by contributing to firm failure (Nkurunziza, 2005) and increase liquidity risk by raising bank funding costs especially for small banks (Brownbridge, 1998).

Misati et al. (2013) pointed out that fuel and food inflation are the key drivers of inflation in Kenya, contributing to over 80% of overall inflation every month. This is because Kenya is a net importer of oil – changes in the international crude oil prices always affect the domestic inflation dynamics. Additionally, frequent food shortages following inadequate rainfall and occasional drought increase inflationary pressure that necessitates food importation. Increases in both oil and food prices depreciate the exchange rate immediately and have a more significant influence on non-food non-fuel inflation than the money supply growth rate. Bohachova (2008) found that high rates of inflation have a negative effect on the earnings of existing borrowers and therefore impair the quality of previously extended loans. Odhiambo (2012) found that the financial sector in developing countries becomes less developed as the inflation rate increases because inflation adversely affects the holding of all classes of financial assets.

Greuning and Bratanovic (2003) explained that medium-sized and large banks in developing countries that maintain correspondent banking relationships with foreign banks or that support customer transactions denominated in foreign exchange are exposed to higher levels of currency risk. This risk is higher for banks that borrow and/or lend in foreign currency, as this may result in open currency positions or maturity mismatches. According to Bohachova (2008), the effect of exchange rate fluctuations on bank risk is dependent on a bank's foreign currency exposure, whereby a domestic currency depreciation can be expected to adversely affect banks whose foreign currency liabilities substantially exceed their foreign currency assets. However, it is the effect of exchange rate levels on the performance of bank borrowers that generally has the primary effect on bank profitability (i.e., the resulting increase in credit risk). On aggregate, a domestic currency depreciation is likely to increase the credit risk for bank loans extended to importers and decrease the credit risk of the exporting sector.

Dunn and Mutti (2004) explained that many governments prefer fixed exchange rates because they encourage price stability. They also prefer an independent monetary policy that can be used to minimize problems arising from domestic business cycles, and they value free capital mobility because it may result in large capital inflows that can accelerate economic growth. However, they point out that according to the impossible trinity proposition – trilemma– in international monetary economics, these three goals cannot all be reached; any two may be available, but the third must be abandoned. O'Connell et al. (2010) explained that Kenya's Vision 2030 anticipates a substantial increase in external capital flows and that one of the key challenges resulting from enlisting foreign capital inflows in support of Vision 2030 projects is the trade-off between internal (maintaining macroeconomic stability) and external (supporting export competitiveness) policy objectives in the context of large capital inflows. However, their study found that though capital mobility in Kenya is substantial, it is not perfect. Consequently, they concluded that the Central Bank of Kenya still has some "limited scope for pursuing interest rate and exchange rate objectives simultaneously."

Empirically, Weller (2001) found that the vulnerability of emerging economies to currency and banking crises increases after capital account liberalization. This, he explains, is because capital account liberalization allows more liquidity to enter an emerging economy, which then finds its way into both productive and speculative projects due to internal financial liberalization. He further explains that in emerging economies where excess credit is observed, increased liquidity is mostly invested in speculative projects due to rising investor confidence and optimism that favors increasingly speculative financing. This growing trend of speculative financing increases the divergence between the real and the financial sectors, thereby increasing the likelihood of a crisis due to borrower default and the resulting capital outflows.

From the literature reviewed, it is evident that banks are exposed to various macroeconomic shocks and that market structure has the potential to either amplify or dampen the effects of these macroeconomic shocks on banking risk. In addition, it is also evident that macroeconomic shocks tend to be correlated. Hellwig (1998) pointed out that financial risks in banking are also correlated with each other since they are driven by common underlying factors. Such exposure was responsible for the American savings and loans crisis after deregulation in the 1980s and the various banking crises during the 1990s in Latin American, Scandinavian, and South East Asian countries. Locally, the aftermath of the currency crisis in 2011 confirmed that a rise in market interest rates increases market risk exposure, liquidity risk exposure, credit risk exposure, and eventually capital risk exposure.

2 Methodology

In banking, the volatility of net cash flows results from the expected and unexpected losses arising from the principal activities of lending and borrowing. In this study, the risk adjusted return on assets (RAROA) will be used to analyze banking risk exposure to the two activities. As pointed out by Hannagan (2007), the RAROA provides an economic view of bank earnings performance by adjusting for the opportunity cost of risk associated with holding the assets. In addition, the RAROA is a commonly used measure of bank performance used for internal reporting that captures the effect of both lending and borrowing risks. The use of this analytical framework is also based on similar studies (Gurbuz et al., 2013; Kohler, 2014) that have used this and other similar risk-adjusted performance measures:

$$RAROA = \frac{EP}{TA} = \frac{PAT - EL}{TA}$$

where EP denotes economic profit, TA total assets, PAT profit after tax, and EL expected loss.[2] The risk associated with lending activities usually takes time to materialize, even though it may be affected by the same macroeconomic risks as the risk associated with borrowing activities. Thus the RAROA cannot capture the effect of both risks following a change in macroeconomic conditions in a specific year. Therefore, the RAROA is broken down into its key income and expense components to derive the two risk measures that will be used to separately analyze the two risks:

$$RAROA = \frac{NII}{TA} + \frac{NIR}{TA} - \frac{OPEX}{TA} - \frac{NPLP}{TA} - \frac{EL}{TA} - \frac{TX}{TA}$$

where NII denotes net interest income, NIR non-interest revenue, OPEX operating expenses, NPLP non-performing loans provision, and TX taxes paid. The risk associated with borrow-

[2]Expected loss is captured by statutory loan loss reserve and financial assets revaluation reserve.

ing activities affects the net interest margin (NIM), while the risk associated with lending activities affects the non-performing loans (NPLs) and expected loss. These three components are exposed to macroeconomic risks and market competition pressures, while the other three components tend to be within the control of bank management. Non-interest revenue is sometimes exposed to macroeconomic risks because it is made up of foreign exchange trading revenue. Therefore, bank risk exposure will be measured by change in NIM ($\frac{NII}{TRWA}$) and change in lending risk exposure (LRE).[3] Where LRE is calculated as the logarithm of the sum of non-performing loans and expected loss (the logarithmic transformation of the data is done to reduce skewness and heteroskedasticity). The net interest margin is calculated using total risk weighted assets (TRWA) instead of total assets because, as pointed out by Peng et al. (2003), TRWA captures interest earning assets and avoids distortions in NIM due to changes in other assets resulting from valuation effects.

The use of NPL instead of NPLP to measure risk exposure to lending activities is due to the fact that a bank's decision to make provisions for bad loans is often discretionary and partially motivated by capital adequacy considerations. The choice of this risk measure is also based on the finding by Rajan (1994) that banks generally charge-off loans (when losses are realized) which reduces loan loss reserves or add to reserves (when the potential for losses are recognized). This reduces earnings, but only when such actions are anticipated by the market. In addition, he also found that banks' provisions/charge-offs are also influenced by the provisions/charge-offs of other banks in the same lines of business. Therefore, he concluded that voluntary loan loss provisions and charge-offs will tend to have limited information effects.

The use of LRE instead of the NPL ratio to measure risk exposure to lending activities is due to the fact that several studies (Serwa, 2013; Coelho and Vivan, 2013) have found that the standard NPL ratio may vary in time for reasons not directly related to credit risks. Some of these reasons include rapid credit growth and the time a loan remains in the NPL condition (before being renegotiated, regularized or written-off). Therefore, modifications in the level of credit risk may be offset by movements in any of these other factors and can be concealed or amplified, which in turn could make the NPL ratio pro-cyclical. Consequently, several adjustments to the standard NPL ratio (that control for changes in credit growth and fluctuations in the term structure of bank loans) have been proposed for countries with rapidly developing banking sectors (such as Kenya). However, these adjustments require data on individual bank loan portfolios that was not readily available.

---

[3]The use of these dependent variables is based on similar studies by Gerlach et al. (2004), Gurbuz et al. (2013) and Ramayandi et al. (2014)

2.1 Data and Model Specification

The aim of this research study is to analyze the effect of macroeconomic shocks and the changing market structure on banking risk in Kenya by estimating the following equation:

$$R_{it} = \delta R_{i,t-1} + \beta_1 X_{it} + \beta_2 Y_t + \beta_3 Z_t + \eta_i + \varepsilon_{it} \tag{1}$$

where R_{it} is a vector of observations on the bank risk measure of bank i at time t, $R_{i,t-1}$ is the lagged bank risk variable, X_{it} is a vector of time-varying bank-specific control variables, Y_t is a vector of time-varying macroeconomic variables, Z_t is a vector of time-varying market structure variables, η_i are the unobservable bank-specific effects, the $\beta's$ are coefficients of the fixed effects that are estimated across banks, δ is the coefficient of the lagged bank risk variable and ε_{it} is the disturbance term. This model specification follows similar specifications by Gerlach et al. (2004), Gurbuz et al. (2013), and Ramayandi et al. (2014).

The following model specification is used to investigate the determinants of risk exposure associated with borrowing activities:

$$\begin{aligned} NIM_{it} &= \delta NIM_{i,t-1} + \beta_1 MSHARE_{it} + \beta_2 DIVERSE_{i,t-k} + \beta_3 LTA_{i,t-k} \\ &+ \beta_4 CONC_t + \beta_5 MSIZE_t + \beta_6 RGDPG_t + \beta_7 INT_t + \beta_8 INFL_t + \beta_9 ER_t \\ &+ \beta_{10} NCF_t + \eta_i + \varepsilon_{it} \end{aligned} \tag{2}$$

The following model specification is used to investigate the determinants of risk exposure associated with lending activities:[4]

$$\begin{aligned} lnLRE_{it} &= \delta lnLRE_{i,t-1} + \beta_1 MSHARE_{it} + \beta_2 lnLOAN_{i,t-k} + \beta_3 CAR_{i,t-k} \\ &+ \beta_4 CONC_{t-1} + \beta_5 MSIZE_{t-1} + \beta_6 RGDPG_{t-1} + \beta_7 INT_{t-1} + \beta_8 INFL_{t-1} \\ &+ \beta_9 ER_{t-1} + \beta_{10} NCF_{t-1} + \eta_i + \varepsilon_{it} \end{aligned} \tag{3}$$

The market structure variables are defined as follows:

- The degree of concentration (CONC) in the banking sector is measured by the percentage share of the assets of the three largest banks in total banking assets for year t. Banks that experience less competition (a high degree of concentration) should theoretically be more risk averse (Hellman et al., 2000).

- The size of the banking market (MSIZE) is measured as the share of domestic credit to the private sector relative to GDP for year t. It will be used as a measure for both financial development and the degree of leverage in the economy. The expected effect

[4] The dynamics of both models will be determined by trying out several lags and then removing the nonsignificant lags.

is not clear – the more financially developed the country is, the lower we anticipate the volatility of macroeconomic variables. The higher the credit ratio, the larger the multiplier effects of a given economic shock (Bremus and Buch, 2015).

Both of the market structure variables enter the LRE equation with a lag to account for the delay with which the changing market structure affects a bank's credit portfolio. The macroeconomic variables used here are based on the discussion in sub-section 1.2 and are defined as follows:[5]

- The annual rate of growth of real GDP (RGDPG) for year t is used as a measure of the business cycle conditions – banking risks increase as the economic conditions worsen.
- The average rate on 91-day treasury bills (INT) for year t is used as a proxy for the short-term interest rate levels. The expected effect on borrowing risk exposure is negative but positive for lending risk exposure.
- The annual inflation rate (INFL), the USD and EUR exchange rate (ER) changes, and the annual net capital flows (NCF) for year t are also included in the model as explanatory variables. The more volatile the inflation rate and exchange rates the higher the risk exposure. The volatility of net capital flows generally depends on the volatility of the inflation rate and the exchange rates.

All of the macroeconomic variables enter the LRE equation with a lag to account for the delay with which macroeconomic shocks affect a bank's credit portfolio. The following bank-specific control variables are used:

- The bank's market share of total banking assets (MSHARE) for bank i in year t is included to proxy for bank size. Large banks are less risky because they are more diversified and have better risk screening models. However, they also enjoy a too big to fail subsidy that may increase their risk-taking incentives (Bremus and Buch, 2015).
- The loans to total assets ratio (LTA) for bank i in year t is used to control for the choices made by bank managers for riskier investments compared to holding government securities. A higher proportion of assets allocated to loans increases credit risk exposure at banks and may therefore result in more problem loans that increase fluctuations in interest income (Love and Ariss, 2013).
- The rate of loan growth (LOG.LOAN) for bank i in year t is used to control for credit portfolio growth. Excessive credit growth fills the bank's balance sheet with more risky assets (Gurbuz et al., 2013).

[5]See Figure 1 for time-series charts of the macroeconomic data used.

- The degree of functional diversification (DIVERSE) for bank i in year t is measured by calculating the share of a bank's non-interest revenue in its total operating revenue. A high ratio of non-interest income improves risk diversification by making banks less dependent on interest income. Non-interest income is usually more volatile than interest income because it is usually more difficult for borrowers to switch their lending relationships (Kohler, 2014).

- The capital adequacy ratio (CAR) for bank i in year t is used to control for the bank's risk profile. Banks with riskier loan portfolios may need higher capital buffers to insure against the resulting credit risks (Bohachova, 2008; Bremus and Buch, 2015).

Banks that grow faster are more likely to increase their exposure to risky assets. Therefore all of the bank-specific variables (with the exception of market share) enter the LRE equation with a lag to account for the delay with which idiosyncratic shocks affect banks' credit portfolios.

Data on market structure variables will be obtained from the CBK Bank Supervision Annual Reports, data on macroeconomic variables will be obtained from the economic surveys and CBK Rates, and data on the bank-specific variables will be obtained from their annual financial statements. The bank sample is drawn from banks that have end-of-year information for the period 2008 to 2013. The bank sample was made up of 32 out of the 43 banks operating at the end of 2013, which accounted for about 95% of the total banking assets.

2.2 Model Estimation

In equation 1, the lagged bank risk variable is included as an explanatory variable. Ramayandi et al. (2014) explained that the persistence of the bank risk variable may reflect the existence of intense competition or the pro-cyclical risk-taking behaviour in line with the business cycle dynamics. The coefficient of the lagged bank risk variable is viewed as the speed of convergence to equilibrium. A statistically significant value of zero implies that bank risk is characterized by a high speed of adjustment, while a value of one means that the adjustment is very slow, and values between zero and one suggest that risk persists but will eventually return to its mean. Consequently, a static model would be biased if bank risk is persistent.

To resolve the estimation problem caused by using the lagged dependent variable as an explanatory variable, the generalized method of moments (GMM) procedure proposed by Arellano and Bond (1991) will be used because it leads to consistent and efficient estimates by using the dynamic endogeneity inherent in the explanatory variables (i.e., lags of endogenous variables) as instruments.[6] Heij et al. (2004) explained that the GMM procedure derives

[6]The risk measure in equation 1 is explained by past values (one lag) of the risk measure; therefore, all lags of this explanatory variable beyond lag one will be used as instruments.

parameter estimates by equating sample moments to unobserved population moments with the assumed statistical distribution and then solving the equations. The first differenced GMM estimator vector is derived as:

$$\hat{\beta^e} = \left[\left(\sum_{i=1}^{N} (\Delta x^e_{i,-1})' Z_i \right) W_N \left(\sum_{i=1}^{N} Z_i' \Delta x^e_{i,-1} \right) \right]^{-1} \times \left[\left(\sum_{i=1}^{N} (\Delta x^e_{i,-1})' Z_i \right) W_N \left(\sum_{i=1}^{N} Z_i' \Delta y_i \right) \right] \quad (4)$$

where Z_i is the instrument matrix, W_N is the weight matrix and the exogenous independent variables are defined as:

$$\beta^e = \begin{bmatrix} \delta \\ \beta_1 \\ \vdots \\ \beta_k \end{bmatrix} \; and \; x^e_{i,-1} = \begin{bmatrix} y_{i,2} & x_{1,i,1} & \cdots & x_{k,i,1} \\ \vdots & \vdots & \ddots & \vdots \\ y_{i,T-1} & x_{1,i,T-2} & \cdots & x_{k,i,T-2} \end{bmatrix}$$

To complement the GMM multivariate analysis and identify the key determinants of risk persistence, a panel vector-autoregression (PVAR) model will be used. The PVAR framework is ideal for this purpose because it simultaneously takes into account interactions between all the macroeconomic variables and bank-specific variables in the model, unlike the separate model specifications used in the GMM multivariate analysis to control for possible multicolinearity of the macroeconomic variables. If there are no unit roots in the underlying time series, GMM estimators can be used to estimate the PVAR model coefficients.

Pfaff (2008) explained that the basic vector auto-regression (VAR) model consists of a set of K endogenous variables $y_t = (y_{1t}, ..., y_{kt})$ for k = 1,...,K and that the VAR(p) process is defined as:

$$y_t = A_1 y_{t-1} + ... + A_p y_{t-p} + CD_t + u_t \quad (5)$$

where A_i are $(K \times K)$ coefficient matrices for i = 1,...,p and u_t is a K dimensional white noise process. The matrix C is the coefficient matrix of potentially deterministic regressors with dimension $(K \times M)$, and D_t is an $(M \times 1)$ column vector holding the appropriate deterministic regressors such as a constant, trend, and/or dummy variables. Canova and Ciccarelli (2013) explained that PVAR models are built on the same structure as VAR models (all variables are assumed to be endogenous and interdependent), with a cross sectional dimension included that makes them well suited for analyzing the transmission of shocks across units and time. Therefore, following Love and Ariss (2013), the PVAR model used to identify the transmission of macroeconomic shocks is defined as:

$$y_{it} = U_i + A(L) y_{it} + e_{it} \quad (6)$$

where A(L) is the lag operator, U_i is used to control for unobserved bank heterogeneity and y_{it} is a vector of macroeconomic and bank-specific variables. Variables that enter first in equation 6 are assumed to be the most exogenous and hence affect subsequent variables both contemporaneously and with a lag. Variables that are ordered later are less exogenous and affect previous variables only with a lag. System GMM is used to estimate the coefficients of the PVAR model.

3 Results

3.1 Descriptive Statistics

The descriptive statistics of the variables used in the study are summarized in Table 1. The bank sample shows a large variability in bank size as measured by market share (MSHARE) and a large variability in bank risk profile as measured by the capital adequacy ratio (CAR), which minimize the potential of sample selection bias. The variability in the bank sample is captured in more detail in the bank descriptive statistics in Table 2.[7]

3.2 Correlation Analysis

Macroeconomic variables are not independent, and therefore multicolinearity may be a problem when using these variables in the same regression equation. Table 3 shows that some of the macroeconomic variables that will be used in the study are highly correlated; thus, multicolinearity is indeed a problem. Though their interdependence reinforces their individual influence on bank risk, it can also make an empirical assessment of their relative importance for bank risk exposure difficult. Additional regressions will be run so that the macroeconomic variables can be included in separate model specifications.

3.3 Panel Unit Root Tests

Panel unit root tests help evaluate the time series property of the data accordingly thus avoiding contradictory results in individual time series. The first two tests will be the augmented Dickey-Fuller (ADF) test and the Phillips-Perron (PP) test. Two other tests – the Elliott-Rothenberg-Stock (ERS) test and the Schmidt-Phillips (SP) test – will also be carried out to address a common shortcoming with the first two tests. Pfaff (2008) explained that the common shortcoming of the ADF and PP tests is their relatively low power if the true data-generating process is an AR (1) process with a coefficient close to one, due to the fact that a unit root process is specified as the null hypothesis.

[7] Large: Total assets market share exceeds 5%; Medium: Between 1% and 5%; Small: Less than 1%

Table 4 presents the results of the panel unit root tests. All the tests reject the presence of unit roots in the panel. However, (MSHARE), (CTI), and (ROE) are not significant at the 1% level, probably due to the effects of rising competition and growing market size on the market shares, managerial efficiency, and shareholder returns at some of the banks.

3.4 Robustness Checks

The validity of the results for all the model specifications is confirmed by the various model diagnostic tests used to evaluate whether the data are consistent with the assumptions of dynamic panel data models. The results are presented in the bottom rows of Table 7 and 8.

The Sargan test of over-identifying restrictions meets the requirement of failing to reject the null hypothesis that the instruments are not correlated with the errors in the first-differenced equation. The AR (1) and AR (2) tests meet the requirements of rejecting the null hypothesis of no first-order serial correlation but fails to reject the null hypothesis of no second-order serial correlation in first-differenced errors. Therefore, the validity of the instruments is guaranteed under the hypothesis that the error terms are not second-order serially correlated. In addition, the results of the Wald test of joint significance show that the coefficients are jointly significant.

3.5 Empirical Results

The empirical analysis proceeds in three steps. The first step involves running a baseline fixed effects regression for the bank-specific control variables. The second step involves running a GMM regression for the borrowing and lending risk exposure models, and the final step involves analyzing the key variables contributing to risk persistence by using a PVAR model to interact the significant variables from the risk exposure models.

Table 5 and 6 present the baseline regression results. The purpose of the baseline specifications is to estimate the within effect of bank-specific control variables on bank risk exposure before conducting regression with the market structure and macroeconomic variables. The large group comprises banks with a market share of total assets in excess of 5% each, those in the medium-sized group have a market share of between 1% to 5%, and those in the small group have a market share of less than 1%.

Table 7 and 8 present the GMM regression results for the NIM model and LRE model respectively. The different columns indicate the separate model specifications for the macroeconomic variables, whereby the macroeconomic variables are included separately to avoid the problems of multicolinearity.

3.5.1 Net Interest Margin

The baseline regression results for all banks in Table 5 indicate a negative and statistically significant estimate for the borrowing risk persistence measure. However, the relationship only applies to small banks which may imply that increased competition in the deposit market is reducing their margins. Nevertheless, this result justifies the choice of a dynamic model. The F-statistic for the large banks model is comparatively smaller and statistically insignificant, which indicates that the regression coefficients are not jointly significant due to a high ratio of unexplained variance. Therefore, this may imply that the effect of macroeconomic and/or market structure variables is more important in explaining the borrowing risk exposure of large banks. The GMM regression results in Table 7 indicate that borrowing risk exposure is not persistent, which may reflect the increased competition (i.e., a high speed of adjustment) in the deposit market.

The degree of concentration (CONC) was found to have a positive effect which implies that increased competition in the deposit market reduces the franchise value of banks by reducing the NIM. The size of the banking market (MSIZE) was also found to have a positive effect, which implies that the higher the credit ratio, the higher the volatility of a given economic shock (in this case the inflation rate, USD exchange rate, and EUR exchange rate). A higher credit ratio implies higher leverage in the economy, which implies larger multiplier effects.

The loan to assets ratio (LTA) was found to have a negative effect that also holds for the previous period's loan to assets ratio. This implies that an increase in the size of the proportion of loans (at medium-sized and small banks, see Table 5) tends to reduce the NIM in the current and following year, probably because the higher liquidity requirements following credit expansion and/or the resulting rise in NPLs increases funding costs. This result is similar to the finding by Love and Ariss (2013) that banks in Egypt with a higher proportion of assets allocated to loans also had higher credit risk exposure, and the resulting problem loans increased fluctuations in interest income. Market share (MSHARE) has no effect and this is consistent with the findings of Bremus and Buch (2015) – bank size does not matter for idiosyncratic fluctuations of banks in low-income countries because the return on assets does not reduce bank-level risk.

The inflation rate (INFL) was found to have a negative effect, which implies that rising inflation increases borrowing risk exposure (reduces NIM). This is consistent with the findings of Ndebbio (2004), who stated that rising rates of inflation tend to induce disintermediation by causing economic agents to hold other assets such as land, physical goods, gold, and foreign currency in preference to domestic currency. Changes in the exchange rates (USD and EUR) were also found to have a negative effect, which implies that depreciation of the domestic currency increases borrowing risk exposure (reduces NIM). The results also indicate that changes in the short-term interest rate (INT) have no effect, which may imply that bank deposit and lending rates are rigid. The interest rate channel in Kenya was found to be ineffective (Misati et al., 2011; Mahasi and Pokhariyal, 2013) because it took between 10 to 24 months to fully transmit monetary policy shocks to the lending and deposit rates. In South Africa, Aziakpono and Wilson (2010) found that banks were more rigid in adjusting their lending rates and deposit rates upward in response to a positive shock in the official rate, thus providing support for the adverse customer reaction hypothesis and the collusive behaviour hypothesis respectively. In Hong Kong, Peng et al. (2003) found that changes in the short-term interest rate had no impact on the intermediation spread.

3.5.2 Lending Risk Exposure

The baseline regression results for all banks in Table 6 indicate a positive and statistically significant estimate for the lending risk persistence measure. The relationship only applies to small and medium-sized banks, but nevertheless justifies the choice of a dynamic model. The GMM regression results in Table 8 also indicate that lending risk exposure is persistent; however, the coefficient is less than one, which means that lending risk exposure will eventually return to its mean. The results also suggest that all the macroeconomic variables used are significant determinants of lending risk exposure for banks in Kenya.

The degree of concentration (CONC) was found to have a positive effect, which implies that reduced competition in the loan market increases the lending risk exposure. The degree of concentration has been declining during the study period; therefore, the positive relationship does not support the franchise value paradigm where the decline in franchise value resulting from competition is expected to lower incentives for making good loans. Therefore, the results imply that bank competition in the loan market increases banking stability. The size of the banking market (MSIZE) was found to have a negative effect, which implies that a larger banking market provides more opportunities to diversify risk. This effect is explained by Bremus and Buch (2015) who stated that the more financially developed a country is, the lower is the volatility of a given economic shock (in this case, the positive shock of net capital flows).

The loan growth rate (LOG.LOAN) was found to have a positive effect, which implies that rapid credit growth (at large and medium-sized banks, see Table 6) fills the bank's balance sheet with more risks. Greuning and Bratanovic (2003) found that rapid credit growth increases credit risk when the bank fails to match its growing loan portfolio with adequate credit risk management capacity. Love and Ariss (2013) found that the effect was due to the relationship between rapid loan growth and adverse selection, which reduces asset quality.

The real GDP growth rate (RGDPG) was found to have a negative effect, which implies that an improvement in economic conditions reduces lending risk exposure in the following period. All the other macroeconomic variables were found to have a positive effect on the following period lending risk exposure, which implies that a sharp rise in their values impairs the quality of previously extended loans. Though the estimated coefficient for net capital flows (NCF) is marginal, the positive relationship may imply that an increase in foreign borrowing may give rise to misallocation of funds and over-investment in the non-tradeable sectors that increases lending risk exposure.[8] This is consistent with the findings of Hansanti et al. (2008). Following financial liberalization in Thailand, both FDI and portfolio inflows switched from industry and trade to the non-tradeable sectors (real estate, short-term loans, and portfolio investments) that were not generating foreign exchange earnings to service the foreign debt. This led to the creation of an asset-price bubble. Similarly, Beck et al. (2013) found that exchange rate depreciations lead to an increase of non-performing loans in countries with a high degree of lending in foreign currencies to unhedged borrowers. Specifically, they found that the depreciation of local currencies against the Swiss Franc and the Euro – in Poland, Hungary, and Croatia where lending in these currencies was widespread – negatively affected bank asset quality via negative balance sheet effects.

3.5.3 Analysis of Risk Persistence

The focus of this study was to analyze the impact of the factors affecting banks' borrowing and lending risk exposure. From the results presented in the preceding sub-sections, it is evident that lending risk exposure is persistent and therefore requires further analysis. This section uses a PVAR model to analyze how the key variables affect lending risk exposure. The PVAR model specification considers three significant macroeconomic variables (real GDP growth rate, short-term interest rate, and the USD/KES exchange rate) and three bank-specific variables (lending risk exposure, loan growth rate, and capital adequacy ratio). Variables that enter first in the PVAR model (equation 6) are assumed to be the most exogenous and hence affect subsequent variables both contemporaneously and with a lag. Variables that are ordered later are less exogenous and affect previous variables only with a lag.

The original shock is assumed to come from changes in the USD exchange rate, which has a contemporaneous effect on the real GDP growth rate, short-term interest rate, and all bank-specific variables. All the other variables affect the USD exchange rate with a lag. For the bank-specific variables, the shock is assumed to come from changes in the lending risk exposure, which affects the loan growth rate and capital adequacy ratio contemporaneously. The loan growth rate and capital adequacy ratio affect the lending risk exposure with a

[8]There has been a growing trend of commercial banks borrowing from foreign financial institutions to meet the rising domestic financing requirements, and this is contributing to the declining trend in commercial banks' net foreign asset position – from a credit balance of KES 50 billion in December 2007 to a debit of KES 109 billion in December 2014. (Source: CBK Depository Corporation Survey)

lag. Love and Ariss (2013) explained that due to the fact that all macroeconomic variables are entered first into the system, they have an immediate effect on bank-specific variables. Feedback from bank-specific variables on macroeconomic variables occurs only with a lag.

Table 9 presents the estimation results showing that most coefficients are found to be statistically significant. From the PVAR results, the key variables affecting the persistence of lending risk exposure are the previous period's loan growth rate and interest rate. They are both positively related with lending risk exposure and the estimated direct effects are 0.075 and 0.037, respectively. Therefore, this implies that bank risk taking at some of the medium-sized and small banks is the key determinant of the persistence of lending risk exposure (see Figures 2 and 3).

There are various factors that influence excessive risk taking by banks. However, several studies (Johnson, 1994; Godlewski, 2007; Abdellaoui et al., 2013) have all found that prospect theory best explains risk-taking decisions that increase risk exposure in banking, such as increased risk taking due to negative or declining returns. Prospect theory, which was developed by Kahneman and Tversky (1979), states that the tendency to over-weigh outcomes that are considered certain relative to outcomes that are probable (the certainty effect) contributes to risk aversion in choices involving sure gains and to risk seeking in choices involving sure losses. Therefore, following Johnson (1994), the risk-return trade-off for banks with above median ROE and below median ROE is depicted in Figure 3. Banks operating above the median ROE tend to cluster around the same level, and there are a couple of outliers for banks operating below the median ROE (especially medium-sized and small banks). This may indicate excessive risk taking in the face of negative or declining target returns. This tendency of excessive risk taking is also depicted in Figure 2, where the few banks with the highest loan growth rate also happen to have an NPL ratio that is above the median.

4 Conclusions

This paper investigated the effect of changing market structure and macroeconomic shocks on the borrowing and lending risk exposure of Kenyan commercial banks using a GMM estimation approach. Borrowing risk exposure was found not persistent, being mainly affected by the degree of concentration and external economic shocks. Interestingly, the results also suggest that changes in the short-term interest rate do not affect the net interest margin, which may imply that bank deposit and lending rates are rigid and that the interest rate channel may be ineffective. Lending risk exposure was found to be persistent, being mostly affected by the degree of concentration, internal economic shocks, and external economic shocks. The positive relationship between the degree of concentration and both borrowing and lending risk exposure supports the concentration-fragility view – the declining franchise value did not lower incentives for making good loans during the study period where the degree of concentration was on a downward trend. Further analysis of the factors contributing to the persistence of lending risk exposure using a PVAR model found that the banks' loan growth rate and the market interest rate were the key determinants. The effect of the loan growth rate was about double the effect of interest rate risk, implying that bank risk taking at some of the medium-sized and small banks is the key determinant of the persistence of lending risk exposure.

These results have important implications as far as bank regulation is concerned. Specifically, the persistence of lending risk exposure can be reduced by improving the capacity of the regulator to monitor overall bank risk taking. The underlying risk posed by the declining net foreign assets of commercial banks due to foreign borrowing also needs to be monitored. This problem was identified by Taylor (1998) as having the potential to increase the overall risk of the financial system's balance sheet in the event of a currency depreciation by being long on domestic assets and short on foreign currency holdings.

The USD exchange rate was found to have a large negative effect the net interest margin. Therefore, the biggest threat to borrowing risk exposure is the USD exchange rate depreciation. According to Moore and Pentecost (2006), one possible mitigating measure involves distinguishing between permanent and transitory shocks on the exchange rate so as to avoid the potentially damaging attempt to stabilize exchange rate changes that are due to structural changes in the economy. This can result in an overvalued currency that can lead to a speculative attack. According to Agenor and da Silva (2013), another possible mitigating measure involves adopting an integrated inflation targeting framework that combines monetary policy with macro-prudential policies, whereby the policy interest rate is also set to respond directly to a pre-defined measure of the private sector credit growth gap, to jointly achieve macroeconomic and financial stability.

The real GDP growth rate was found to have a large negative effect on lending risk exposure. Therefore, the biggest threat to lending risk exposure is a negative shock in any of the key economic sectors. It is thus prudent for policy makers to continue monitoring the potential for such developments to ensure that the existing institutional structure can dampen such fluctuations and that timely mitigating measures can be implemented to reduce the persistence of the ensuing gap between actual and potential output.

Acknowledgements

My gratitude goes to Prof. Francis Mwega, Ms. Laura Barasa and to two anonymous referees for their insightful comments and suggestions during the research process. I acknowledge with thanks the helpful criticisms and suggestions from Dr. Bethuel Kinyanjui, Dr. Thomas

Ongoro, Prof. Jane Mariara, Prof. Leopold Mureithi and Mr. George Macharia during the proposal presentation seminar. I am also grateful to Mr. E. P. Kipsitet, Mr. Luke Plapan and Ms. Irene Rugiri of the Central Bank of Kenya for facilitating the financial statement data collection process.

References

Abdellaoui, M., Bleichrodt, H., and Kammoun, H. (2013). Do financial professionals behave according to prospect theory? An experimental study. *Theory and Decision*, 74:411–429.

Acemoglu, D., Johnson, S., Robinson, J., and Thaicharoen, Y. (2003). Institutional causes, macroeconomic symptoms: Volatility, crises and growth. *Journal of Monetary Economics*, 50:49–123.

Agenor, P.-R. and da Silva, L. P. (2013). Inflation Targeting and Financial Stability: A Perspective from the Developing World. *Banco Central do Brasil Working Paper*. No 324.

Agenor, P.-R. and Montiel, P. J. (2008). *Development Macroeconomics*. Princeton, NJ: Princeton University Press, 3rd edition.

Agosin, M. R. and Huaita, F. (2011). Capital flows to emerging economies: Minsky in the tropics. *Cambridge Journal of Economics*, 35:663–683.

Allen, F., Babus, A., and Carletti, E. (2009). Financial Crises: Theory and Evidence. *Annual Review of Financial Economics*, 1:97–116.

Allen, F. and Gale, D. (2004). Competition and Financial Stability. *Journal of Money, Credit and Banking*, 36(3):453–480.

Arellano, M. and Bond, S. (1991). Some Tests of Specification for Panel Data: Monte Carlo Evidence and an Application to Employment Equations. *Review of Economic Studies*, 58(2):277–297.

Aziakpono, M. J. and Wilson, M. K. (2010). Interest Rate Pass-Through and Monetary Policy Regimes in South Africa. In *Paper presented during the CSAE conference held at Oxford University from 21-23 March 2010*.

Beck, R., Jakubik, P., and Piloiu, A. (2013). Non-performing loans: What matters in addition to the economic cycle? *European Central Bank Working Paper*. No 1515.

Bohachova, O. (2008). The impact of macroeconomic factors on risks in the banking sector: A cross-country empirical assessment. *IAW Discussion Paper*. No 44.

Boyd, J. H. and De Nicolo, G. (2005). The Theory of Bank Risk Taking and Competition Revisited. *Journal of Finance*, 60(3):1329–1343.

Bremus, F. and Buch, C. M. (2015). Banking Market Structure and Macroeconomic Stability: Are Low Income Countries Special? *Pacific Economic Review*, 20(1):73–100.

Brownbridge, M. (1998). The Causes of Financial Distress in Local Banks in Africa and Implications for Prudential Policy. *UNCTAD Discussion Paper*. No 132.

Canova, F. and Ciccarelli, M. (2013). Panel Vector Autoregressive Models: A Survey. *European Central Bank Working Paper*. No 1507.

Central Bank of Kenya (2003). *Bank Supervision Annual Report 2003*. Nairobi: Central Bank of Kenya.

Coelho, R. L. P. and Vivan, G. F. A. (2013). Converting the NPL Ratio into a Comparable Long Term Metric. *Banco Central do Brasil Working Paper*. No 309.

Degryse, H. and Ongena, S. (2005). Competition and Regulation in the Banking Sector: A Review of the Empirical Evidence on the Sources of Bank Rents. Tilburg University, mimeo.

Demirguc-Kunt, A. and Detagiache, E. (1998). The Determinants of Banking Crises in Developing and Developed Countries. *IMF Staff Papers*, 45(1):81–109.

Demirguc-Kunt, A. and Detragiache, E. (2001). Financial Liberalization and Financial Fragility. In Caprio, G., Honohan, P., and Stiglitz, J. E., editors, *Financial Liberalization: How Far, How Fast?*, pages 96–122. New York: Cambridge University Press.

Dunn, R. M. and Mutti, J. H. (2004). *International Economics*. New York: Routledge, 6th edition.

Esch, L., Kieffer, R., and Lopez, T. (2005). *Asset and Risk Management*. West Sussex: Wiley.

Gerlach, S., Peng, W., and Shu, C. (2004). Macroeconomic Conditions and Banking Performance in Hong Kong: A Panel Data Study. *HKMA Research Memorandum*. No 05/2004.

Godlewski, C. J. (2007). An Empirical Investigation of Bank Risk-Taking in Emerging Markets within a Prospect Theory Framework. *Banks and Bank Systems*, 2(2):35–43.

Goodhart, C., Hofmann, B., and Segoviano, M. (2004). Bank Regulation and Macroeconomic Fluctuations. *Oxford Review of Economic Policy*, 20(4):591–615.

Government of Kenya (2007). *Kenya Vision 2030.* Nairobi: Government of Kenya.

Greuning, H. V. and Bratanovic, S. B. (2003). *Analyzing and Managing Banking Risk.* Washington, D.C.: International Bank for Reconstruction and Development, 2nd edition.

Gurbuz, A. O., Yanik, S., and Ayturk, Y. (2013). Income Diversification and Bank Performance: Evidence from Turkish Banking Sector. *BDDK Bankacilik ve Finansal Piyasalar*, 7(1):9–29.

Hannagan, T. A. (2007). Capital-Based Profitability Measurement. *Bank Accounting and Finance*, pages 21–28. August-September.

Hansanti, S., Islam, S. M. N., and Sheehan, P. (2008). *International Finance in Emerging Markets.* Heidelberg: Physica-Verlag.

Hausmann, R. and Gavin, M. (1996). Securing Stability and Growth in a Shock Prone Region: The Policy Challenge for Latin America. *Inter-American Development Bank Working Paper.* No 315.

Heffernan, S. (2005). *Modern Banking.* West Sussex: Wiley.

Heij, C., de Boer, P., Franses, P. H., Kloek, T., and van Dijk, H. K. (2004). *Econometric Methods with Applications in Business and Economics.* Oxford: Oxford University Press.

Hellman, T. F., Murdock, K. C., and Stiglitz, J. E. (2000). Liberalization, Moral Hazard in Banking, and Prudential Regulation: Are Capital Requirements Enough? *American Economic Review*, 90(1):147–165.

Hellwig, M. (1995). Systemic Aspects of Risk Management in Banking and Finance. *Swiss Journal of Economics and Statistics*, 131(4):723–737.

Hellwig, M. (1998). Banks, Markets, and the Allocation of Risk in an Economy. *Journal of Institutional and Theoretical Economics*, 154:328–351.

Johnson, H. J. (1994). Prospect Theory in the Commercial Banking Industry. *Journal of Financial and Strategic Decisions*, 7(1):73–89.

Kahneman, D. and Tversky, A. (1979). Prospect Theory: An Analysis of Decision under Risk. *Econometrica*, 47(2):263–292.

Kilishi, A. A., Mobolaji, H. I., Yaru, M. A., and Yakubu, A. T. (2013). Institutions and Economic Performance in Sub-Saharan Africa: A Dynamic Panel Data Analysis. *Journal of African Development*, 15(2):91–119.

Kohler, M. (2014). Does non-interest income make banks more risky? Retail versus investment-oriented banks. *Review of Financial Economics*, 23(4):182–193.

Laeven, L. (2011). Banking Crises: A Review. *Annual Review of Financial Economics*, 3:17–40.

Love, I. and Ariss, R. T. (2013). Macro-Financial Linkages in Egypt: A Panel Analysis of Economic Shocks and Loan Portfolio Quality. *IMF Working Paper*. No WP/13/271.

Mahasi, J. and Pokhariyal, G. P. (2013). Two Stage Interest Rate Pass Through in Kenya. *Journal of Emerging Trends in Economics and Management Sciences*, 4(1):54–61.

Misati, R. N., Nyamongo, E. M., and Kamau, A. W. (2011). Interest rate pass-through in Kenya. *International Journal of Development Issues*, 10(2):170–182.

Misati, R. N., Nyamongo, E. M., and Mwangi, I. (2013). Commodity price shocks and inflation in a net oil-importing economy. *OPEC Energy Review*, 37(2):125–148.

Moore, T. and Pentecost, E. J. (2006). The Sources of Real Exchange Rate Fluctuations in India. *Indian Economic Review*, 41(1):9–23.

Mwega, F. M. (2011). The Competitiveness and Efficiency of the Financial Services Sector in Africa: A Case Study of Kenya. *African Development Review*, 23(1):44–59.

Ndebbio, J. E. U. (2004). Financial deepening, economic growth and development: Evidence from selected Sub-Saharan African countries. *AERC Research Paper*. No 142.

Ngugi, R. W. and Kabubo, J. W. (1998). Financial sector reforms and interest rate liberalization: The Kenya experience. *AERC Research Paper*. No 72.

Nkurunziza, J. D. (2005). Credit Can Precipitate Firm Failure: Evidence from Kenyan Manufacturing in the 1990s. *CSAE Working Paper*. No WPS/2005-04.

O'Connell, S. A., Maturu, B. O., Mwega, F. M., Ndung'u, N. S., and Ngugi, R. W. (2010). Capital mobility, monetary policy, and exchange rate management in Kenya. In Adam, C. S., Collier, P., and Ndung'u, N., editors, *Kenya: Policies for Prosperity*, pages 172–208. Oxford: Oxford University Press.

Odhiambo, N. M. (2012). The Impact of Inflation on Financial Sector Development: Experience from Zambia. *Journal of Applied Business Research*, 28(6):1497–1508.

Peng, W., Lai, K., Leung, F., and Shu, C. (2003). The Impact of Interest Rate Shocks on the Performance of the Banking Sector. *HKMA Research Memorandum*. No 07/2003.

Pfaff, B. (2008). *Analysis of Integrated and Cointegrated Time Series with R*. New York: Springer.

Rajan, R. G. (1994). Why Bank Credit Policies Fluctuate: A Theory and Some Evidence. *Quarterly Journal of Economics*, 109(2):399–441.

Ramayandi, A., Rawat, U., and Tang, H. C. (2014). Can Low Interest Rates be Harmful: An Assessment of the Bank Risk-Taking Channel in Asia. *Asian Development Bank Working Paper*. No 123.

Serwa, D. (2013). Measuring non-performing loans during (and after) credit booms. *Central European Journal of Economic Modelling and Econometrics*, 5:163–183.

Stiglitz, J. E. and Weiss, A. (1981). Credit Rationing in Markets with Imperfect Information. *American Economic Review*, 71(3):393–410.

Taylor, L. (1998). Lax Public Sector, Destabilizing Private Sector: Origins of Capital Market Crises. *CEPA Working Paper*. No 6.

Weller, C. E. (2001). Financial Crises After Financial Liberalisation: Exceptional Circumstances or Structural Weakness? *Journal of Development Studies*, 38(1):98–127.

Figure 1: Macroeconomic Variables

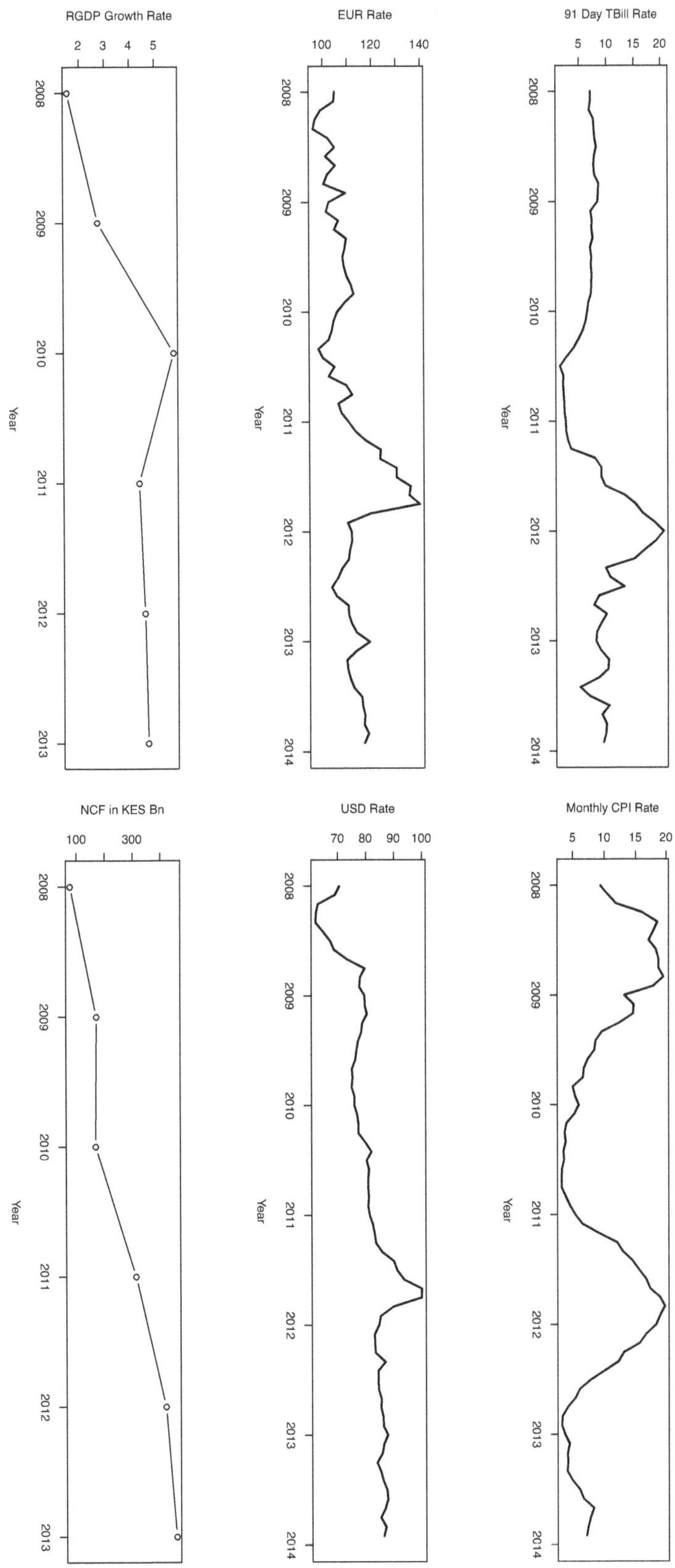

Figure 2: NPL Ratio depending on log-loan

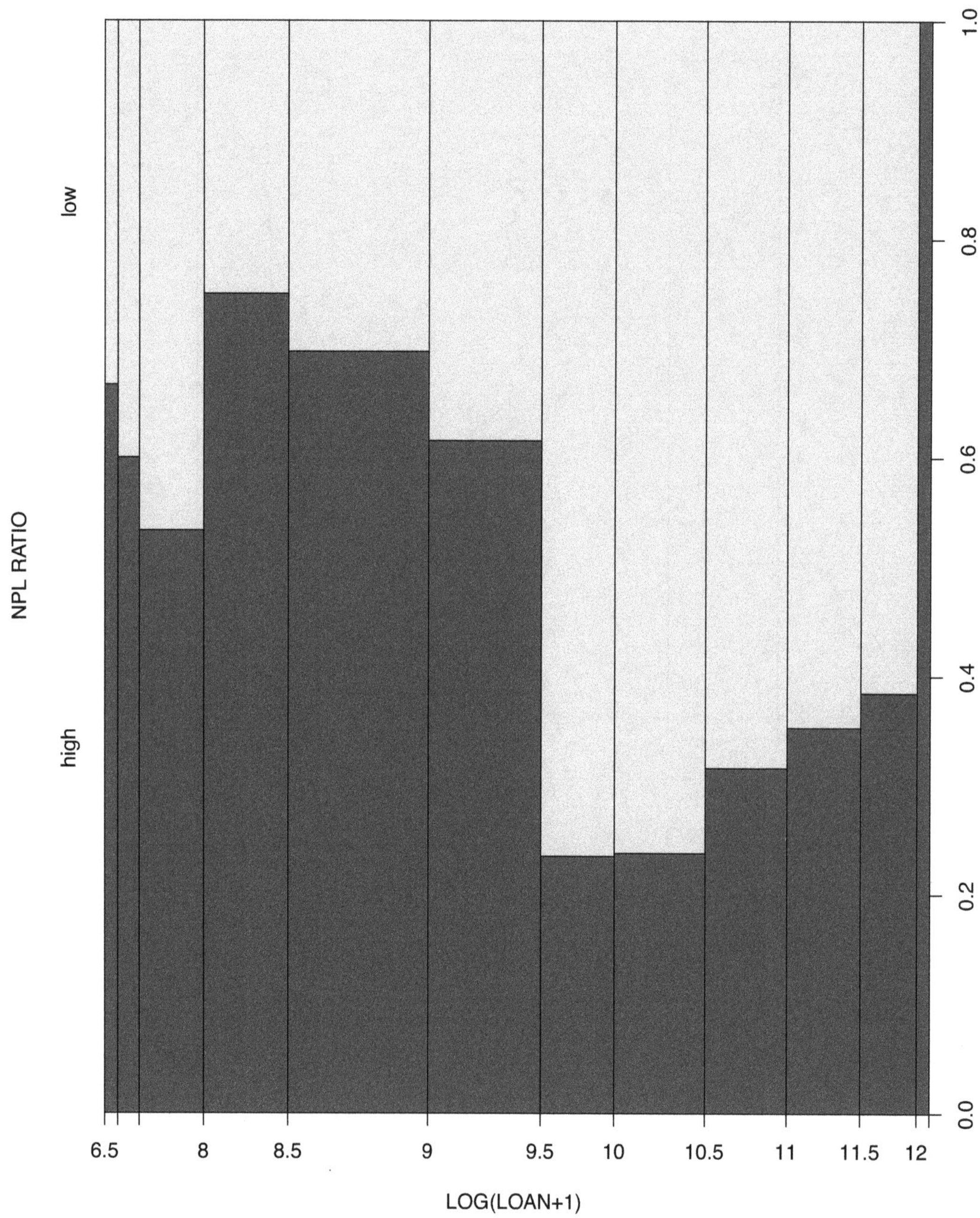

Figure 3: Distance from median ROE

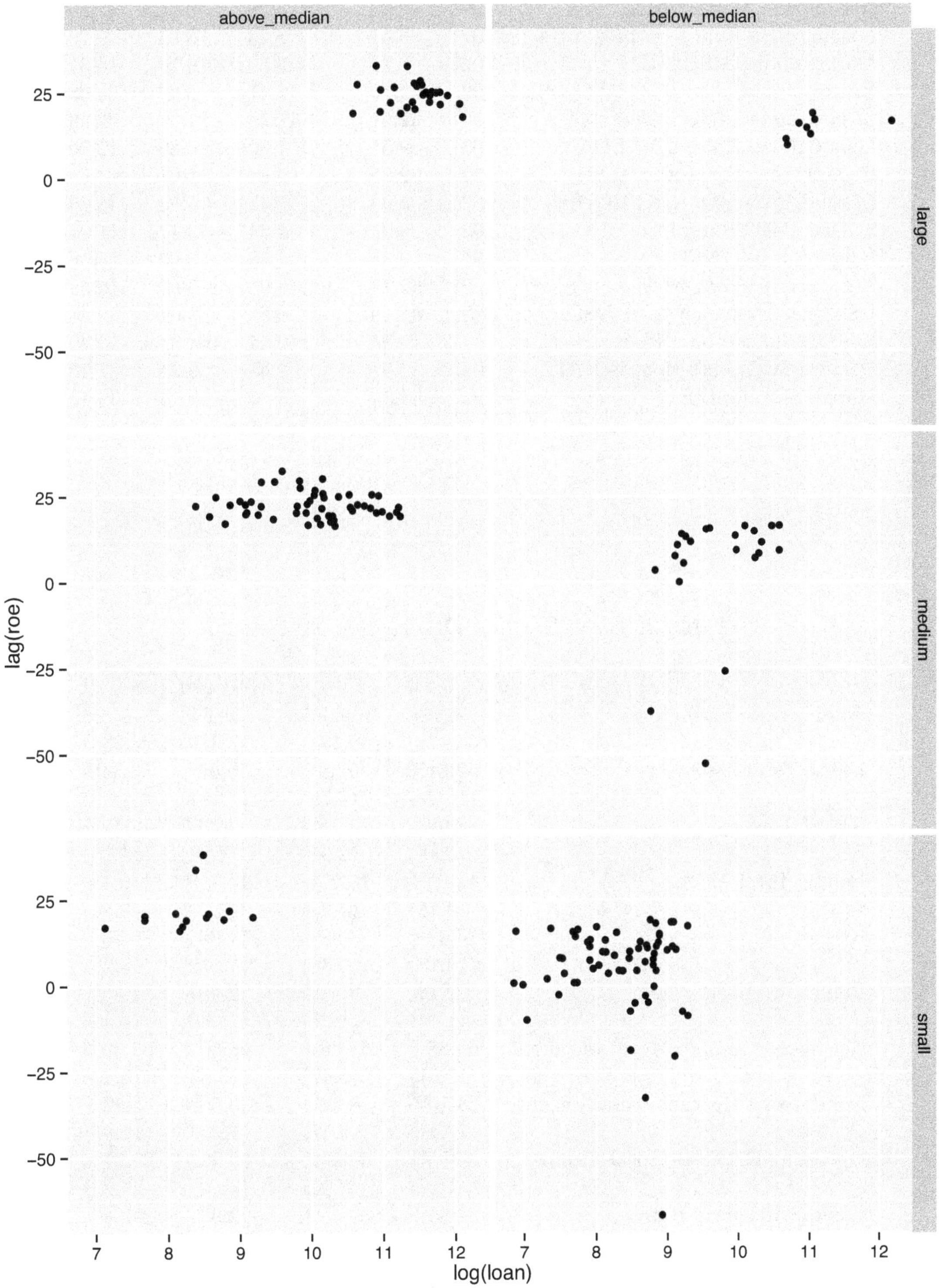

Table 1: Descriptive Statistics

Statistic	N	Mean	St. Dev.	Min	Max
Net Interest Margin, NIM	192	9.63	3.98	0.23	25.89
Lending Risk Exposure, LOG.LRE	192	6.61	1.23	3.64	9.70
Market Share, MSHARE	192	3.13	3.59	0.10	15.31
Degree of Diversification, DIVERSE	192	34.15	12.41	6.90	94.98
Loan to Assets Ratio, LTA	192	52.61	11.24	21.01	75.66
Loan Growth Rate, LOG.LOAN	192	9.54	1.30	6.86	12.20
Capital Adequacy Ratio, CAR	192	22.85	9.36	8.87	64.78
Real GDP Growth Rate, RGDPG	192	3.95	1.41	1.53	5.76
91-Day T-Bill Rate, INT	192	8.06	2.64	3.17	11.01
Inflation Rate, INFL	192	9.81	4.58	3.80	16.58
Net Capital Flows, NCF	192	262.10	143.93	100.61	514.39
US Dollar Exchange Rate, USD	192	81.19	6.55	69.62	89.44
Euro Exchange Rate, EUR	192	110.86	6.44	104.03	123.29
Degree of Concentration, CONC	192	32.57	2.65	29.24	37.40
Market Size, MSIZE	192	34.33	3.86	29.13	39.42

Table 2: Bank Sample Descriptive Statistics

	All	Large	Medium	Small
Total Assets in Mn	55,188	169,665	48,943	9,108
	(65,878)	(60,184)	(27,670)	(4,283)
Loans/Total Assets	52.61%	55.58%	50.47%	53.34%
	(11.24)	(6.78)	(11.81)	(11.99)
NPL/Loans	7.62%	4.78%	4.33%	12.12%
	(8.68)	(2.91)	(4.81)	(11.10)
Equity/Total Assets	14.63%	15.27%	14.11%	14.84%
	(4.78)	(4.23)	(3.70)	(5.84)
Return on Equity	14.92%	23.08%	17.08%	9.10%
	(13.18)	(5.36)	(13.12)	(13.23)
Return on Assets	2.21%	3.58%	2.48%	1.33%
	(1.74)	(1.28)	(1.69)	(1.48)
Net Interest Income/Total Income	65.88%	61.36%	66.50%	67.33%
	(12.61)	(6.47)	(13.53)	(13.43)
Non-Interest Revenue/Total Income	34.15%	38.64%	33.50%	32.73%
	(12.41)	(6.47)	(13.53)	(12.97)
Operating Expenses/Total Income	65.55%	59.26%	58.20%	75.57%
	(31.23)	(8.94)	(38.43)	(27.22)
Capital Adequacy Ratio	22.85%	21.45%	22.03%	24.28%
	(9.36)	(5.95)	(9.06)	(10.71)

Note: Means and Standard Deviations (in brackets) for the period 2008–13.

Table 3: Correlation of Macroeconomic Variables

	RGDPG	INT	INFL	NCF	USD	EUR
RGDP	1					
INT	-0.16	1				
INFL	-0.72	0.53	1			
NCF	0.58	0.41	-0.27	1		
USD	0.74	0.47	-0.27	0.82	1	
EUR	0.30	0.67	0.25	0.67	0.83	1

Table 4: Panel Unit Root Tests Results

Variable	ADF Test	PP Test	ERS Test	SP Test
RGDPG	11.86***	3.81***	−0.66***	3.86***
	(0.02)	(0.30)	(0.09)	(0.42)
INT	24.20***	8.09***	−2.93***	8.04***
	(1.16)	(0.62)	(0.14)	(0.84)
INFL	29.44***	14.34***	−0.10***	14.23***
	(0.77)	(0.70)	(0.04)	(1.12)
NCF	783.48***	274.21***	−0.92***	273.40***
	(44.15)	(21.76)	(0.13)	(37.29)
USD	242.40***	70.65***	−0.26***	70.87***
	(11.01)	(5.85)	(0.07)	(6.00)
EUR	332.50***	143.17***	−0.75***	143.20***
	(17.13)	(7.73)	(0.12)	(7.84)
CONC	97.04***	32.56***	−0.52***	32.48***
	(5.02)	(2.37)	(0.10)	(2.46)
MSIZE	102.80***	24.25***	−0.88***	24.30***
	(3.86)	(2.41)	(0.12)	(2.52)
NIM	3.80***	3.46***	−0.32***	5.15***
	(0.95)	(0.58)	(0.07)	(1.01)
LOG.LRE	1.85***	1.48***	−0.15***	1.94***
	(0.40)	(0.31)	(0.04)	(0.42)
MSHARE	0.49*	0.29**	−0.04*	1.02**
	(0.29)	(0.14)	(0.02)	(0.48)
DIVERSE	11.05***	15.01***	−0.25***	11.91***
	(2.98)	(2.19)	(0.07)	(2.86)
CTI	13.99**	30.01***	−0.24***	15.89***
	(5.19)	(4.43)	(0.07)	(6.08)
LTA	11.90***	15.76***	−0.28***	15.18***
	(2.92)	(2.78)	(0.06)	(3.05)
LOG.LOAN	2.23***	1.74***	−0.17***	2.51***
	(0.54)	(0.42)	(0.05)	(0.55)
CAR	11.17***	7.42***	−0.30***	9.00***
	(2.12)	(1.31)	(0.06)	(2.06)
ROE	5.98**	6.11***	−0.29***	13.05***
	(2.32)	(1.16)	(0.07)	(2.94)

Note: *,**,*** denote significance at 10%, 5% and 1% levels.

Table 5: Baseline Two-Way Fixed Effects Regression for NIM

	All	**Large**	**Medium**	**Small**
L1.NIM	−0.153*	0.229	0.133	−0.490***
	(0.083)	(0.279)	(0.125)	(0.138)
DIVERSE	−0.128***	−0.049	−0.103***	−0.086*
	(0.025)	(0.061)	(0.030)	(0.046)
MSHARE	−0.206	0.400	−0.232	−10.060**
	(0.318)	(0.258)	(0.565)	(4.327)
LTA	−0.156***	−0.048	−0.198***	−0.192***
	(0.039)	(0.054)	(0.056)	(0.070)
Observations	160	30	66	64
R^2	0.267	0.245	0.395	0.393
Adjusted R^2	0.201	0.131	0.264	0.264
F Statistic	10.954***	1.298	7.196***	6.970***
	(df = 4; 120)	(df = 4; 16)	(df = 4; 44)	(df = 4; 43)

Note: *,**,*** denote significance at 10%, 5% and 1% levels. Standard errors in brackets.

Table 6: Baseline Two-Way Fixed Effects Regression for LRE

	All	**Large**	**Medium**	**Small**
L1.LOG.LRE	0.351***	0.111	0.244*	0.388**
	(0.083)	(0.202)	(0.130)	(0.144)
L1.CAR	−0.001	0.033**	−0.009	−0.011
	(0.007)	(0.015)	(0.014)	(0.012)
MSHARE	0.004	−0.110	0.116	0.911
	(0.066)	(0.098)	(0.141)	(0.828)
L1.LOG.LOAN	0.848***	2.061***	0.878**	0.265
	(0.226)	(0.613)	(0.329)	(0.434)
Observations	160	30	66	64
R^2	0.361	0.602	0.378	0.370
Adjusted R^2	0.270	0.321	0.252	0.249
F Statistic	16.923***	6.043***	6.693***	6.325***
	(df = 4; 120)	(df = 4; 16)	(df = 4; 44)	(df = 4; 43)

Note: *,**,*** denote significance at 10%, 5% and 1% levels. Standard errors in brackets.

Table 7: GMM Regression Results for Net Interest Margin

	(1)	(2)	(3)	(4)	(5)	(6)
L1.NIM	−0.149	−0.149	−0.128	−0.067	−0.097	−0.095
	(0.151)	(0.149)	(0.152)	(0.121)	(0.147)	(0.146)
DIVERSE	−0.145***	−0.144***	−0.147***	−0.142***	−0.148***	−0.148***
	(0.028)	(0.028)	(0.028)	(0.027)	(0.028)	(0.028)
L1.DIVERSE	0.014	0.013	0.023	0.028	0.030	0.031
	(0.025)	(0.025)	(0.024)	(0.025)	(0.024)	(0.024)
MSHARE	−0.389	−0.391	−0.369	−0.343	−0.348	−0.346
	(0.385)	(0.384)	(0.385)	(0.360)	(0.381)	(0.381)
LTA	−0.168***	−0.170***	−0.158***	−0.166***	−0.153***	−0.153***
	(0.045)	(0.045)	(0.044)	(0.044)	(0.044)	(0.044)
L1.LTA	−0.072*	−0.072*	−0.076*	−0.081*	−0.080*	−0.080*
	(0.043)	(0.042)	(0.044)	(0.043)	(0.045)	(0.045)
CONC	0.953	1.062*	1.207**	−0.325	1.420**	1.121*
	(0.636)	(0.579)	(0.578)	(1.213)	(0.598)	(0.590)
MSIZE	0.329	0.394	0.456*	0.077	0.682**	0.452*
	(0.305)	(0.267)	(0.266)	(0.364)	(0.293)	(0.271)
RGDPG	0.073					
	(0.140)					
INT		−0.009				
		(0.041)				
INFL			−0.049*			
			(0.026)			
NCF				−0.009		
				(0.007)		
USD					−0.130**	
					(0.065)	
EUR						−0.049**
						(0.025)
Num. obs.	192	192	192	192	192	192
Num. obs. used	128	128	128	128	128	128
Sargan Test: p-value	0.936	0.933	0.946	0.922	0.945	0.944
AR (1) Test: p-value	0.005	0.005	0.007	0.008	0.008	0.008
AR (2) Test: p-value	0.237	0.249	0.190	0.217	0.181	0.182
Wald Test: p-value	0.000	0.000	0.000	0.000	0.000	0.000

Note: *,**,*** denote significance at 10%, 5% and 1% levels. Standard errors in brackets.

Table 8: GMM Regression Results for Lending Risk Exposure

	(1)	(2)	(3)	(4)	(5)	(6)
L1.LOG.LRE	0.506**	0.501**	0.641***	0.651***	0.651***	0.680***
	(0.202)	(0.202)	(0.195)	(0.210)	(0.210)	(0.201)
CAR	0.001	0.001	0.001	0.003	0.003	0.002
	(0.006)	(0.006)	(0.007)	(0.007)	(0.007)	(0.007)
MSHARE	−0.029	−0.027	−0.093	−0.111	−0.110	−0.117
	(0.070)	(0.070)	(0.075)	(0.081)	(0.081)	(0.079)
LOG.LOAN	0.821**	0.813**	1.010**	0.935**	0.933**	1.019**
	(0.365)	(0.361)	(0.450)	(0.427)	(0.427)	(0.455)
L1.LOG.LOAN	−0.067	−0.064	−0.063	0.101	0.102	0.020
	(0.316)	(0.315)	(0.333)	(0.309)	(0.311)	(0.326)
L1.CONC	0.020	0.061*	0.022	0.131***	0.205***	0.128***
	(0.036)	(0.035)	(0.036)	(0.048)	(0.079)	(0.044)
L1.MSIZE	0.019	−0.011	−0.031	−0.058*	−0.007	−0.003
	(0.017)	(0.017)	(0.019)	(0.035)	(0.018)	(0.017)
L1.RGDPG	−0.116***					
	(0.032)					
L1.INT		0.043***				
		(0.012)				
L1.INFL			0.032***			
			(0.009)			
L1.NCF				0.003**		
				(0.001)		
L1.USD					0.045**	
					(0.022)	
L1.EUR						0.020***
						(0.007)
Num. obs.	192	192	192	192	192	192
Num. obs. used	128	128	128	128	128	128
Sargan Test: p-value	0.999	0.999	0.997	0.999	0.998	0.997
AR (1) Test: p-value	0.057	0.060	0.021	0.025	0.025	0.020
AR (2) Test: p-value	0.804	0.811	0.616	0.716	0.715	0.693
Wald Test: p-value	0.000	0.000	0.000	0.000	0.000	0.000

Note: *,**,*** denote significance at 10%, 5% and 1% levels. Standard errors in brackets.

Table 9: Coefficient Estimates for the PVAR Model

	USD_t	INT_t	$RGDPG_t$	$LOG.LRE_t$	$LOG.LOAN_t$	CAR_t
USD_{t-1}	1.150***	0.020***	0.075***	0.002	0.007***	0.216**
	(0.024)	(0.005)	(0.002)	(0.005)	(0.002)	(0.088)
INT_{t-1}	−1.657***	0.114***	−0.075***	0.037**	−0.020***	−0.248
	(0.027)	(0.007)	(0.003)	(0.015)	(0.006)	(0.170)
$RGDPG_{t-1}$	−1.361***	1.347***	−0.041***	−0.012	−0.013	−1.306***
	(0.073)	(0.016)	(0.006)	(0.030)	(0.011)	(0.453)
$LOG.LRE_{t-1}$	0.320	−0.161**	0.039	0.863***	−0.002	−0.921*
	(0.213)	(0.070)	(0.033)	(0.038)	(0.019)	(0.493)
$LOG.LOAN_{t-1}$	0.598***	0.175***	−0.107***	0.075**	0.990***	0.108
	(0.126)	(0.057)	(0.025)	(0.035)	(0.014)	(0.431)
CAR_{t-1}	0.080***	−0.006	−0.003	−0.005	−0.001	0.768***
	(0.017)	(0.006)	(0.002)	(0.004)	(0.002)	(0.055)

Note: *,**,*** denote significance at 10%, 5% and 1% levels. Standard errors in brackets.

2

Does Forward Guidance Matter in Small Open Economies? Examples from Europe

Jakub Rybacki[*♣]

[♣]Collegium of Economic Analysis, SGH Warsaw School of Economics

---

ABSTRACT: The effect of forward guidance on interest rate expectations in small, open economies is often described as heterogeneous. There are examples when financial markets adjusted term structure to reflect interest rate forecasts provided in the projections published by the central banks. On the other hand, medium-term expectations can persistently deviate from trajectories presented by decision-makers, influenced by foreign monetary policy. Our aim is to find the maximal forecast horizon where the domestic forward guidance of local banks in European economies affects market interest rate expectations strongly as compared to the ECB policy. We analyzed the term structure of interest rates in Sweden, Norway, and the Czech Republic. Central banks in these three economies provide the most mature forward guidance, e.g., regularly publishing interest rate forecasts with detailed discussions. The three-month interbank rate path calculated with the Nelson-Siegel model was contrasted with both the trajectory of policy rates presented in central bank projections and that implied by the three-month EURIBOR. We found that interest rate expectations were more influenced by ECB policy than by domestic assumptions when the forecast horizon exceeds four quarters.

Keywords: forward guidance, interest rate projections, Nelson-Siegel model, Diebold-Mariano test

[*]Corresponding Author. Email: jr70663@sgh.waw.pl

Introduction

In the aftermath of the subprime crisis, major central banks were forced to stimulate the economy with unconventional policies after achieving an effective lower bound on interest rates. In order to lower yields on financial instruments with longer duration (e.g. Treasury Bonds), policymakers responded with greater transparency in communicating their assumptions about the term structure of interest rates to market participants. Despite solid theoretical support (e.g., Eggertsson and Woodford, 2003), the effects of the new tools were mixed (Swanson, 2017).

The subject literature describes a problem termed the *forward guidance puzzle* (Giannoni et al., 2015). The introduction of forward guidance policy was accompanied by high confidence of monetary authorities e.g. in the United States or the Eurozone. Theoretical dynamic stochastic general equilibrium (DSGE) models overestimated the response of the output gap and inflation related to interest rate expectations shocks. This class of models predicts rapid expansion of activity, when interest rate expectations are anchored below the natural rate level.

Empirical evidence showed neither the full adjustment of markets interest rate expectations to the levels declared by the monetary authorities nor strong macroeconomic feedback. Policymakers' declarations of no policy change in the two-year horizon failed to lower yields on instruments with a duration greater than five years (Swanson, 2017). Communication policies has only modest positive effects on long-term interest rate. Introduction of the forward guidance by Fed lowered sensitivity of rate expectations to economic surprises and market volatility (e.g., Raskin, 2013).

The problem of managing expectations is much more complex in small, open economies. Central banks are required to account for real exchange rates in their reaction function (Ball, 1999). They cannot anchor interest rate expectations at a lower or higher level than the leading bank in the region without consequences for foreign exchange rates. In order to lower long term interest rates, monetary authorities need to convince the markets that the currency should systematically depreciate.

Our hypothesis states that market expectations regarding exchange rates and interest rates are not that flexible. Therefore, the term structure should adapt only to short-term central bank commitments (e.g., in the horizon up to one year) and not to long-term ones. Market expectations about interest rates in the longer horizon should, rather, converge toward the expected rates set by the central banks of the leading economies in a region.

Our goal is to find if there exists some common horizon in three European economies, when expectations about ECB policy become predominant over domestic forward guidance in navigating market expectations about future short-term interest rates (e.g., after six quarters or two years). The research outcome should help design communication policies for the central banks, which so far have not applied forward guidance and do not provide regular information about policymakers' expectations (i.e., with publication of a monetary policy report). The outcome of this analysis is important as credible forward guidance is expected to lower the cost of money by exhausting the risk premia related to uncertainty about policymakers' future decisions (e.g., Campbell et al., 2012).

We conducted our investigation based on market expectations regarding developments of three-month interbank rates in three European economies: Norway, Sweden, and the Czech Republic. Central banks in these selected countries provide the most mature forward guidance worldwide. Their inflation reports are published least frequently on a quarterly basis and contain forecasts with fan chart projections and detailed discussions about changes in the projections.

We analyzed market expectations regarding central bank policies using the following methodology. Implied future interest rates were derived from the market interest rate swap curve using the Nelson-Siegel model (Diebold and Li, 2006). The actual increases or decreases in these future interest rates were contrasted with changes in the policy rates in the local central bank projections and with changes in the three-month interbank rate expectations in the Eurozone (also calculated using the Nelson-Siegel approach).

We found limited impact of domestic forward guidance on market expectations based on the entire period considered in the research (2007-2018). The conclusion changes after 2012, when financial market started to play greater attention to central banks' communication. We found that Eurozone monetary policy played a superior role for horizons of six quarters or more, whereas domestic forward guidance played a superior role only in the short horizon (less than four quarters).

This paper is structured as follows. The next section reviews the literature analyzing the effectiveness of forward guidance in a small, open economy. Section 2 briefly discusses interest rate forecasts published by the central banks in Europe. Section 3 presents the research methodology. Section 4 describes the results of the analysis. Section 5 concludes the paper.

1 Literature Review

In this section, we present findings of research on forward guidance in small economies. The expected benefit from implementing this new communication policy is, due to greater transparency, the exhaustion of the risk premia related to uncertainty about rate policy. But even on the theoretical front, there is no accepted consensus on the optimal scope of monetary policy transparency in an open economy. The optimal communication policy should, to the greatest extent, help execute the statutory mandate of central banks, e.g., by anchoring inflation expectations at the targeted level.

The literature does not provide evidence that the publishing of interest rate forecasts by the central banks improves the predictability of monetary policy, e.g., inflation, interest rates, etc., for market participants (Rudebusch and Williams, 2008). Furthermore, the policy could have negative consequences: the major risks include miscommunication (i.e., treating commitment as unconditional by public opinion) and overconfidence in the central bank forecasts relative to other sources of information.

The empirical literature describes the effect of forward guidance on market rates in small economies as heterogeneous. Svensson (2015) described experiences of Sweden and New Zealand. This author pointed out that market expectations converged directly to the Swedish Riksbank projections during the phase of lowering the policy rate in 2009. Yet, in the period 2011-2012, the Swedish central bank frequently failed to push market expectations. Markets did not believe in the rapid tightening of monetary conditions announced by the Riksbank's executive board. The experiences of the Reserve Bank of New Zealand (RBNZ) were less discouraging, although its projections sometimes misled the markets regarding the scale of interest rate changes, i.e., central bank behavior was different than stated in the previous projection, despite no significant macroeconomic surprises.

Quantitative event studies confirm that publishing new projections drives market expectations. However, these studies also report significant problems with convergence of the term structure to the trajectory expected by monetary authorities. Brubakk et al. (2017) employed the Gürkaynak et al. (2005, further termed as GSS) framework to identify the effects of publishing new interest rate projections in Sweden. The proposed method decomposed monetary policy shocks into surprises related to the present level of policy rates and expectations about their future trajectory. The authors presented evidence that shifts in the policy path expected by the executive board are positively correlated with changes in market expectations, yet major moves typically occur prior to the publication of a new report.

In their study of New Zealand, Detmers and Nautz (2012) provided evidence that interest rate projections only have a significant impact on short-term market rates. Based on a method similar to GSS, the authors also highlighted the weakening effect of forward guidance during the global financial crisis when major rate moves actually occurred. Interestingly, Detmers and Nautz concluded that shortening rate projections to one year would be the most desirable policy because the long-term projections were more likely to destabilize, rather than pinpoint, expectations.

Other studies reflect the failures of forward guidance to affect market consensus forecasts. There is strong evidence that forward guidance fails to improve the predictability of interest rates. Kool and Thornton (2015) reported no change in the unconditional forecast error of the market consensus median after the introduction of forward guidance in Sweden and Norway (with New Zealand as an exception). The performance of predictions in these countries was not different from the random walk process. Furthermore, economies where central banks do not communicate their future policies achieved similar forecast errors for short-term interest rates. These findings were confirmed by Jain and Sutherland (2018), who also highlighted no reduction in disagreement between forecasters on their projections of the future interest rate path. The single benefit of communicating future expected policy rates was a lower frequency of interest rates forecasts revisions, compared to the period prior to introducing forward guidance (Winkelmann, 2016).

The literature provides a solid description of the forward guidance effects on consensus forecasts and the yields curve. On the other hand, the economic research seems to be silent on the impact of foreign policy spillovers on the effectiveness of local forward guidance, even though it is clear that international monetary policy spillovers affect the behavior of local banks in small, open economies (e.g., Gajewski et al., 2018). Therefore, it seems reasonable to analyze how the monetary policies of leading central banks in the region influence the effectiveness of local forward guidance. Before introducing the methodology of our research, we will briefly discuss the content of the inflation reports in selected economies.

2 A Brief History of Forward Guidance in Small Economies

This section summarizes the data used in this research and presents a brief history of the publishing of policy rate projections in inflation reports by central banks worldwide. The concept of expectations management with forward guidance through interest rate projections became popular in the academic literature after the U.S. Federal Reserve introduced *dot-plot* charts of future policy rates and expressed the macroeconomic conditions required to increase interest rates in 2012. A *dot-plot* is a chart reflecting interest rate forecasts for the next three years and the long run as provided by each individual Federal Open Market Committee's (FOMC) member. It remains one of the policy tools used today.

However, the history of navigating financial market expectations through projection rates published by central banks goes back much further. In 1997, the RBNZ introduced the market interest rate as one of the projected variables it publishes on a quarterly basis. At the beginning, the bank presented forecasts for the 90-day interbank rate. Then it forecasted the official cash rate (OCR) directly set by monetary authorities. Despite the long history of forward guidance in New Zealand, we decided not to analyze the RBNZ case, as its policy is affected by the decisions of three central banks (U.S. Federal Reserve, Reserve Bank of Australia, and People's Bank of China). Accounting for all three foreign central banks would significantly complicate our analysis.

Our paper is focused on Europe and interactions with the European Central Bank (ECB). Amongst central banks in this region, Norges Bank was the first to start publishing its forecasts, which it did in 2005. The first releases contained projections of annual indicators. The project achieved maturity in 2009 when a fan chart with quarterly forecasts was introduced. The key policy rate in this economy describes the interest rate on banks' reserves up to a specified quota. The projection contains forecasts for approximately the next three-year window-i.e., the next 12 to 16 quarters, depending on the publication period.

The idea of publishing policy rate forecasts has swiftly found followers. In 2007, policy rate projections were introduced by the Sveriges Riksbank and the Bank of Israel (BoI). From the beginning, Swedish authorities have been publishing detailed fan charts with quarterly forecasts of average policy rates in a given quarter. The Swedish policy rate defines the cost of borrowing or depositing funds at the Riksbank for a period of seven days. Forecasts for the next 12 to14 quarters are presented.

The policy of the BoI is less transparent. Even today, the BoI provides only annual indicators. The bank's macroeconomic forecast report contains fan charts with quarterly indicators (including bank rate), yet the data are not publicly available. For this reason, from among the above-mentioned central banks, only the Scandinavian ones are deeply scrutinized in this paper. The strong motivation for our policy analysis of the two Scandinavian economies also comes from their deep interlinkages with the Eurozone.

Finally, the Czech National Bank (CNB) has been publishing projected market and policy rates since 2008 (the sole country in Central Europe to do so). Similar to the RBNZ approach, the first projections were dedicated to interbank interest rates (initially PRIBOR1Y, then PRIBOR3M). The bank started publishing forecasts for two-week repo rates directly set by monetary authorities (presented as a quarterly average) in 2013. The CNB publishes a decomposition of factors affecting interest rate projections, including expert judgments. The projection window of the CNB is much shorter than that of the Scandinavian central banks. The trajectory for the next 7 to 10 quarters is forecasted.

Our aim is to examine whether expectations of the future policy rate path derived from the interbank rates of the STIBOR, NIBOR, and PRIBOR (up to 12-months) and swap rates in those economies (longer tenors) are converging closer to the trajectories forecasted by the national central banks, rather than to the shape of the Eurozone yield curve expected by markets. We use changes in swap rates to measure market reactions to monetary policy shocks because those instruments do not contain a substantial credit risk premium (only interest, no capital is transferred) or accrued interest related to coupon payments. Therefore, interest rate swap prices should more accurately reflect the perception of interest rate risk.

3 Methodology

The aim of this section is to present the methodology of our research. Our goal is to analyze whether the expected change in short-term interest rates in a small economy (derived from the current yield curve) is better predicted by the national central bank's forward guidance or by a similarly defined shift in expectations regarding ECB policy.

The first step in our analysis was to approximate the yield curve with the standard Nelson-Siegel (NS) formula for daily data readings. Realized interest rates were transformed to logarithmic form. We used the following equation to represent the NS model (Diebold and Li, 2006):

$$R_t(m) = \beta_{1,t} + \beta_{2,t} \cdot \left(\frac{1 - e^{-\varphi_t \cdot m}}{\varphi_t \cdot m}\right) + \beta_{3,t} \cdot \left(\frac{1 - e^{-\varphi_t \cdot m}}{\varphi_t \cdot m} - e^{-\varphi_t \cdot m}\right), \tag{1}$$

where R_t denotes the interbank interest rate or the swap rate for a term of m months at time t. $\beta_{1,t}$, $\beta_{2,t}$, and $\beta_{3,t}$ are the weights of the three estimated latent dynamic factors. The decay parameter (φ_t) was set to 0.0609, in line with recommendations in the literature (Diebold and Li, 2006). The beta parameters were estimated using the ordinary least squares method.

Our aim was to use estimated parameters in an event study. We focused on observations directly following the publication of inflation and/or monetary policy reports by the three central banks of interest (Riksbank, Norges Bank, and Czech National Bank). For example, if the monetary policy report was published by one of these central banks on December 15, we used interest rate data for December 16 (the next trading day). We assume that after one day the financial markets should be able to price in all information from interest rate projections and at the same time, the risk that market participants' expectations would be changed by other events (e.g., economic surprises) is minimized. Calculations were conducted independently for each central bank.

Based on the yield curve estimates, we computed bootstrapped three-month interbank forward rates for the next h months ($h = 3$, 6, 9 etc.) to mimic market expectations of future policy paths.[1] We decided to use the three-month tenor as it is the most commonly forecasted by private entities, as well as being used in the surveys of professional forecasters provided by various central banks. Furthermore, it mostly prices expectations related only to the outcome of the most recent Monetary Policy Council (MPC) or executive board meetings. In recent

[1]The term *bootstrapping* in this paper refers to the financial meaning of this word, i.e., implying current expectations about interest rates in the future, using the information about term structure. *Bootstrapping* also has a different statistical meaning describing inference based on randomly selected subsamples. Such analyses, however, were not carried out as part of this work.

years, central banks in developed economies have preferred to use a gradual approach during policy tightening, linking important decisions with publications of monetary policy reports (usually provided on a quarterly basis). Using longer (e.g., two-year) tenors would require us to decompose changes in interest rates into two factors: the effect directly dedicated to MPC decisions in the forecast horizon, and the effects of changes in the yield curve after subsequent meetings. We used the following formula to bootstrap forward interest rates expected at time t (Rubaszek, 2016):

$$R_{t,3m}{}^{f}(h) = \frac{(3+h)\cdot R_t(3+h) - h\cdot R_t(h)}{h}. \tag{2}$$

$R_{t,3m}{}^{f}(h)$ is a bootstrapped three-month forward rate computed for the period h months after time t (i.e., the day directly following the publication of an inflation report). $R_t(m)$ is the current m-month short-term rate implied by the NS model (based on parameters estimated with equation 1). For example, to compute the three-month rate one quarter after the December 15, 2016 publication of the monetary policy report, we would need to input the spot six-month rate $R_{t=2016/12/16}(3+3)$ and the spot three-month rate $R_{t=2016/12/16}(3)$ into equation (2).

The central banks' inflation projections typically provide forecasts of an average policy rate or a short-term interbank rate in the next quarters. To provide a consistent estimate of market expectations, we set the forecast horizon h to the middle of the quarter corresponding to the central bank projections. For example, when a central bank provides a policy rate projection for the first quarter of the year, the horizon date h is set to be February 15; for the second quarter, h equals May 15, etc.

We used the following formula to calculate the expected change in the three-month market interest rate between the horizon date h and the day t following publication of the inflation report:

$$\Delta R_{t,3m}{}^{f}(h) = R_{t,3m}{}^{f}(h) - R_{t,3m}{}^{f}(0). \tag{3}$$

Calculations presented in formulas (1), (2), and (3) were also repeated for the Eurozone three-month EURIBOR to derive expected changes between the period $t+h$ and t. All calculations were done for the periods when central banks published monetary policy reports in these tree economies (Sweden, Norway, and the Czech Republic). We also calculated the shift in the local central bank projections, $\Delta R_{t,3m,projection}{}^{f}(h)$, using formula (3).

We directly compare changes in the money market rate in small, open economies with changes in the policy rate in the respective central bank projections and with similarly defined changes in the Eurozone interbank rates. Calculations are described by the following equations:

$$\begin{array}{l} e_{1,t}(h) = \Delta R_{t,3m,interbank}{}^{f}(h) - \Delta R_{t,3m,projection}{}^{f}(h) \\ e_{2,t}(h) = \Delta R_{t,3m,interbank}{}^{f}(h) - \Delta R_{t,3m,ECBrates}{}^{f}(h) \end{array}, \tag{4}$$

where $\Delta R_{t,3m,interbank}{}^{f}(h)$ denotes the expected change in the three-month interbank rate in the small economy h months on from time t. $\Delta R_{t,3m,projection}{}^{f}(h)$ describes the shift in a policy rate (or an interbank rate if applicable) in the central bank projections. Finally, the $\Delta R_{t,3m,ECBrates}{}^{f}(h)$ is the expected change in the bootstrapped three-month EURIBOR, based on a similarly defined NS model h months on from time t.

In order to verify which trajectory has a greater impact on rate expectations, we calculate root mean squared error statistics (i.e., RMSE) and the results of the two-sided and one-sided Diebold-Mariano (DM) tests (Diebold and Mariano, 1995; Harvey et al., 1997). The RMSE formulas are given as follows:

$$\begin{cases} RMSE_{projection}(Q) = \sqrt{\frac{\Sigma_{t=1}^{n}(\Delta R_{t,3m,interbank}{}^{f}(Q) - \Delta R_{t,3m,projection}{}^{f}(Q))^2}{n}} \\ RMSE_{ECBrates}(Q) = \sqrt{\frac{\Sigma_{t=1}^{n}(\Delta R_{t,3m,interbank}{}^{f}(Q) - \Delta R_{t,3m,ECBrates}{}^{f}(Q))^2}{n}} \end{cases} \tag{5}$$

where the numerator contains one of the error series calculated using formula (4) and n is the number of observations in the available sample. To highlight our interest in quarterly forecasts, we used index Q instead of h.

We define $Q1$ as the period following the quarter when the inflation report containing forward guidance was published, $Q2$ as the next quarter afterward, and so on. For example, if the document was published in February, the middle day of the second quarter of the year (April-June) will be denoted as $Q1$, and the middle day of the third quarter (July-September) as $Q2$. Based on prediction errors, we calculated the DM test statistics.

The basic DM test assumes calculation of differentials between two error series. We use symmetrical squared-error loss transformations. The differential (d) formula is presented in equation (6):

$$d = g(e_{1t}) - g(e_{2t}), \qquad g(e_{it}) = e_{it}^2 \tag{6}$$

The null hypothesis states that the expected value of the differential is zero, implying a similar accuracy of forecasts. We provide results of both one-sided and two-sided tests. The alternative hypothesis for the one-sided test particularly points out which forecast is better (either domestic central bank projection or term structure describing market expectations regarding ECB policy). In the case of two-sided test alternative test states only that the predictive accuracy between these two sources is different. Test statistics were computed with the Harvey et al. (1997) correction for small samples. The formula is given as follows:

$$\text{HLNDM} = \sqrt{\frac{T + 1 - 2h + h \cdot (h-1)}{T}} \cdot \frac{d}{V(d)} \tag{7}$$

where T denotes sample size, h the forecast horizon, and $V(d)$ is an estimate of variance related to the differential d. The HLNDM statistic has a normal distribution under the null hypothesis, implying equal precision of forecasts.

4 Estimation Results

In this section, we present the expected changes in short-term interest rates derived with the methodology described above. We also calculate root mean squared error statistics (RMSE) from predictions regarding interest rate changes Q quarters ahead for each central bank as well as DM test statistics.

Calculations were performed on two different samples: 1) the full sample with all available quarterly observations (starting from 2007 in Sweden, 2009 in Norway, and 2008 in the Czech Republic), and 2) the subsample of quarterly observations starting from late 2012–the date corresponding to the introduction of the dot-plot by the U.S. Federal Reserve and the publication of the pioneering article written by Campbell et al. (2012) highlighting the importance of navigating markets through transparent communication of future rates. Although these two events did not explicitly change the behavior of central banks in Scandinavia or the Czech Republic, we argue that market attention to published forecasts has increased as this type of communication has become widespread amongst central banks. Therefore, we expect the projections become more relevant to the investors' decisions from 2012 onward. Both samples end in May 2018.

Sweden

The first country analyzed is Sweden. The expected change in the three-month STIBOR through time (11 quarters), the corresponding change in policy rate in the Riksbank projections, and the corresponding expected change in the EURIBOR 3M are presented in Figure 1. The largest changes in interest rate levels, which also imply a greater volatility, occur in cases of instruments with longer maturity. The standard deviation of expectations increases with the forecast horizon and becomes greatest at the longest Q11 horizon. Therefore, sensitivity of interest rate changes does not differ from patterns reported by Gürkaynak et al. (2005); there is no visible volatility reduction as reported, for example, by Raskin (2013) for the U.S. economy.

There are three significant episodes in the discussed period (2007-2018). First, the Riksbank projections successfully managed expectations during the financial crisis of 2008-2009, although the forward guidance to a great extent mirrored the behavior of the Eurozone yield curve over that time frame. Second, the central bank failed to convince the markets in late 2011 and 2012 that financial tightening of monetary policy was likely to occur in the two-year horizon. Market expectations in Sweden have most likely adapted to those observed in the Eurozone. Finally, during 2015 and 2016, the Swedish market expected a steeper yield curve than given by the Riksbank projections, again following expectations about the Eurozone policy. Shift in expectation did not occur, despite the central bank using large scale asset purchases (LSAP). Thus, the use of other unconventional instruments did not trimmed expectations for rate hikes.

Based on the RMSE statistics, the change in the policy rate derived from the Riksbank projections turned out to be a less accurate predictor of Sweden's interbank rate term structure than changes in the Eurozone yield curve for every forecast horizon. We interpret this as evidence that expectations about local interest rates tend to converge to market assumptions regarding changes in global monetary policy. Especially in the medium term (more than one year), coordination between central banks' decisions is expected (see, e.g., Taylor (2013)). The results of the RMSE calculations are presented in Figure 2 and in Table 1.

Underperformance of Riksbank rate projections in relation to Eurozone market expectations is visible in both selected samples. However, the RMSE statistics were significantly lower from 2012 onward as interest rate volatility diminished, compared with the period directly following the Lehman Brothers collapse (2008-2010). In 2008 and 2009, the Riksbank initially projected further rate hikes, then benign cuts. Instead, much greater policy easing was delivered.

The results of the DM test confirm that the Riksbank's interest rate projections in general provided less accurate guidance for local interest rates than the expectations regarding the EURIBOR increase (Table 2). Statistically significant outcomes are visible in the very short (up to two-quarter) and far (beyond two-year) horizons.

The results change for the period when major central banks put greater emphasis on communication. In the 2012-2018 period, the investigated projections have similar powers of steering local market interest rates for the first six-quarter horizons. For longer horizons, the rate expectations converge toward the path followed by the Eurozone interest rate swap curve.

Norway

The next country analyzed is Norway. The expected change in the three-month NIBOR calculated with the NS model, the change in policy rate in the Norges Bank projection, and the corresponding change in the three-month EURIBOR are presented in Figure 3.

In contrast with Sweden, the greatest deviation of expectations in Norway occurs in the forecast horizon of seven to eight quarters. There were two major events worth mentioning: Lehman Brothers collapse and monetary easing during 2014-2016 periods.

The Norges Bank made a major communication mistake after the Lehman Brothers collapse: projections assumed tightening, while market expectations priced imminent rate cuts by 200 bp. Therefore, discrepancy between market participants and policymakers interest rates expectations reached the historically highest level.

Incorrect decisions of the central bank could result from the backward-looking approach to the major inflation index increase i.e. CPI-ATE. which describes consumer prices dynamics adjusted for tax changes and shifts in cost of energy products. In 2007 mentioned index overshoot both central bank target and 90% confidence interval of macroeconomic projections. Monetary authorities likely were afraid of an another surprise in a row. Norges Bank also underestimated the financial crisis effects.

For further information, please see the text boxes titled *Evaluation of the projections for 2008* in Norges Bank (2009) and *Changes in the interest rate path* in Norges Bank (2008). We excluded observations from December 2008 from the RMSE calculations so as not to distort the final conclusions.

Finally, the Norges Bank tended to provide forecasts of a much flatter yield curve compared to the interbank expectations during the 2014-2016 period. However, the Norwegian central bank failed to convince the markets as stronger rate increases in the Eurozone were priced by bond investors.

Research on the Norges Bank policy revealed similar results to those from Sweden. Based on the RMSE statistics, Norway's central bank projections have a lower predictive accuracy than the ECB rate expectations after exceeding the six-quarter horizon in both time frames. Taking into account the period of 2009-2018, the Norges Bank projections seem to have systematically worse guidance compared with the Eurozone expected interest rate fluctuations over all the forecast horizons (Table 3, Figure 4a). This likely resulted from an overestimated tightening pace after communication mistakes prior to the Lehman Brothers collapse. The Norway central bank projected further rate hikes before the U.S. recession, but it instead delivered cuts afterward. On the other hand, during the more recent period (2012-2018), the Norges Bank projections outperformed ECB expectations in the short-term horizon (up to four quarters). The possible reason for the change is the increase in the importance of forecasts published by the central bank; however, the methodology used in this study does not allow us to answer this question.

As in the Swedish case, the DM tests for Norway indicate a similar accuracy when changes in the Norges Bank policy rate (in the projection) and the expectations regarding EURIBOR rates were compared in the full sample. The hypothesis of equal accuracy is not rejected at the $\alpha = 0.05$ confidence level (Table 4).

Shortening the sample to the 2012-2018 period leads to the same conclusion for Norway as for Sweden. One-sided DM tests indicate a greater performance of domestic central bank projections in the two-quarter ahead horizon (yet at a higher confidence level, $\alpha = 0.1$). On the other hand, market expectations regarding changes in the ECB policy perform better for horizons longer than six quarters. Both two-sided and one-sided tests reject the null hypothesis for Q8-Q11 forecast horizons.

The Czech Republic (Czechia)

Finally, we analyzed the case of the Czech Republic, qualified as a European emerging economy according to the MSCI or JP Morgan bond indices. The projections presented by the executive board of the Czech National Bank (CNB) have shorter horizons as compared to their Scandinavian peers. The balanced panel consists of forecasts for up to six quarters ahead.

The interest rate forecasts in the CNB projections are much more volatile compared to its Scandinavian peers. Similar to Norway, the Czech central bank projected more excessive tightening compared to financial market expectations after the 2008 financial crisis and an overly accommodative trajectory during the 2013-2015 period. Detailed information is provided in Figure 5.

Taking into account all the available history, the CNB projections generate larger errors than predictions derived from market interest rate swap instruments in the euro currency. The projection errors fell after 2012 (see Table 5, Figure 6). The central bank's forward guidance outperforms the foreign policy impact in the first three-quarter window in the sample covering the period 2012-2018.

Similar to the cases of the Norges Bank and Riksbank, the DM test indicates that interest rate projection accuracy does not divert strongly from the ECB expectations after 2012. The p-value for the null hypothesis drops regularly with longer forecast horizons (for 6 quarters ahead it is equal to 0.09) when the alternative hypothesis states that the ECB interest rate changes are more accurate in predicting the changes of the local yield curve than the forward guidance.

5 Conclusions

Based on the examples of Sweden, Norway, and the Czech Republic, we find very limited evidence that forward guidance in small and open economies persistently provides solid indication of expected changes in the market rate term structure. The investigation based on the shorter sample (2012-2018) suggests that the communication policy is effective in a horizon shorter than four quarters and neutral in the horizon of another additional two quarters. Commitments with a longer time horizon seem to be unproductive.

Expectations for longer tenors (above two years) are more likely to converge toward the shape of market rates in the Eurozone. This implies lower effectiveness of the expectation management policies used by the small open economy central banks compared to leading regional peers like the U.S. Federal Reserve or European Central Bank. In order to affect longterm interest rates (e.g., 10-year government bonds), central banks are required to mix the forward guidance policy with a strong impulse from alternative unconventional instruments, i.e., large-scale asset purchases. Implementation of such policies is subject to adverse economic risk resulting from distortion of market structure, e.g., an increased propensity to debt issuance by non-financial enterprises after introducing a corporate asset purchase program, and credit risk problems (see Klein, 2017).

Evidence from Norway, and to some extent from the Czech Republic, for the period 2012-2018 suggests the superior role of local monetary authorities only for short-term (less than one year) interest rates. This confirms the conclusions of Detmers and Nautz (2012) regarding the optimal duration of forward guidance (four quarters). In our results, the explanatory power of central bank projections was similar to the trajectory of predictions based on the euro yield curve in the forecast horizons up to six quarters ahead. Afterward, the latter factor played a superior role. The response of financial investors to central bank communications seems to be focused mainly on the prediction for forthcoming policy meetings (e.g., in the next six months).

Finally, the relevance of the central banks' forward guidance is likely to be different during periods of financial stress. We found that our test conclusions changed when managing interest rate expectations gained popularity in the major central banks (from 2012 onward). Test results provided no evidence of supremacy of the ECB policy when the samples were extended to the period directly following the Lehman Brothers collapse. This observation may imply a significant role for central banks in directing market expectations during turning points of business cycles (cf. the example of Sweden discussed by Svensson (2015)). Future policy events will surely provide more evidence to verify this hypothesis.

References

Ball, L. M. (1999). *Monetary policy rules*, chapter Policy rules for open economies., pages 127–156. National Bureau of Economic Research, Inc.

Brubakk, L., ter Ellen, S., and Xu, H. (2017). Forward guidance through interest rate projections: does it work? Working Paper 2017/6, Norges Bank.

Campbell, J., Evans, C., Fisher, J., and Justiniano, A. (2012). Macroeconomic effects of Federal Reserve forward guidance. Working Paper Series WP-2012-03, Federal Reserve Bank of Chicago.

Detmers, G.-A. and Nautz, D. (2012). The Information Content of Central Bank Interest Rate Projections: Evidence from New Zealand. *The Economic Record*, 88(282):323–329.

Diebold, F. and Li, C. (2006). Forecasting the term structure of government bond yields. *Journal of Econometrics*, 130(2):337–364.

Diebold, F. and Mariano, R. (1995). Comparing Predictive Accuracy. *Journal of Business and Economic Statistics*, 13(3):253–63.

Eggertsson, G. and Woodford, M. (2003). Optimal Monetary Policy in a Liquidity Trap. NBER Working Papers 9968, National Bureau of Economic Research, Inc.

Gajewski, K., Jara, A., Kang, Y., Mok, J., Moreno, D., and Serwa, D. (2018). International spillovers of monetary policy: lessons from Chile, Korea, and Poland. NBP Working Papers 290, Narodowy Bank Polski, Economic Research Department.

Giannoni, M., Patterson, C., and Del Negro, M. (2015). The Forward Guidance Puzzle. 2015 Meeting Papers 1529, Society for Economic Dynamics.

Gürkaynak, R., Sack, B., and Swanson, E. (2005). Do Actions Speak Louder Than Words? The Response of Asset Prices to Monetary Policy Actions and Statements. *International Journal of Central Banking*, 1(1).

Harvey, D., Leybourne, S., and Newbold, P. (1997). Testing the equality of prediction mean squared errors. *International Journal of Forecasting*, 13(2):281–291.

Jain, M. and Sutherland, C. S. (2018). How Do Central Bank Projections and Forward Guidance Influence Private-Sector Forecasts? Staff working papers, Bank of Canada.

Klein, M. C. (2017). Just how much money did the ECB lose on its Steinhoff investment? *Financial Times*, December 6.

Kool, C. and Thornton, D. (2015). How Effective Is Central Bank Forward Guidance? *Review*, 97(4):303–22.

Norges Bank (2008). Monetary Policy Report 3/2008.

Norges Bank (2009). Monetary Policy Report 1/2009.

Raskin, M. (2013). The effects of the Federal Reserve's date-based forward guidance. Finance and Economics Discussion Series 2013-37, Board of Governors of the Federal Reserve System (US).

Rubaszek, M. (2016). Forecasting the Yield Curve With Macroeconomic Variables. *Econometric Research in Finance*, 1(1):1–21.

Rudebusch, G. and Williams, J. (2008). Revealing the Secrets of the Temple: The Value of Publishing Central Bank Interest Rate Projections. In *Asset Prices and Monetary Policy*, pages 247–289. National Bureau of Economic Research, Inc.

Svensson, L. (2015). Day One Keynote Address: Forward Guidance. *International Journal of Central Banking*, 11(4):19–64.

Swanson, E. (2017). Measuring the Effects of Federal Reserve Forward Guidance and Asset Purchases on Financial Markets. NBER Working Papers 23311, National Bureau of Economic Research, Inc.

Taylor, J. (2013). International monetary policy coordination: past, present and future. BIS Working Papers 437, Bank for International Settlements.

Winkelmann, L. (2016). Forward guidance and the predictability of monetary policy: a wavelet-based jump detection approach. *Journal of the Royal Statistical Society Series C*, 65(2):299–314.

Figure 1: Implied change in three-month STIBOR, three-month EURIBOR, and change of policy rate in the Riksbank projection

(1a) Change in three-month STIBOR rate implied by the Swedish swap curve (1 denotes 100 basis points[bp])

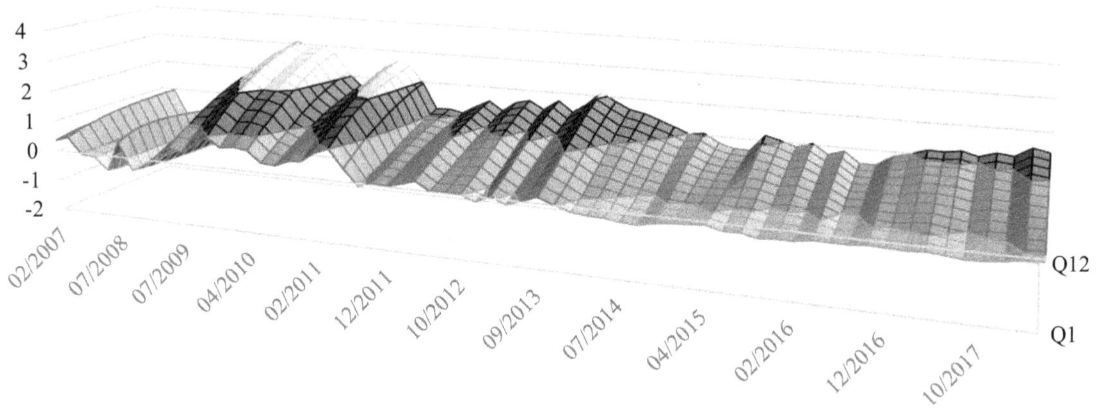

(1b) Change in policy rate in the Riksbank projections (1=100bp)

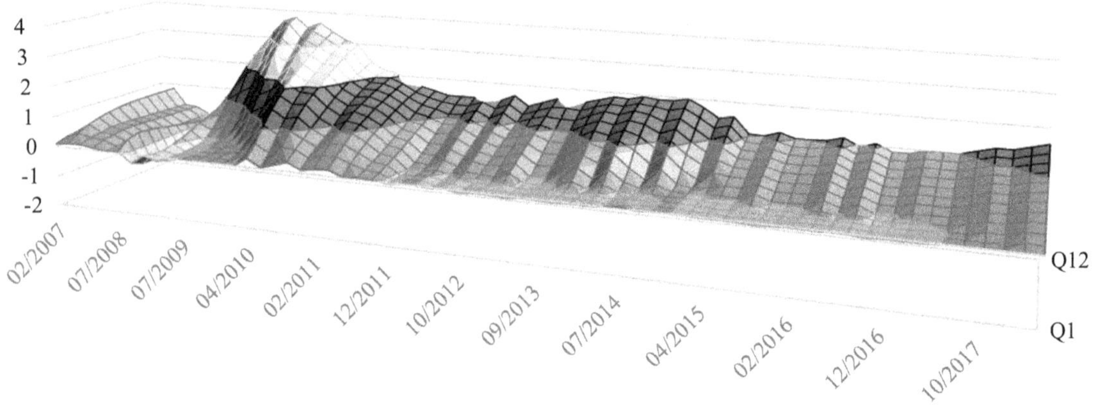

Continued on the next page

Figure 1: Implied change in three-month STIBOR, three-month EURIBOR, and change of policy rate in the Riksbank projection (Continued)

(1c) Change in three-month EURIBOR rate implied by the Eurozone swap curve (1=100bp)

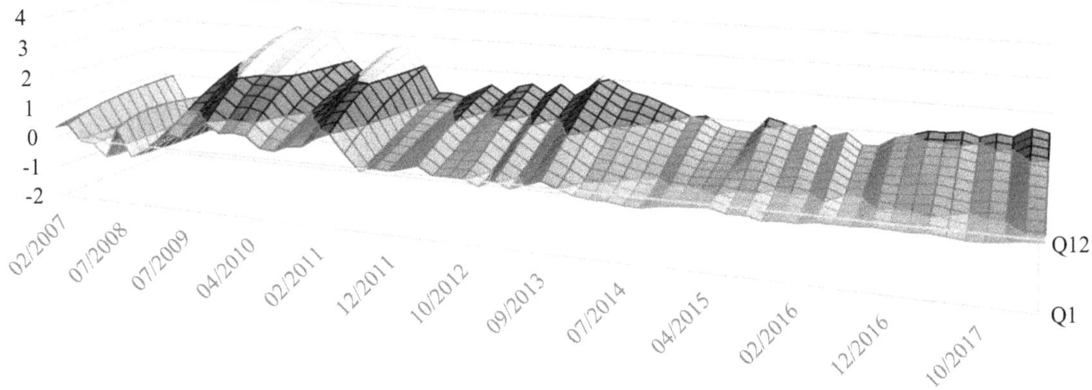

Source: Author's calculations.

Note: The chart presents the expected changes in interest rates in forthcoming quarters during the period of 2007-2018. The x-axis presents the timeframe. The y-axis presents the forecast horizon (Q1 = next quarter, Q12 = end of forecast horizon). Finally, the z-axis is the number of basis points by which interest rates are expected to increase or decrease. The aim of the graph is to visualize the similarity between market rate expectations in Sweden (panel 1) and the Riskbank projection (panel 2) or the expectations in the Eurozone (panel 3). The changes in the three-month market rates were calculated using the Nelson-Siegel model. See the methodology section for further information. The EURIBOR chart uses data corresponding to the monetary policy report publication dates. Its shape will be different for every central bank.

Figure 2: Predictive accuracy of expected change in the STIBOR three-month rate-comparison between the central bank projection and the EURIBOR3M expectations

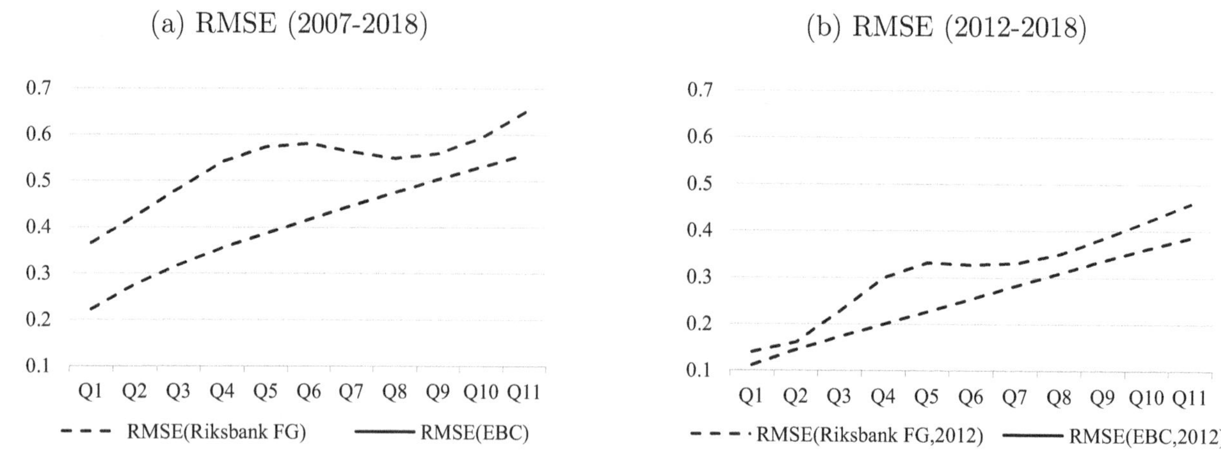

Source: Author's calculations.
Note: The dotted line denotes root mean square error statistics for central bank projections, calculated with formula (5). Error is defined as the difference between expected change in the three-month rate in Sweden and forecasted change in policy rate in the Riksbank projections. The solid line depicts similarly defined statistics, where error is defined as the difference between expected short-term rate increases in Sweden and the Eurozone (EURIBOR 3M). Q1, Q2, ... denote next forecast horizons; see the methodology section for further information.

Figure 3: Implied change in the three-month NIBOR, three-month EURIBOR, and change in policy rate in the Norges Bank projections

(3a) Change in the three-month NIBOR rate implied by the Norway swap curve (1 denotes 100 basis points [bp]).

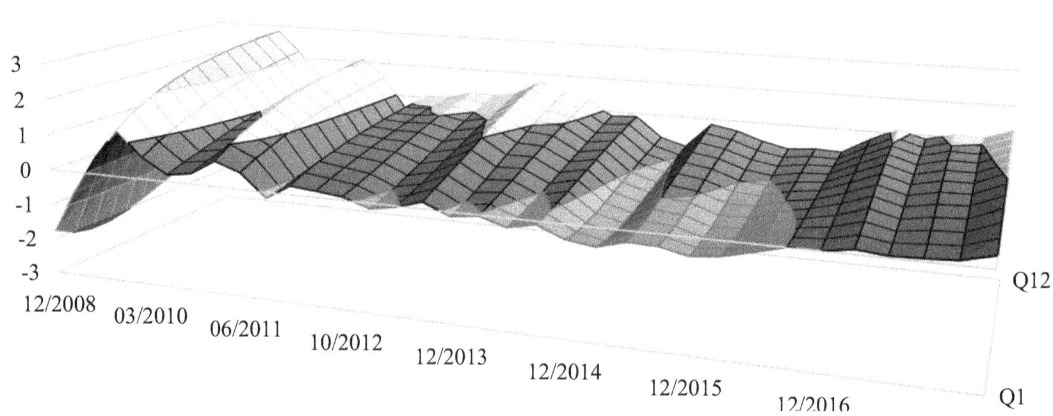

Continued on the next page

Figure 3: Implied change in the three-month NIBOR, three-month EURIBOR, and change in policy rate in the Norges Bank projections (Continued)

(3b) Change in policy rate in the Norges Bank projection (1=100bp)

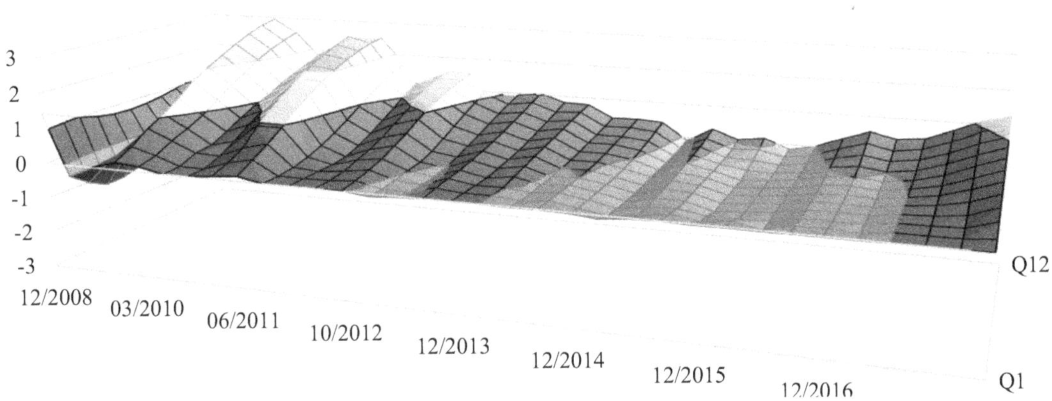

(3c) Change in the three-month EURIBOR rate implied by the Eurozone swap curve (1=100bp)

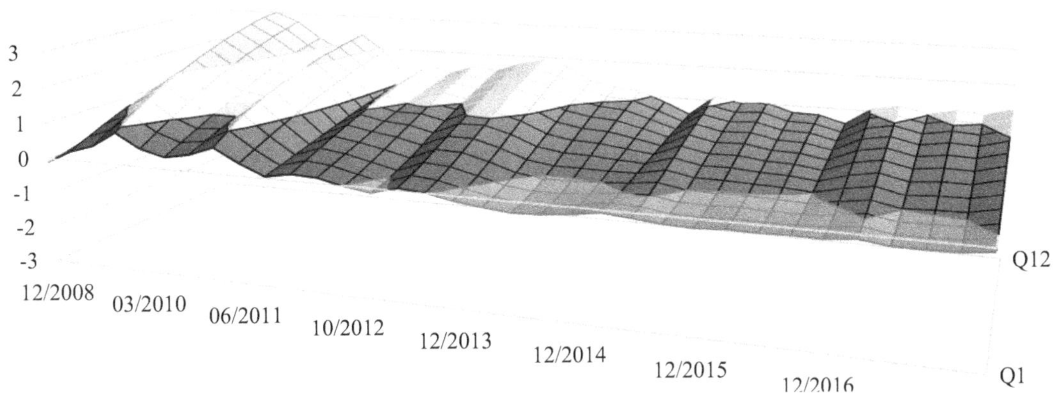

Source: Author's calculations.

Note: The chart presents the expected change in interest rates in forthcoming quarters during the period of 2008-2018. The x-axis presents the timeframe. The y-axis presents the forecast horizon (Q1 = next quarter, Q12 = end of forecast horizon). Finally, the z-axis is the number of basis points by which interest rates are expected to increase or decrease. The aim of the graph is to enable visualization of the similarity between market rate expectations in Norway (panel 1) and the Norges Bank projection (panel 2) or the expectations in the Eurozone (panel 3).
The changes in the three-month market rates were calculated using the Nelson-Siegel model. See the methodology section for further information. The EURIBOR chart uses data corresponding to the monetary policy report publication date. Its shape will be different for every central bank.

Figure 4: Predictive accuracy of expected change in the NIBOR three-month rate-comparison between central bank projection and the EURIBOR3M expectations

(a) RMSE (2009-2018) (b) RMSE (2012-2018)

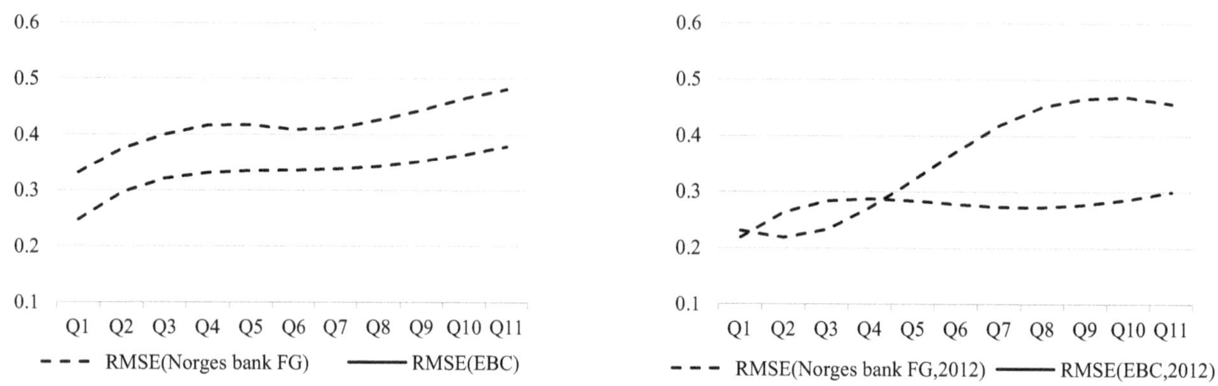

Source: Author's calculations.

Note: The dotted line denotes root mean square error statistics for central bank projections, calculated with formula (5). Error is defined as the difference between expected change on the three-month rate in Norway and forecasted change in policy rate in the Norges Bank projections. The solid line describes similarly defined statistics, where error is defined as the difference between expected short-term rate increases in Norway and the Eurozone (EURIBOR 3M). Q1, Q2, ... denote the next forecast horizons; see the methodology section for further information.

Figure 5: Implied change in the three-month PRIBOR, three-month EURIBOR, and change in policy rate in the CNB projection

(5a) Change in the three-month PRIBOR rate implied by the Czechia swap curve (1 denotes 100 basis points; further bp)

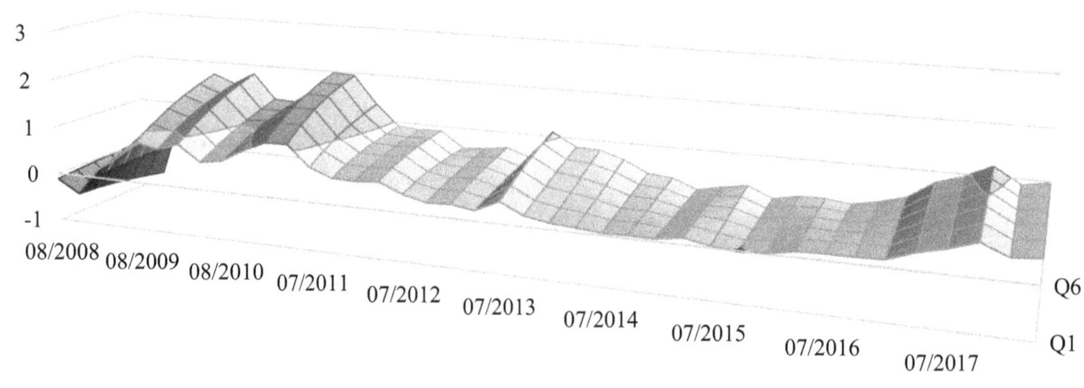

Continued on the next page

Figure 5: Implied change in the three-month PRIBOR, three-month EURIBOR, and change in policy rate in the CNB projection (Continued)

(5b) Change in policy rate in the CNB projection (1=100 bp)

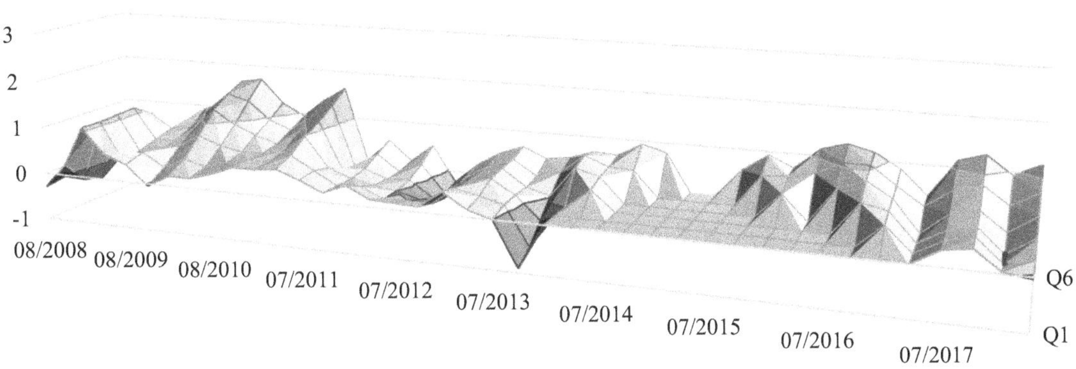

(5c) Change in the three-month EURIBOR rate implied by the eurozone swap curve (1=100 bp)

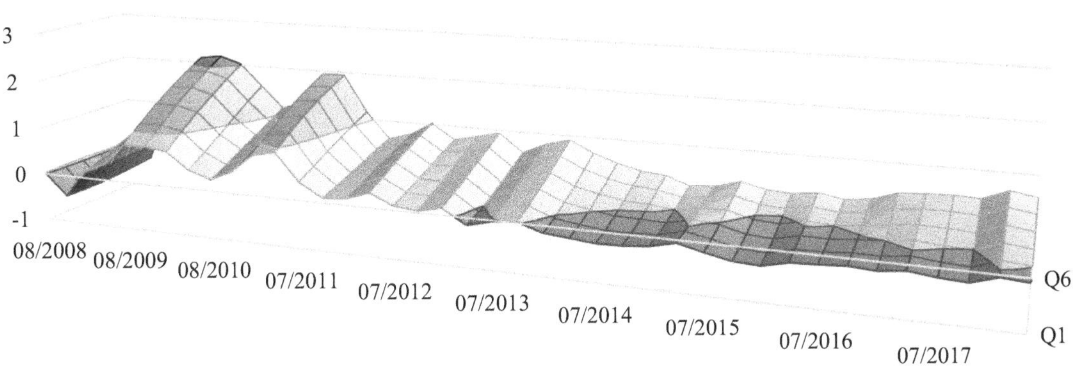

Source: Author's calculations.

Note: The chart presents the expected changes in interest rates in forthcoming quarters during the period of 2008-2018. The x-axis presents the timeframe. The y-axis presents the forecast horizon (Q1 = next quarter, Q6 = end of forecast horizon). Finally, the z-axis is the number of basis points by which interest rates are expected to increase or decrease. The aim of the graph is to enable visualization of the similarity between market rate expectations in Czechia (panel 1) and the CNB bank projection (panel 2) or the expectations in the Eurozone (panel 3).
The changes in the three-month market rates were calculated using the Nelson-Siegel model. See the methodology section for further information. The EURIBOR chart uses data corresponding to the monetary policy report publication date. Its shape will be different for every central bank.

Figure 6: Predictive accuracy of expected change in the PRIBOR three-month rate-comparison between central bank projection and the EURIBOR3M expectations

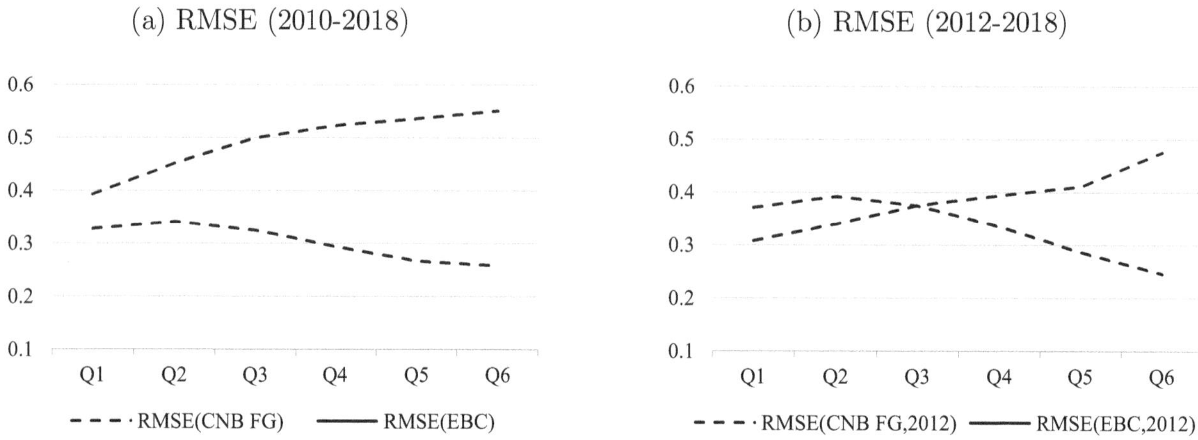

Source: Author's calculations.

Note: The dotted line denotes root mean square error statistics for central bank projections, calculated with formula (5). Error is defined as the difference between expected change in the three-month rate in Czechia and forecasted change in policy rate in CNB projections. The solid line describes similarly defined statistics, where error is defined as the difference between expected short-term rate increases in Czechia and the Eurozone (EURIBOR 3M). Q1, Q2, ... denote the next forecast horizons; see the methodology page for further information.

Table 1: Sweden - RMSE

	Q1	Q2	Q3	Q4	Q5	Q6	Q7	Q8	Q9	Q10	Q11	Q12
Timeframe: 2007.02 - 2018.6												
Riksbank projection	0.37	0.42	0.48	0.54	0.57	0.58	0.56	0.55	0.56	0.59	0.65	#N/A
ECB pol. expectations	0.22	0.28	0.32	0.35	0.39	0.42	0.45	0.48	0.50	0.53	0.56	0.58
Timeframe: 2012.10 - 2018.6												
Riksbank projection	0.14	0.16	0.23	0.30	0.33	0.33	0.33	0.35	0.38	0.42	0.46	#N/A
ECB pol. expectations	0.11	0.14	0.17	0.20	0.23	0.25	0.28	0.31	0.34	0.36	0.39	0.41

Source: Author's calculations.

Note: The table presents detailed data used to create Figure 2. See figure footnote for further information.

Table 2: Results of Mariano-Diebold test for Sweden–comparison of predictive accuracy between change in central bank projection and the EURIBOR expectations

	Q1	Q2	Q3	Q4	Q5	Q6	Q7	Q8	Q9	Q10	Q11
Timeframe: 2007.02 - 2018.6											
Diebold-Mariano test statistic	3.17	1.39	1.02	0.95	0.91	0.82	0.73	0.67	0.83	1.86	2.20
P-value: Two-sided test	0.00	0.17	0.31	0.35	0.37	0.42	0.47	0.51	0.41	0.07	0.03
P-value: One-sided test - alternative ECB less accurate	0.90	0.63	0.75	0.85	0.94	0.99	0.95	0.94	1.00	1.00	1.00
P-value: One-sided test - alternative ECB more accurate	0.00	0.09	0.16	0.17	0.18	0.21	0.24	0.25	0.21	0.03	0.02
Timeframe: 2012.10 - 2018.6											
Diebold-Mariano test statistic	1.30	0.34	0.69	1.06	1.58	2.68	1.67	1.57	2.79	4.80	4.23
P-value: Two-sided test	0.21	0.73	0.50	0.30	0.13	0.01	0.11	0.13	0.01	0.00	0.00
P-value: One-sided test - alternative ECB less accurate	0.90	0.63	0.75	0.85	0.94	0.99	0.95	0.94	1.00	1.00	1.00
P-value: One-sided test - alternative ECB more accurate	0.10	0.37	0.25	0.15	0.06	0.01	0.05	0.06	0.00	0.00	0.00

Source: Author's calculations.
Note: The test hypothesis assumes equal accuracy of both the Riksbank projection and ECB expectations. The alternative hypothesis in the two-sided test assumes a different forecasting performance. The one-sided test explicitly indicates which projections are statistically less/more accurate.

Table 3: Norway - RMSE

	Q1	Q2	Q3	Q4	Q5	Q6	Q7	Q8	Q9	Q10	Q11	Q12
Timeframe: 2009.03 - 2018.6												
Norges Bank projection	0.33	0.37	0.40	0.42	0.42	0.41	0.41	0.43	0.44	0.46	0.48	#N/A
ECB pol. expectations	0.25	0.30	0.32	0.33	0.33	0.34	0.34	0.34	0.35	0.36	0.38	0.40
Timeframe: 2012.10 - 2018.6												
Norges Bank projection	0.23	0.22	0.23	0.27	0.32	0.37	0.42	0.45	0.47	0.47	0.46	#N/A
ECB pol. expectations	0.22	0.26	0.28	0.29	0.28	0.28	0.27	0.27	0.28	0.29	0.30	0.32

Source: Author's calculations.
Note: The table presents detailed data used to create Figure 4. See figure footnote for further information.

Table 4: Results of the Mariano-Diebold test for Norway–comparison of predictive accuracy between change in central bank projection and the EURIBOR expectations.

	Q1	Q2	Q3	Q4	Q5	Q6	Q7	Q8	Q9	Q10	Q11
Timeframe: 2009.03 - 2018.6											
Diebold-Mariano test statistic	1.18	0.763	1.03	1.11	1.32	1.26	0.881	0.866	0.99	1.13	1.43
P-value: Two-sided test	0.25	0.45	0.31	0.28	0.20	0.22	0.39	0.39	0.33	0.27	0.16
P-value: One-sided test - alternative ECB less accurate	0.88	0.77	0.84	0.86	0.90	0.89	0.81	0.80	0.84	0.87	0.92
P-value: One-sided test - alternative ECB more accurate	0.12	0.23	0.16	0.14	0.10	0.11	0.19	0.20	0.17	0.13	0.08
Timeframe: 2012.10 - 2018.6											
Diebold-Mariano test statistic	0.36	-1.43	-1.09	-0.16	0.34	0.85	1.69	2.60	3.85	2.50	2.26
P-value: Two-sided test	0.72	0.17	0.29	0.88	0.74	0.41	0.11	0.02	0.00	0.02	0.03
P-value: One-sided test - alternative ECB less accurate	0.64	0.08	0.14	0.44	0.63	0.80	0.95	0.99	1.00	0.99	0.98
P-value: One-sided test - alternative ECB more accurate	0.36	0.92	0.86	0.56	0.37	0.20	0.05	0.01	0.00	0.01	0.02

Source: Author's calculations.
Note: Detailed information about the test construction is provided in Table 2.

Table 5: Czechia - RMSE calculations

	Q1	Q2	Q3	Q4	Q5	Q6	Q7	Q8	Q9	Q10	Q11	Q12
Timeframe: 2008.10 - 2018.6												
CNB projection	0.39	0.45	0.50	0.52	0.54	0.55	#N/A	#N/A	#N/A	#N/A	#N/A	#N/A
ECB pol. expectations	0.33	0.34	0.32	0.29	0.27	0.26	0.28	0.32	0.37	0.43	0.49	0.55
Timeframe: 2012.10 - 2018.6												
CNB projection	0.31	0.34	0.38	0.39	0.41	0.48	#N/A	#N/A	#N/A	#N/A	#N/A	#N/A
ECB pol. expectations	0.37	0.39	0.37	0.34	0.29	0.25	0.23	0.24	0.28	0.33	0.39	0.45

Source: Author's calculations.
Note: The table presents detailed data used to create Figure 2. See figure footnote for further information.

Table 6: Results of the Mariano-Diebold test for Czechia–comparison of predictive accuracy between change in central bank projection and the EURIBOR expectations.

	Q1	Q2	Q3	Q4	Q5	Q6
Timeframe: 2008.10 - 2018.6						
Diebold-Mariano test statistic	0.97	1.40	1.99	2.20	2.23	3.11
P-value: Two-sided test	0.34	0.17	0.05	0.03	0.03	0.00
P-value: One-sided test - alternative ECB less accurate	0.83	0.92	0.97	0.98	0.98	1.00
P-value: One-sided test - alternative ECB more accurate	0.17	0.08	0.03	0.02	0.02	0.00
Timeframe: 2012.10 - 2018.6						
Diebold-Mariano test statistic	-0.67	-0.58	0.01	0.71	0.85	1.36
P-value: Two-sided test	0.51	0.57	0.99	0.49	0.40	0.19
P-value: One-sided test - alternative ECB less accurate	0.26	0.29	0.50	0.76	0.80	0.91
P-value: One-sided test - alternative ECB more accurate	0.74	0.71	0.50	0.24	0.20	0.09

Source: Author's calculations.
Note: Detailed information about the test construction is provided in Table 2.

3

Determination of Long and Short Run Demand for Money in the West African Monetary Zone (WAMZ) Countries: A Panel Analysis

Agya Atabani Adi *♣ and **Joshua Sunday Riti** †♠

♣Federal University Wukari

♠University of Jos

ABSTRACT: This paper examines demand for real money balances in six West African countries from 1985–2014 using a panel cointegration technique. Real income and inflation rate positively affect demand for money, whereas interest rate spread, real effective exchange rate, and the U.S. real interest rate negatively affect broad money demand in the long run. Income elasticity is greater than unity in the long term and less than unity in the short term. All the variables examined are significant except effective exchange rate. Both the currency substitution and capital mobility hypotheses hold for the long run, but only the capital mobility hypothesis holds in the short run. We recommend that monetary aggregate grow more slowly than economic growth to maintain price stability. Countries should maintain a stable exchange rate and ensure a market driven interest rate policy.

Keywords: demand for money, interest rate spread, capital mobility, currency substitution, panel analysis

*Corresponding Author. Address: Department of Economics, Faculty of Humanities, Social and Management Sciences, Federal University Wukari, Taraba State, PMB 1020, Nigeria. Email: atabaniadi@yahoo.com

†Address: Department of Economics, Faculty of Social Sciences, University of Jos, Plateau State, 930001, Nigeria

Introduction

Monetary integration and adoption of indirect monetary policy instruments in economic management have brought a new paradigm shift in the formulation and implementation of monetary policy in West African countries, especially among West African Monetary Zone (WAMZ) member countries. On the one hand, regional economic corporations require monetary authorities to shift their focus from national to regional macroeconomics management. The adoption of indirect policy instruments, on the other hand, introduces market forces to regional financial markets and makes the effects of monetary policy more difficult to predict. The formulation of effective and efficient money demand functions cannot be overemphasized in the design and implementation of monetary policy in developed and developing economies alike. Disequilibrium in demand for money might undermine the effectiveness of interest rate transmission mechanisms in the long run through its effect on inflation and output in developing countries.

Concerted efforts have been devoted to this issue in the recent past due to its importance in modern macroeconomics. Despite the huge interest, research related to issues in demand for money in sub-Saharan Africa have been limited (Jenkins, 1999; Rother, 1999; Nachega, 2001; Pedroni, 2004). Understanding demand for money is a necessary, important, and significant prerequisite for the formulation of stabilization and economic adjustment programs in developing countries, where limits are set on the expansion of domestic credit to be consistent with growth in demand for money.

Policy makers and economists analyse and estimate money demand functions for at least two reasons. First, the income elasticity of money demand tells us the rate of monetary expansion that is consistent in the long run. Second, the interest elasticity of money demand allows policy makers to determine the long term welfare cost of inflation on the economy. Demand for money is considered an important instrument of stabilization policies where such policy depends on the capacity to adjust money supply to equal demand, in order to prevent monetary distortion from affecting real variables. It is believed that the relationship between money supply and income, prices, and balance of payments is determined by demand for money. This relationship plays an important role in macroeconomic issues such as economic growth, price stability, unemployment, and the balance of payments in any nation.

The efficacy of monetary policy regimes depends on the strength of monetary transmission mechanisms and the velocity of money in an economy. When these relationships are subject to unintended shifts, monetary targets lose their transparency and are less able to accurately provide signals for the appropriate stance of monetary policy. This has been the reason for the switch to inflation targeting, which does not rely on the stability of demand for money and instead uses a broad range of information to assess monetary policy stance (Mishkin, 1999).

Although many studies have been done on money demand functions in individual countries, sub-regions, and Africa as a whole, there have not been any studies done on sub-regional WAMZ countries. None of the studies used interest rate spreads other than single interest rates, which do not really capture the opportunity costs of holding real money balances. Furthermore, none of them examined currency substitution and capital mobility for the WAMZ member countries. Hence the need for this paper to shed light on this important policy tool - interest rate spread, now that these countries are moving towards homogenous monetary policy when the currency union in WAMZ countries comes alive.

This paper employs interest rate spread to examine the effect of interest rate on demand for money in the WAMZ countries, albeit with the single interest rate used in previous studies and recognizing that with financial sector deregulation and innovation, the single interest rate does not adequately capture the opportunity costs of money. We investigated empirically whether the so-called currency substitution and capital mobility hypotheses hold in this region, and determined which variable has the greater effect on real money demand. The objective was to empirically determine the plausibility of the null hypothesis that income elasticity equals unity in the short run, and whether foreign real interest rate, inflation rate, and effective real exchange rate negatively affect real money demand.

The subsequent part of this paper is structured as follows: Section 1 provides a brief review of relevant empirical research in the literature. Section 2 details the econometric methodology employed and Section 3 presents an econometric analysis of the results obtained. The last section offers some concluding remarks on our research.

1 Literature review

The subject of money demand in developing and developed countries is well documented for many different time periods. Most literature on sub-Saharan Africa indicates that money demand is stable: this view is supported by Suliman and Dafaalla (2011); Bahmani-Oskooee (2009); Hamori et al. (2008); Salisu et al. (2013). Bitrus (2011) used annual time series spanning 26 years to examine narrow and broad money, income, interest rate, exchange rate, and the stock market. He found a stable demand for money function in Nigeria, with income as the most significant determinant of demand for money. He also found that stock market instruments improved the demand for money function. Kovanen et al. (2011) adopted bounds testing procedures to test the stability of long run money demand in Ghana. They found a strong, stable long run demand for money function in spite of substantial changes in the financial markets, and deviations from equilibrium were short lived. Kumar et al. (2013) investigated the stability of money demand in Nigeria from 1960 to 2008. They employed canonical and alternative specifications by proxy for the cost of holding money. They found that the Nigerian regime shift in 1986 improved demand for money marginally, and that demand for money was stable overall. They concluded that broad money stock can be used effectively as an instrument of monetary policy. Bahmani (2008) found stable demand for money in the majority of Middle East countries. Rother (1999) analyzed demand for money across the entire West African Economic and Monetary Union (WAEMU), the six smaller member countries and Côte d'Ivoire, finding a stable aggregate money demand function in the sub-region. In contrast to the findings above, some studies indicate the instability of money demand in transition and developing countries. For example, Kararach (2002) found no evidence of a stable money demand in Uganda, and Dekle and Pradhan (1997) found money demand to be unstable in Asian countries. Tahir (1995) attributed instability of money demand functions to financial innovation leading to fundamental change in-and possibly the instability of-money demand. Similarly, Arrau et al. (1995) stated that taking financial innovation into account in money demand functions could help solve auto-correlation errors, persistent over-prediction, and incredible parameter estimate problems in money demand functions. Nell (1999) examined stable long run demand for money in South Africa using annual data spanning the period of 1965-1997. He found a stable long run money demand function for M3 in South Africa, while the M1 and M2 money demand functions showed unstable parameters after financial reforms in 1980. Nell (1999)'s results support the use of M3 money stock as the nominal anchor for the South African Reserve Bank's monetary policy.

Ogunsakin and Awe (2014) employed multivariate cointegration methods to estimate the relationship between M1, M2, and domestic inflation, gross domestic product, foreign interest rate, exchange rate, savings deposit and Treasury bill rates. There were two cointegrating vectors: income elasticity was positive and significant in the long run, and inflation, foreign interest, and domestic interest rates were statistically significant and correctly signed. The speed of adjustment was 34 percent and 56 percent for M2 and M1, respectively. They concluded that financial liberalization has not altered money demand stability and monetary aggregate remains a valuable policy instrument in Nigeria.

Tano (2011) investigated stability of money and money demand for Côte d'Ivoire, finding a long run equilibrium relationship between M1 (or M2) and its determinants – real income and expected inflation. The income elasticity with respect to M2 was 1.40 while income elasticity with respect to M1 was 0.94 (i.e. less than unity). Herve and Shen (2011) examined money supply (M2) and its main determinants (real income and interest rate) in Côte d'Ivoire from 1980 to 2007 using the Juselius and Johansen cointegration test. They found that long run relationships exist and the independent variables significantly affected the dependent variable with a correct sign. Niyimbanira (2013) examined whether there is a stable long run equilibrium relationship between real demand for money and independent variables in South

Africa. The cointegration test confirmed the existence of stable equilibrium relationships and the error correction model (ECM) showed that monetary policy is effective in South Africa.

Hamori et al. (2008) empirically examined demand for money functions in the sub-Saharan African region, using non-stationary variables in a panel data analysis for 35 countries spanning from 1980 to 2005. He found cointegration relationships exist for money demand functions in the sub-Saharan African region. Valadkhani and Alauddin (2003) examined determinants of demand for real money balances in eight developing countries by pooling cross-country and time series data from 1979 to 1999. They found an increase in real income had significant positive effects, whereas an increase in interest and inflation rates negatively affected real demand for money.

2 Methodology

Following Arize et al. (1999), Agénor and Khan (1996), and Bahmani-Oskooee and Rhee (1994), this paper *complements* the traditional demand for money function with interest rate spread (the difference between the time deposit and lending rates), real effective exchange rate (REER), and the U.S. real interest rate (R_{US}). The demand for real money balances as a function of real income, inflation rate, REER, interest rate spread, and the RUS R_{US} as follows:

$$M2/P = f(Y, RD - LR, P, REER, R_{US}) \tag{1}$$

Equation (1) is stated in econometric form as

$$\begin{aligned} ln(M2_i/P_i)_t &= \delta_{0i} + \delta_1 ln(Y_i)_t + \delta_2(RD_i - LR_i)_t + \\ &+ \delta_3 \Delta ln(P_i)_t + \delta_4 ln(REER_i)_t + \delta_5 R_{US,t} + \varepsilon_{it} \end{aligned} \tag{2}$$

where i denotes a specific country and varies from 1 to 6; t is time, with the time series spanning from 1980 to 2014; $M2$ is the stock of broad money; P is the GDP deflator; Y is the real GDP as a proxy for transactions and precautionary demand for money; RD is the time deposit interest rate (i.e. the interest rate on time deposits); RL is the lending interest rate (i.e. a proxy measuring the rate of return on assets other than money); R_{US} is the U.S. real interest rate; and $REER$ is the real effective exchange rate. The R_{US} is used to test the capital mobility hypothesis and $REER$ is used for testing the currency substitution hypothesis.

The expected sign and elasticity of the income (Y) coefficient is as follows: if $\delta_1 = 1$, the quantity theory applies; if $\delta_1 = 0.5$, the Baumol-Tobin inventory theoretic approach is applicable; and if δ is greater than 1, money can be considered a luxury or some neglected wealth effects are present. An income elasticity of less than unity has several implications for monetary policy. For example, it may be concluded that the Friedman rule is not optimal and money supply must grow more slowly than output to achieve price stability objectives (Ball, 2000, pp.36). For a comprehensive discussion of the controversy around quantity theory see Hoffman and Rasche (2001), Laidler (1993), and Laidler (1991). We also expected negative coefficient signs for all other variables in the model (i.e. δ_2, δ_3, δ_4, and $\delta_5 < 0$). The inflation rate, $\Delta ln(P_t) = ln(P_t) - ln(P_{t-1})$, is a proxy for measuring the return on holdings of goods and its coefficient should be negative (i.e. $\delta_3 < 0$). Goods such as real estate and shares are substitutes for holding domestic currency.

The real effective exchange rate, $\ln(REER)$, and the U.S. real interest rate, R_{US}, are expected to be negatively signed (i.e. δ_4 and $\delta_5 < 0$). This means that the currency substitution and capital mobility hypotheses hold. Furthermore, this also means that the depreciation of domestic currency and the rise in the U.S. real interest rate will lead to a higher propensity to invest in foreign currency, as a result of international capital mobility due to capital account liberalization in the globalization era.

We began our estimation by assuming homogeneity of all model parameters across countries and then estimated a fixed effect to capture cross-country heterogeneities by varying the intercept 0 across all countries. By estimating different intercept terms (i.e. 01, 02, 03,... 06), the within mean is subtracted from each variable and the transformed data is estimated using the OLS method. After identifying the heterogeneities across countries, we estimated income specific elasticities across countries. Based on our desired objective and the importance of income elasticity in the demand for money equation, both the intercept (0) and income elasticity (1) were allowed to vary across countries in the long run model.

Equation (2) is restated as follows to allow both the interecept and income elasticity to vary across countries:

$$\begin{aligned} ln(M2_i/P_i)_t = \delta_{0i} + \delta_{1i} ln(Y_i)_t + \delta_2(RD_i - LR_i)_t + \\ + \delta_3 \Delta ln(P_i)_t + \delta_4 ln(REER_i)_t + \delta_5 R_{US,t} + \varepsilon_{it} \end{aligned} \tag{3}$$

Allowing δ_{0i} and δ_{1i} to take specific values for each country entails a loss of degrees of freedom. This involves a trade-off between the lost degrees of freedom and the gain in terms of country-specific parameters, as well as an enhanced goodness of fit estimate. However, it is imperative to test the functional forms of equations (2) and (3) to determine the appropriate model to be employed. Therefore, (i) the common intercept term hypothesis can be stated as $H_{1,0}$: $\delta_{0i} = 0$, and (ii) the common income elasticity hypothesis can be stated as $H_{2,0}$: $\delta_{1i} = 1$, where i = 1, 2,..., 6. If these two hypotheses are rejected, the use of equation (3) will be justified (the gains in identifying country heterogeneity outweighing the loss of degrees of freedom). This is equivalent to testing for redundant fixed effects.

After stating the long run model, we proceeded by modelling a short run model based on Engle-Granger's two step procedure. The estimate of a panel vector error correction (VEC) model which captures short run dynamics of demand for money is stated as follows:

$$\begin{aligned}\Delta ln(M2_i/P_i)_t = \phi_{0i} + \phi_1 \Delta ln(Y_i)_t + \phi_2 \Delta(RD_i - LR_i)_t + \phi_3 \Delta ln(P_i)_t + \\ + \phi_4 \Delta ln(REER_i)_t + \phi_5 \Delta R_{US,t} + \phi_6 \Delta ln(M2_i/P_i)_{t-1} + \phi_7 ECM_{it-1} + \nu_{it}\end{aligned} \tag{4}$$

where ϕ_i are the estimated short-term coefficients; ϕ_7 is the speed of adjustment, which measures the speed of adjustment of short-term dynamic convergence to the long run equilibrium path; and we added lagged dependent variables to ensure the residuals ν_t are white noise.

We applied principle of parsimony to the short run model by removing insignificant variables in equation (4) based on the battery of maximum likelihood tests. The empirical results for the parsimonious model captured short run dynamics for money demand.

2.1 Panel Cointegration Test

We implemented panel cointegration tests by applying the seven cointegration tests proposed by Pedroni (1999). The estimated relationship is as follows:

$$y_{it} = \alpha_i + \gamma_{it} + \theta t + \beta_1 x_{1,it} + ... + \beta_k x_{k,it} + \varepsilon_{it} \tag{5}$$

where k is the number of regressors and β_1, β_2, ..., β_k are the elasticities. The deterministic elements are defined as above and θt are common time effects.

2.2 Unit root tests

Pooled time series data, like univariate time series data, usually exhibit a time trend which is non-stationary. Hence, direct application of OLS or GLS to non-stationary data produces regression results that are spurious or misspecified (Engle and Granger, 1987).

This paper adopts the methodologies of Levin et al. (2002), Breitung (2000), Hadri (1999), and Im et al. (2003) for panel unit root tests that are similar to tests carried out on an individual series. However, this paper will not discuss the econometric derivation of the equation as this is beyond the scope of our research.

3 Data and empirical results

GDP, GDP deflator (P), broad money supply ($M2$), the U.S. interest rate, and interest rate spread data were obtained from the World Bank. Except for Ghana and Guinea, interest rate spread was obtained from individual countries while real effective exchange rates were obtained from the United Nations Conference on Trade and Development (UNCTAD).

Table 1 shows the descriptive statistics for real money balance, income, interest spread, price and U.S. interest across the six countries. The real effective exchange rate has the highest mean, median, and maximum values, while price has the lowest mean, median, and maximum values. Using the standard deviation of these variables from their means as a measure of volatility shows the real effective exchange rate was the most volatile and price the least volatile of all the variables.

Table 2 presents the IPS test results and Table 3 presents the LLC test results of equations (4) and (5), showing that all variables (dependent and independent) were not stationary. This indicates that the variables were differenced once and became stationary, implying that the variables are integrated of order one.

There are seven Pedroni's tests: four are based on 'within dimension' (panel cointegration tests) and three are based on 'between dimension' (group mean panel cointegration tests). The tests' statistics are based on the null hypothesis of no cointegration for all countries i, while the alternative hypothesis is that there is cointegration for all countries i. However, the group mean panel cointegration statistics allow for heterogeneity across countries under the alternative hypothesis. Table 4 displays the results of Pedroni's tests; all panel and group mean statistics reject the null hypothesis of no cointegration at the 5% significance level. Therefore, we conclude that the variables are cointegrated, meaning there is a long run relationship among the variables.

3.1 Functional Form Test

The first step in panel estimation is to determine the appropriate functional form of the model. This involves determination of the homogeneity or heterogeneity of the cross section involved to decide whether pooled or fixed effect estimation is the appropriate method to use. Table 5 shows the results of the fixed effect test. With a p-value of 0.0000, we reject the null hypothesis of the redundancy of fixed effects, and conclude that the fixed effects model in equation (3) is an appropriate model to use for the estimates.

Table 6 shows estimates of the parameters from equations (2) and (3) for pooled annual data from 1985 to 2014 for Guinea, Ghana, Gambia, Liberia, Sierra Leone, and Nigeria. We proceeded further by testing the two null hypotheses discussed in our methodology (i.e. $H_{1,0} : \delta_{0,i} = 0$ and $H_{2,0} : \delta_{1,i} = 1$). The tests' results are also presented in Table 6. Both hypotheses were rejected at the 5% significance level. This justified the use of country specific coefficients for intercept and income elasticity. Both Schwartz's information criterion and Akaike's information criterion indicate equation (3) is better than equation (2). The residuals are stationary (white noise) and normally distributed, as shown in the Jarque-Bera normality test for equation (3) where both intercept and income elasticity are country specific.

The coefficients estimated for equations (2) and (3) are shown in Table 5. All variables have the expected signs, except the interest spread and income elasticity for Guinea in equation 3 which has the opposite sign and is not statistically significant. Other variables are highly significant in determining the real money demand functions in the WAMZ member countries, and are consistent with a priori expectations regarding the sign and the magnitude of the coefficients.

Both equations are robust in terms of goodness of fit ($R^2 = 0.995$ and 0.993, respectively), but only equation 3 has white noise residuals. The results presented in Table 5 are consistent with theories of demand for money. Real income and inflation rate positively affect demand for money, whereas the interest rate spread, real effective exchange rate, and U.S. real interest rate negatively affect broad money demand. However, the estimated long run country specific income elasticities in Table 4 had values higher than unity in three countries: Guinea – 3.60, Gambia – 1.95, and Sierra Leone – 2.38, the elasticities in while three other countries had values less than unity: Ghana – 0.89, Liberia – 0.58, and Nigeria – 0.62. The elasticity of income greater than unity could be attributed to political inference and shallow financial development in these three countries.

In 6, we observe that the inflation rate (representing the opportunity cost of holding monetary assets relative to real estate assets or other assets excluding financial assets such as gold and foreign currencies) has a positive significant coefficient ($\delta_3 = 0.091$), implying that demand for money has influenced portfolio decisions in these countries. This makes the shallow development of the stock market, or its nonexistence, in some countries in the region unsurprising.

In comparison to the interest rate spread, real effective exchange rate, and the U.S. real interest rate, the inflation rate has relatively higher effects on the real money balance in the long run. This implies that an increase in the rate of inflation discourages investors from investing in financial assets and encourages them to diversify their portfolios by acquiring real assets (Valadkhani, 2008).

The estimated coefficients for the interest rate spread (δ_2), the real effective exchange rate (δ_4), and the U.S. real interest rate (δ_5), are all negative (as shown in Table 6), indicating that the demand for real money balances is negatively affected by these three variables. All things being equal, a rise in the domestic interest rate spread or U.S. real interest rate, or currency depreciation will lead to a significant decrease in the demand for real money balances. In these circumstances, rational economic agents will diversify their portfolios in the economy by substituting foreign currencies (e.g. USD, EUR, etc.) for domestic currency in their financial portfolios or by acquiring other financial and/or real assets (e.g. real estate property, gold, and shares).

Table 7 shows the estimated short run dynamics of real demand for money. The estimated coefficients are consistent with our expectations, with changes in inflation rate and interest rate spread reflecting the rate of return on non-financial assets and having negative coefficients of -0.125 and -0.007, respectively. Changes in the U.S. interest rate will lead to capital outflows from domestic economies to foreign countries by 2.3% in the short run; this implies that economic agents will substitute their domestic asset holdings with foreign ones. Moreover, changes in real income exert positive effects (0.40) on money demand functions. Additionally, the ECM term is highly significant, reinforcing earlier cointegration relationships in long run money demand models. The estimated coefficients for ECM indicate an excess demand for real money balance in the last period (year) will be reduced by 39% in each subsequent year. The real effective exchange rate was removed because it was not statistically significant in the short run model.

We summarize the principal findings as follows. First, all things being equal, the long run income elasticity is greater than unity and short run income elasticity is 0.40. We reject the null hypothesis that short run income elasticity equals unity (i.e., $\delta_1 = 1$), because $F(1, 159) = 22.20$ with p-value $= 0.00$. The implication of this result is that – to maintain price stability in this region – the monetary aggregate growth rate must be slower than the rate of economic growth. Second, inflation has a relatively large effect on demand for money, both in the long and short run. The coefficient for inflation has the second largest magnitude, only lower than real income. Rising inflation encourages agents to diversify their portfolios away from money by acquiring real assets such as real estate property. Third, a change or rise in interest rate spread has more effect on money demand functions in the short run than it does in the long run. Fourth, both real effective exchange rate and U.S. real interest rate determine the long run demand for money. However, only the U.S. real interest rate is significant in the short run. Hence, we can conclude that the currency substitution hypothesis holds only for the long term, whereas the capital mobility hypothesis holds in both the short and long term.

Conclusion and policy implications

The formulation of effective and efficient money demand functions cannot be overemphasized in the design and implementation of monetary policy in developing economies, whether the central banker's major policy target variable is quantitative (stock of money), interest rate, or inflation.

This paper examines the long and short run determinants of demand for real money balances within the WAMZ region, pooling cross-sectional time series data spanning the years 1985 to 2014 for six countries, and implementing various fixed effects regression models to estimate long and short run demand for real money balances.

The Levin et al. (2002) tests for unit roots show that all variables in the models are $I(1)$. Both the Pedroni panel and Engle-Granger's two step procedures were employed to test for cointegration. The results of the tests showed that there is a long run relationship (cointegration) among the variables in the model.

We conclude that an increase in real income or inflation rate has a positive effect on demand for money, whereas the real effective exchange rate, the U.S. real interest rate, and a rise in interest rate spread all have a negative effect on demand for money in this region. This implies that real broad money supply (M2) is a predictable monetary aggregate in the region. The estimated long run income elasticity from the pooled estimation is higher than unity. Although some fixed effect models are greater than unity, others are less than unity for some countries. The implication is that, to maintain price stability in this region, the monetary aggregate growth rate must be slower than the rate of economic growth.

The dynamic error correction term, measuring the speed of adjustment of the short run dynamics of money demand to its long run path, was highly significant. The estimated coefficients for income, inflation rate, interest rate spread, and the U.S. real interest rate in this model are highly significant and consistent with a priori expectations of the direction of the signs. The estimated error correction model indicates that short run changes in income, the rate of inflation, the interest rate spread, and the U.S. real interest rate are statistically significant in determining changes in demand for money. The real effective exchange rate was statistically insignificant. One can conclude that, in this region, both the currency substitution and capital mobility hypotheses hold for the long term, whereas only the capital mobility hypothesis holds in the short term. We recommend that the monetary aggregate should grow more slowly than economic growth to maintain price stability. Countries in this region should try to maintain stable exchange rates and ensure market driven interest rate policies.

References

Agénor, P.-R. and Khan, M. S. (1996). Foreign currency deposits and the demand for money in developing countries. *Journal of Development Economics*, 50(1):101–118.

Arize, A. C., Malindretos, J., and Shwiff, S. S. (1999). Structural breaks, cointegration, and speed of adjustment Evidence from 12 LDCs money demand. *International Review of Economics and Finance*, 8(4):399 – 420.

Arrau, P., Gregorio, J. D., Reinhart, C. M., and Wickham, P. (1995). The demand for money in developing countries: Assessing the role of financial innovation. *Journal of Development Economics*, 46(2):317 – 340.

Bahmani, S. (2008). Stability of the Demand for Money in the Middle East. *Emerging Markets Finance and Trade*, 44(1):62–83.

Bahmani-Oskooee, M. (2009). How stable is the demand for money in African countries? *Journal of Economic Studies*, 36(3):216–235.

Bahmani-Oskooee, P. M. and Rhee, H.-J. (1994). Long-Run Elasticities of the Demand for Money in Korea:Evidence from Cointegration Analysis. *International Economic Journal*, 8(2):83–93.

Bitrus, Y. P. (2011). The demand for money in Nigeria. *European Journal of Business and Management*, 3(6):63–85.

Dekle, M. R. and Pradhan, M. (1997). Financial liberalization and money demand in ASEAN countries: implications for monetary policy. Working Paper 97/36, International Monetary Fund.

Engle, R. F. and Granger, C. W. J. (1987). Co-Integration and Error Correction: Representation, Estimation, and Testing. *Econometrica*, 55(2):251–276.

Hamori, S. et al. (2008). Empirical analysis of the money demand function in Sub-Saharan Africa. *Economics Bulletin*, 15(4):1–15.

Herve, D. B. G. and Shen, Y. (2011). The Demand for Money in Cote d'Ivoire: Evidence from the Cointegration Test. *International Journal of Economics and Finance*, 3(1):188.

Hoffman, D. L. and Rasche, R. H. (2001). *Aggregate money demand functions: Empirical applications in cointegrated systems*. Boston:Kluwer Academic Publishers.

Im, K. S., Pesaran, M., and Shin, Y. (2003). Testing for unit roots in heterogeneous panels. *Journal of Econometrics*, 115(1):53 – 74.

Jenkins, C. (1999). Money demand and stabilisation in Zimbabwe. *Journal of African Economies*, 8(3):386–421.

Kararach, G. (2002). Evidence on the demand for money function in Uganda. Technical Report WP No. 2002-01, Zimbabwe, Policy Analyst-UNICEF and others, EconWPA.

Kovanen, A., Dagher, J., et al. (2011). On the Stability of Money Demand in Ghana; A Bounds Testing Approach. Working Paper WP/11/273, International Monetary Fund.

Kumar, S., Webber, D. J., and Fargher, S. (2013). Money demand stability: A case study of Nigeria. *Journal of Policy Modeling*, 35(6):978 – 991.

Laidler, D. (1991). The Quantity Theory Is Always and Everywhere Controversial–Why? *The Economic Record*, 67(199):289–306.

Laidler, D. (1993). The demand for money: theories, evidence and problems. *Forth Edition, Harper Collins College Publishers*, page 56.

Levin, A., Lin, C.-F., and James Chu, C.-S. (2002). Unit root tests in panel data: asymptotic and finite-sample properties. *Journal of Econometrics*, 108(1):1–24.

Mishkin, F. S. (1999). International Experiences with Different Monetary Policy Regimes. Working Paper 6965, National Bureau of Economic Research.

Nachega, J.-C. (2001). A Cointegration Analysis of Broad Money Demand in Cameroon. IMF Working Papers 01/26, International Monetary Fund.

Nell, K. S. (1999). The Stability of Money Demand in South Africa, 1965-1997. Studies in Economics Discussion Papers 9905, School of Economics, University of Kent.

Niyimbanira, F. (2013). Stability Of Money Demand In A Developing Economy: Empirical Evidence From South Africa. *The International Business and Economics Research Journal*, 12(5):565.

Ogunsakin, S. and Awe, A. (2014). Impact of financial liberalization on the stability of Nigerian money demand function. *International Journal of Economics, Business and Finance*, 2(1):1–18.

Pedroni, P. (1999). Critical Values for Cointegration Tests in Heterogeneous Panels with Multiple Regressors. *Oxford Bulletin of Economics and Statistics*, 61(S1):653–670.

Pedroni, P. (2004). Panel Cointegration: Asymptotic And Finite Sample Properties Of Pooled Time Series Tests With An Application To The Ppp Hypothesis. *Econometric Theory*, 20(03):597–625.

Rother, P. (1999). Money demand in the West African economic and monetary union - the problems of aggregation. *Journal of African Economies*, 8(3):422–447.

Salisu, A., Ademuyiwa, I., and Fatai, B. (2013). Modelling the Demand for Money in Sub-Saharan Africa (SSA). *Economics Bulletin*, 33(1):635–647.

Suliman, Z. S. and Dafaalla, H. A. (2011). An econometric analysis of money demand function in Sudan, 1960 to 2010. *Journal of Economics and International Finance*, 3(16):793–800.

Tahir, J. (1995). Recent Developments in Demand for Money Issues: Survey of Theory and Evidence with Reference to Arab Countries. Working Papers 9530, Economic Research Forum.

Tano, G. G. (2011). Money Demand Estimation using SAS®. Paper SA01-2011, Southern Illinois University Carbondale.

Valadkhani, A. (2008). Long- and Short-Run Determinants of the Demand for Money in the Asian-Pacific Countries: An Empirical Panel Investigation. *Annals of Economics and Finance*, 9(1):77–90.

Valadkhani, A. and Alauddin, M. (2003). Demand for M2 in Developing Countries: An Empirical Panel Investigation. School of Economics and Finance Discussion Papers and Working Papers Series 158, School of Economics and Finance, Queensland University of Technology.

Table 1: Descriptive statistics

Statistics	$M2/P$	Y	$RD - LR$	$REER$	P	R_{US}
Mean	19.643	21.826	11.336	768.332	3.641	4.401
Median	18.575	21.324	11.000	35.958	4.214	4.906
Maximum	26.128	25.997	35.759	7014.119	6.265	7.191
Minimum	9.088	18.776	-2.250	0.005	-2.351	1.161
Standard deviation	4.148	1.807	5.989	1543.369	1.741	1.953
Cross sections	6	6	6	6	6	6

Table 2: The Im, Pesaran, and Shin (2003) unit root test results

Variables	Intercept Only	q (optimal lags length)	Both intercept and trend	q (optimal lags length)
$ln(M2_i/P_i)_t$	2.449	2	-0.386	2
	(0.992)		(0.349)	
$\Delta ln(M2_i/P_i)_t$	-5.282	6	-9.520	0
	(0.000)		(0.000)	
$ln(Y_i)_t$	6.226	5	3.6382	6
	(1.000)		(0.999)	
$\Delta ln(Y_i)_t$	-2.748	4	-3.495	4
	(0.003)		(0.000)	
$(RD_i - LR_i)_t$	-2.101	6	-1.349	1
	(0.017)		(0.088)	
$\Delta(RD_i - LR_i)_t$	-8.440	5	-6.330	5
	(0.000)		(0.000)	
$(P_i)_t$	12.296	1	6.479	1
	(1.000)		(1.000)	
$\Delta ln(P_i)_t$	-3.170	2	-6.285	3
	(0.000)		(0.000)	
$ln(REER_i)_t$	6.257	3	0.214	1
	(1.000)		(0.585)	
$\Delta ln(REER_i)_t$	-0.747	2	-7.424	2
	(0.000)		(0.000)	
$R_{US,t}$	-0.542	1	-1.482	1
	(0.293)		(0.069)	
$\Delta R_{US,t}$	-2.427	0	-1.738	0
	(0.007)		(0.041)	

Notes: * The SIC and the Newey-West bandwidth selection method based on the Bartlett kernel are used in the test procedure. Figures in the parentheses represent the corresponding p-values.
Source: Authors' estimation.

Table 3: The Levin et al. (2002) unit root test results

Variables	Intercept only	q (optimal lags length)	Both intercept and trend	q (optimal lags length)
$ln(M2_i/P_i)_t$	3.811	2	-1.023	2
	(0.99)		(0.153)	
$\Delta ln(M2_i/P_i)_t$	-1.846	6	-8.801	0
	(0.032)		(0.000)	
$ln(Y_i)_t$	3.132	5	1.387	6
	(0.999)		(0.917)	
$\Delta ln(Y_i)_t$	-3.428	4	-4.237	4
	(0.000)		(0.000)	
$(RD_i - LR_i)_t$	-0.768	6	-0.365	1
	(0.221)		(0.357)	
$\Delta(RD_i - LR_i)_t$	-7.470	5	-3.578	5
	(0.000)		(0.000)	
$ln(P_i)_t$	11.733	1	6.479	1
	(1.000)		(1.000)	
$\Delta ln(P_i)_t$	-3.478	2	-6.416	3
	(0.000)		(0.000)	
$ln(REER_i)_t$	4.658	3	-1.080	1
	(1.000)		(0.140)	
$\Delta ln(REER_i)_t$	-7.739	2	-6.417	2
	(0.000)		(0.000)	
$R_{US,t}$	-1.046	1	-1.647	1
	(0.147)		(0.049)	
$\Delta R_{US,t}$	-2.986	0	-2.480	0
	(0.001)		(0.006)	

Notes: * The SIC and the Newey-West bandwidth selection method based on the Bartlett kernel are used in the test procedure. Figures in the parentheses represent the corresponding p-values.
Source: Authors' estimation.

Table 4: Pedroni panel cointegration tests

Panel Cointegration Tests				Group Mean Cointegration Tests		
v-Stat	rho-Stat	PP-Stat	ADF-Stat	rho-Stat	PP-Stat	ADF-Stat
1.84121	2.05173	3.88595	2.15473	1.89627	3.66798	4.12761
(0.0328)*	(0.0035)*	(0.0025)*	(0.0047)*	(0.0467)*	(0.0039)*	(0.0368)*

Note: p-values are stated in parentheses; * denotes rejection of null hypothesis at the 5% critical level (p-value less than 0.05).
Source: Authors' estimation.

Table 5: Redundant fixed effects tests

Effects Test	Statistic	d.f.	Prob.
Cross-section F	93.35	(5,168)	0.0000
Cross-section Chi-square	237.94	5	0.0000

Table 6: Long run determinants of demand for the real balances

Independent Variables	Fixed effect model with country specific intercept			Fixed effect model with country specific intercept and income elasticity		
	Coefficient	t–ratio	p–value	Coefficient	t–ratio	p–value
Country specific intercept						
Guinea	6.317	2.55	0.01	99.711	2.06	0.04
Ghana	-0.396	-0.16	0.88	-3.025	-0.46	0.65
Gambia	1.729	0.79	0.43	-22.155	-3.37	0.00
Liberia	-1.715	-0.78	0.43	2.134	0.63	0.53
Serra-Leone	7.819	3.30	0.00	-27.164	-1.84	0.07
Nigeria	5.712	2.06	0.04	9.319	1.35	0.18
$ln(Y_i)_t$	0.765	6.91	0.00	-	-	-
Country specific income elasticity						
Guinea	-	-	-	-3.603	-1.60	0.11
Ghana	-	-	-	0.878	2.97	0.00
Gambia	-	-	-	1.956	5.889	0.00
Liberia	-	-	-	0.585	3.46	0.00
Sierra Leone	-	-	-	2.387	3.38	0.00
Nigeria	-	-	-	0.617	2.22	0.03
$(RD_i - LR_i)_t$	-0.009	-2.46	0.02	-0.008	2.07	0.04
$ln(P_i)_t$	0.134	4.51	0.00	0.091	2.43	0.01
$ln(REER_i)_t$	-0.001	-9.85	0.00	-0.004	-2.22	0.03
$R_{US,t}$	-0.086	-4.04	0.00	-0.044	-2.03	0.04
R^2	0.995			0.993		
Adjusted R^2	0.995			0.993		
AIC	3.861			3.809		
SIC	4.060			4.100		
F-statistics	3284		0.00	71.17		0.00
Unit root test for residual term using IPS test	0.962		0.83	-2.22		0.01
Jarque-Bera normality test	3.601		0.34	2.780		0.72
$H_0^1 : \delta_{i0} = \delta_0$ F (5,163)	709.3		0.00			
$\chi^2(5)$	3.601		0.34	2.780		0.72
$H_0^2 : \delta_{i1} = \delta_1$ F (5,158)				17.31		0.00
$\chi^2(5)$				86.57		0.00

Note: * the White cross-section standard errors and covariance are used in the estimation of the t-ratios.
Source: Authors' estimation.

Table 7: Short run determinants of demand for the real balances

Panel Cointegration Tests	Group Mean Cointegration Tests		
	Coefficient	t-ratio	p-value
1.84121	2.05173	3.88595	2.15473
(0.0328)*	(0.0035)*	(0.0025)*	(0.0047)*

Note: p-values are stated in parentheses; * denotes rejection of null hypothesis at the 5% critical level (p-value less than 0.05).
Source: Authors' estimation.

4

The Effect of Central Bank Communication on the Capital Buffer of Banks: Evidence from an Emerging Economy

Rodolfo Tomás da Fonseca Nicolay[*♣♠],
Claudio Oliveira de Moraes[◊♠], and **Bruno Pires Tiberto**[◊]

[♣]Catholic University of Petrópolis
[♠]Candido Mendes University
[◊]Central Bank of Brazil

ABSTRACT: The global financial crisis has revealed that the coordination between monetary policy and financial stability should be part of economic policy. This study examines the effects of monetary policy on the capital buffer (financial stability proxy) in the Brazilian economy and, in particular, how communication about both monetary policy and normative macroprudential policy affect the capital buffer maintained by banks. The study presents three main results: i) banks react strongly to monetary policy changes by increasing (reducing) the capital buffer in response to an increase (decrease) in the interest rate; ii) banks increase (decrease) the capital buffer when the central bank monetary policy communication signals an increase (decrease) in interest rates; and iii) banks use the capital buffer to accommodate the new measures of regulatory capital: the announcement of restrictive (liberalizing) capital measures reduces (increases) the capital buffer.

Keywords: central bank communication; capital buffer; monetary policy; financial stability

[*]Corresponding Author. Email: r-nicolay@hotmail.com

Introduction

Financial stability is fundamental to the performance of the economy. Prior to the global financial crisis (GFC), policymakers viewed financial stability as a typical regulatory problem. The monitoring of bank behavior was not regarded as part of macroeconomic environment analyses (Woodford, 2010). The GFC challenged the assumptions of financial stability and created an environment of uncertainty with potential effects on the conduct of macroeconomic policies. In particular, the GFC has given rise to a new point of view in which the coordination between monetary policy and financial stability is seen as a necessary part of economic policy (Poloz, 2015).

Regarding the financial stability issue, the aftermath of the GFC was the highlight received by new macroprudential policies. In this sense, policymakers face the need to incorporate new macroprudential instruments into the set of policy concerns (Galati and Moessner, 2013). Among the alternatives, the literature identifies the capital buffer as the main macroprudential instrument for financial stability management (Borio, 2011). Capital buffers are capital holdings of banks that exceed the regulatory minimum. The capital buffer can be explained as insurance against the risk of breaching the minimum capital requirement, because (i) banks cannot instantly adjust their capital; and (ii) breach of minimum regulatory capital requirements triggers supervisory actions, which can lead to a high cost penalty for banks (Jokipii and Milne, 2008; Stolz and Wedow, 2011). Furthermore, Carvallo et al. (2015) argue that maintaining the capital buffer above the required minimum is a way to signal financial soundness to the market as well as to take advantage of profitable market opportunities.

One strand of the empirical literature on the capital buffer is concerned with analyzing the effect of business cycle fluctuations on banks' capital buffers. The findings of this literature are mixed about the effect of capital buffers on the business cycle (Ayuso et al., 2004; Lindquist, 2004; Jokipii and Milne, 2008; Stolz and Wedow, 2011; Shim, 2013). Another strand of the empirical literature examines the effect of the capital buffer on the risk-taking of banks. Overall, the literature reveals that banks with a higher capital buffer take less risk than less capitalized banks (Konishi and Yasuda, 2004; Repullo, 2005; Jokipii and Milne, 2011; Guidara et al., 2013). In addition, since the GFC, several empirical studies have investigated the link between monetary policy and financial stability through banks' behavior and the risk-taking channel (Altunbas et al., 2009; Borio and Zhu, 2012; Montes and Scarpari, 2015). Other studies extended this analysis to explain the connection between monetary policy and regulatory capital (de Moraes et al., 2016).

The analysis of the relationship between macroprudential instruments (e.g., the capital buffer) and monetary policy is a new challenge for policymakers. The policy design problem for central banks is how to set multiple instruments to meet multiple stabilization goals. There are theoretical advancements on the interplay between macroprudential and monetary policy that may help in addressing this problem. For example, DSGE models incorporate financial frictions in order to analyze coordination problems between monetary and macroprudential policies (Rubio and Carrasco-Gallego, 2014; Quint and Rabanal, 2014; Paoli and Paustian, 2017). However, empirical analyses of the relationship between capital buffers and monetary policy, as well as the effect of central bank communications on capital buffers, are still rare. Basel Committee on Banking Supervision (2010) points out that central banks do consider the effect of buffer communication on market expectations, on the behavior of their own capital buffer, and on financial stability. Born et al. (2012) highlight the importance of central bank communication to macroprudential supervision and show that the financial market reacts to central bank communication on financial stability issues.

We examine the effects of monetary policy on capital buffers (financial stability proxy) in the Brazilian economy and, in particular, how communication about both monetary policy and normative macroprudential policy affect the capital buffer maintained by banks. Brazil is an important case because it is an emerging economy in which the Central Bank of Brazil (CBB) explicitly aims at price stability and financial stability. In order to evaluate the effect of monetary policy, we use the basic interest rate in Brazil. For documenting the effect of central bank communication, we use two indicators: monetary policy communication and normative macroprudential policy communication. The first, extracted from the Monetary Policy Committee (COPOM) minutes, helps predict the next monetary policy decision of the CBB. The second represents a novel approach to measuring the effect of capital regulatory measures on financial stability.

To our knowledge, this is the first work that analyzes the relationship between the capital buffer, monetary policy, and central bank communication. Our work differs from the existing literature in several aspects. First, we investigate the relationship between monetary policy and financial stability in a different way. Whereas the literature is concerned with analyzing only the effect of monetary policy on bank risk-taking, this study examines the effect of monetary and macroprudential policies on the capital buffer. Second, we analyze the effect of communication about monetary policy and normative macroprudential policy on the capital buffer.

Our work has three main results that contribute to the empirical literature on the capital buffer, monetary policy, and central bank communication. First, the results indicate that banks react strongly to monetary policy changes by increasing (reducing) the capital buffer in response to an increase (decrease) in the interest rate. Second, we present evidence that banks increase (decrease) the capital buffer when the central bank monetary policy communication signals an increase (decrease) in interest rates, affecting more significantly the banks with riskier positions. Third, the central bank normative macroprudential policy communication does not have the desired effect on soundness and safety of the financial system because banks use the capital buffer to accommodate the new measures of regulatory capital: the announcement of restrictive (liberalizing) capital measures reduces (increases) the capital buffer.

The remainder of this work is organized as follows. The next section provides the data and methodology used in this work. Section 2 presents empirical evidence regarding the impact of monetary policy and of communication about both monetary policy and normative macroprudential policy on capital buffers. The last section concludes the work.

1 Data and Methodology

In this section, we present the data and methodology used to provide empirical evidence on the relationships among capital buffers, monetary policy, and central bank communication. The period of analysis runs from January 2006 to December 2016.[1] We gather the monthly data series used in this study from the CBB site.[2] The data used in this work are country-wide and the bank data represent the entire Brazilian banking sector.

The idea of the capital buffer, brought by Basel III, is to use a buffer of capital to protect the banking sector from periods of excess aggregate credit growth that have often been associated with a build-up of system-wide risks (Basel Committee on Banking Supervision, 2010). On the other hand, as pointed out by Carvallo et al. (2015), when banks are unable to build up a capital buffer in times of economic expansion, they can fail to meet the minimum capital requirements during an economic recession. This cyclical behavior of banks amplifies the effect of shocks on economic and financial stability because, in order to meet the minimum capital requirement, banks are forced to deleverage assets and reduce lending to the market (Borio and Zhu, 2012).

The capital buffer ($BUFFER$) is defined in our model as the excess capital held by banks in relation to regulatory capital. It is calculated by taking the difference between the capital adequacy ratio (CAR) disclosed by CBB and the minimum capital requirement in force in Brazil. The higher the $BUFFER$, the more solvent are the banks and the greater is the financial stability.

The benchmark model considers some macroeconomic variables that help to explain the capital buffer held by banks. The return on equity (ROE) is an indicator of the banks' profitability and represents the cost of capital. Generally, the capital buffer is accumulated through retained earnings. As pointed out by Stolz and Wedow (2011), high profits may reflect high charter values and, hence, the ability to consistently generate high profits and increase capital buffers through retained earnings. In this sense, in accordance with Milne

[1]The database begins in January 2006 due to the availability of liquidity index data.
[2]Table A.1 presents descriptive statistics.

and Whalley (2001), high profit banks have less need to hold substantial capital buffers as an insurance against a possible violation of the regulatory minimum. Therefore, it is expected that an increase in ROE implies a reduction of the $BUFFER$.

We also include output gap (GDP_GAP) as a proxy for the business cycle. It corresponds to the difference between the GDP accumulated in 12 months at current values and the potential output (Hodrick-Prescott filter). Some studies show that an increase in GDP_GAP results in a reduction of $BUFFER$, indicating that in a scenario of economic expansion (contraction), banks assume more (less) risks (Ayuso et al., 2004; Lindquist, 2004; Jokipii and Milne, 2008).

The credit gap ($CRED\_GAP$) corresponds to the difference between the credit-to-GDP ratio and the trend of long-term credit (Hodrick-Prescott filter). According to Basel Committee on Banking Supervision (2010), in times of economic expansion, banks are more risk prone and increase the supply of credit. Therefore, it is expected that an increase in $CRED\_GAP$ results in a reduction of the $BUFFER$.

Liquidity (LIQ) measures the volume of liquid assets that Brazilian banks keep available for the "programmed" and "not programmed" cash flow of the next 30 days (21 workdays), under a severe stress scenario. According to the findings of (Stolz and Wedow, 2011), it is expected that greater volumes of liquid assets increase the capital buffer.

Basic interest rate (IR) is the main instrument of monetary policy for inflation targeting in Brazil. We use the natural logarithm of the SELIC annualized interest rate. Montes and Scarpari (2015) showed that banks react to an increase in interest rates with an increase in risk aversion, demonstrated by increasing provisions to mitigate risk. As one of the provisions, the capital buffer is a proxy for bank risk aversion. Therefore, it is expected that an increase in IR will result in an increase of $BUFFER$, indicating that in a scenario of monetary tightening (easing), banks assume less (more) risk.

We also construct two dummy variables to measure the events that affect the capital buffer. $SUBPRIME\ CRISIS$ is a dummy variable for the period prior to the subprime crisis. It is equal to 1 in the period from January 2006 to July 2009 and 0 otherwise. $POLITICAL\ CRISIS$ is a dummy variable for the period of political instability in Brazil. It assumes value 1 in the period from December 2015 to December 2016 and 0 otherwise.

The dummy variables of the monetary policy communication are constructed according to the methodology developed by Rosa and Verga (2007). We apply the methodology using the COPOM minutes (see Table A.2). The COPOM minute is the main document released after each COPOM meeting to decide the basic interest rate. The minutes present information about the economic outlook, the monetary policy decision, and the path of the interest rate. When the central bank indicates an increase to the basic interest rate, the variable D_UP is equal to 1 and 0 otherwise. In turn, when the central bank indicates a reduction in the basic interest rate, the variable D_DOWN is equal to 1 and 0 otherwise.

We build the dummy variables of the normative macroprudential policy communication based on the regulatory capital measures published by the CBB whose purpose is to change the method for calculating the minimum requirement of regulatory capital (see Table A.3). This indicator represents a new methodology for measuring the effect of capital regulatory measures on financial stability. In the months when there are published regulatory capital measures indicating a reduction in the regulatory capital requirement, the variable D_LIB is equal to 1 and 0 otherwise. In turn, in the months when there are published regulatory capital measures indicating an increase in the regulatory capital requirement, the variable D_RES is equal to 1 and 0 otherwise.

The empirical analyses apply ordinary least squares (OLS), one-step generalized method of moments (GMM 1-STEP) with HAC covariance matrix, two-step generalized method of moments (GMM 2-STEP) with Windmeijer (2005) covariance matrix, and quantile regression (QREG). These methods allow straight observation and interpretation of the signal and statistical significance of all the estimated coefficients.

The OLS estimates use the Newey-West covariance matrix to account for the potential problems of heteroscedasticity and autocorrelation of the model. We present the adjusted R^2 statistic, F statistic, and Ramsey's RESET test. Whereas the adjusted R^2 reveals the explanatory power of the model, the F statistic shows the joint significance of the explanatory variables in the model. In addition, the RESET test evaluates whether the model is well specified. The RESET is a general test with the null hypothesis that the linear functional form is appropriate (Ramsey, 1969; Wooldridge, 2009).

The GMM estimator is recommended because it provides robust estimations even in the presence of endogeneity and simultaneity, common in time series analysis (Hansen, 1982). The empirical model developed in this study is subject to these problems. The presence of reverse causality is possible, for example, in the relation between capital buffer and ROE, as well as in the relation between liquidity and ROE.

In order to obtain a more efficient GMM estimator than OLS, it is important to observe the overriding conditions and the orthogonality of the instruments (Wooldridge, 2001). The coefficients estimated by GMM are consistent only if the instrumental variables used in the analysis are exogenous. Therefore, the hypothesis of exogeneity of instruments requires that these variables do not directly affect the dependent variable. We follow the methodology of Johnston (1984) to select the instruments on GMM estimation, that is, the instruments were dated to the period $t-1$ or earlier to assure exogeneity. We calculate the J-statistic to check the instruments' validity. We also present the Durbin (1954), Wu (1974), and Hausman (1978) test of endogeneity of the regressors. The one-step GMM estimations with HAC covariance matrix address robust standard errors in the presence of autocorrelation and heteroskedasticity of unknown form. Moreover, we apply the Windmeijer covariance matrix correction in the two-step GMM estimations to address small-sample downward biases on standard errors.

Finally, the QREG developed by Koenker and Bassett (1978) divides the distribution such that a given proportion of observations is located below the quantile and allows one to observe the estimated coefficient for different levels of the dependent variable. The QREG is a non-parametric technique (no distributional assumptions are required to optimally estimate the parameters) and is adequate for analyzing the relations for a set of variables, presenting more robust coefficients for outliers and non-normality than the OLS regressions (Brooks, 2014). We estimate the QREG with the moving blocks bootstrap (MBB), which provides robust standard errors to heteroskedasticity and autocorrelation of unknown form (Fitzenberger, 1998).

A first condition to analyze previous estimates is to check if the series are stationary. Thus, the augmented Dickey-Fuller test (ADF), Phillips-Perron test (PP), and Kwiatkowski-Phillips-Schmidt-Shin test (KPSS) were performed. As observed in Table A.4, all series analyzed are stationary, except LIQ whose result indicates that the use of the series in first difference would be more adequate. As the communication variables representing monetary policy and normative macroprudential policy are dummy variables that assume values of 0 or 1, unit root tests are not necessary, and the variables are stationary.

2 Estimates and Results

In order to verify the effects of monetary policy on financial stability, we estimate the baseline model taking into account the effects of macroeconomic variables on the capital buffer.

$$\begin{aligned} BUFFER_t = \alpha_1 + \alpha_2 ROE_t + \alpha_3 GDP\_GAP_t + \alpha_4 CRED\_GAP_t + \\ + \alpha_5 \Delta LIQ_t + \alpha_6 IR + \varepsilon_{1,t} \end{aligned} \tag{1}$$

The CBB has two economic policy objectives: price stability and financial stability. Blinder et al. (2008) argue that central bank communication is fundamental to economic policy management. However, Born et al. (2012) warn of the differences in central bank communication on monetary and macroprudential policies. Thus, to capture the effect of different forms of central bank communication on financial stability, communication dummy variables were included in the baseline model. Equation 2 includes the monetary policy communication dummy variable and equation 3 includes the normative macroprudential policy communication dummy variable.

$$BUFFER_t = \alpha_7 + \alpha_8 ROE_t + \alpha_9 GDP\_GAP_t + \alpha_{10} CRED\_GAP_t + \\ + \alpha_{11} \Delta LIQ_t + \alpha_{12} IR + \alpha_{13} COM\_MONETARY_t + \varepsilon_{2,t} \tag{2}$$

$$BUFFER_t = \alpha_{14} + \alpha_{15} ROE_t + \alpha_{16} GDP\_GAP_t + \alpha_{17} CRED\_GAP_t + \\ + \alpha_{18} \Delta LIQ_t + \alpha_{19} IR + \alpha_{20} COM\_MACROPRU_t + \varepsilon_{3,t} \tag{3}$$

where $COM\_MONETARY_t$ refers to D_UP and D_DOWN; $COM\_MACROPRU_t$ refers to D_LIB and D_RES; and $\varepsilon_{i,t}$, $i = 1, 2, 3$, are random error terms.

Table 1 presents the estimation results. Due to autocorrelation and heteroskedasticity, the reported t-statistics for the OLS regression are calculated using the Newey-West covariance matrix. Regarding OLS estimates, the F-statistic of all equations indicates the regressions are significant. Furthermore, the outcomes of the Ramsey RESET test indicate the estimations do not present problems of model misspecification. Regarding the GMM estimations, the J-statistic and the Durbin-Wu-Hausman test indicate we cannot reject the hypothesis that the model is correctly specified.

The positive and significant relation between IR and $BUFFER$ indicates that the effect of monetary policy on capital buffers cannot be neglected. The results reveal that banks react significantly to monetary policy changes by increasing (decreasing) their buffers when the central bank increases (decreases) the interest rate. One possible interpretation for this conservative behavior is that banks display forward-looking behavior and are anticipating a deterioration of the credit market in the face of a tightening in the monetary policy.

In relation to the effect of central bank communication on financial stability, the estimates reveal that monetary policy communication affects the capital buffer. The signals of the coefficients D_UP and D_DOWN, having statistical significance in all GMM models, show that when there is an indication of an increase (decrease) in the interest rate, banks respond in a forward-looking manner with an increase (decrease) of their buffers, revealing higher (lower) risk aversion. The reason for this result is similar to that given to the effect of monetary policy changes on capital buffer. That is, banks react proactively to the anticipated future behavior of the credit market based on inferences obtained through central bank communications on monetary policy.

Regarding the effects of normative macroprudential policy communication on the capital buffer, the results show that central bank communications indicating an increase in regulatory capital requirement ($D\_RES = 1$) generate a reduction in the capital buffer held by banks, signaling that banks use the capital buffer to meet new regulatory constraints. On the other hand, central bank communications indicating a reduction in the regulatory capital requirement ($D\_LIB = 1$) generate an increase in the capital buffer maintained by banks, indicating that banks do not reduce their risk aversion due to regulatory capital changes. An explanation for this result is that banks use their own capital excess over the regulated capital requirement (their buffer) to accommodate new capital regulatory measures. This result corroborates the study by Nier and Baumann (2006) for a set of countries in which the capital buffer has an accommodative character for shocks on capital.

Finally, in relation to the coefficients for ROE, $CRED\_GAP$, and GDP_GAP, it is observed that they have statistical significance and the signs are positive. As pointed out by Milne and Whalley (2001), high profit banks can hold lower capital buffers as insurance against a violation of the regulatory capital minimum. The coefficients on $CRED\_GAP$ confirm the view highlighted by Basel Committee on Banking Supervision (2010) that during an economic boom, banks increase credit and reduce the capital buffer, thereby increasing the risk exposure of the entire financial system. In addition, the positive and significant coefficients for GDP_GAP denote that the business cycle exerts pressure to decrease capital buffers. This result is in line with the argument by Ayuso et al. (2004), Lindquist (2004), and Jokipii and Milne (2008) that banks reduce (increase) the capital buffer and increase (reduce) their exposure to risk in times of economic expansion (contraction). Furthermore, the findings regarding LIQ reveal that $BUFFER$ is sensitive to the liquidity conditions of banks. An increase in LIQ variation contributes to an increase in $BUFFER$. One explanation for this result is that more liquid banks tend to take on less risk.

Additionally, we estimate the models using QREG to obtain further evidence on the effect on the capital buffer of monetary policy and central bank communication about both monetary policy and normative macroprudential policy. This estimation method allows measurement of whether the bank's response to macroeconomic issues or central bank communication remains in different quantiles. In this sense, different from the OLS and GMM estimation methods, it is possible through QREG to observe the effect of the control variables and, in particular, the effect of IR, D_UP, D_DOWN, D_LIB, and D_RES on different levels of $BUFFER$.

Table 2 presents the estimates of the quantile regression.[3]Regarding the effect of monetary policy on the different levels of capital buffer, the estimates show that IR is significant in most quantiles of $BUFFER$, being more responsive in the middle quantiles. In general, banks react more strongly to changes in monetary policy in high quantiles. With respect to the effect of monetary policy communication on capital buffer, the results suggest that the indication of an increase in the interest rate ($D\_UP = 1$) is able to affect the $BUFFER$ in low quantiles when the banks present riskier positions. On the other hand, the results do not

[3]Estimates for $CONSTANT$, $SUBPRIME\ CRISIS$, and $POLITICAL\ CRISIS$ were omitted. In all models, these variables presented statistical significance in most quantiles and robust signals with the previously reported OLS and GMM estimates.

show statistical significance for the cases in which the central bank indicates a reduction in the interest rate ($D\_DOWN = 1$).

Regarding the effect of normative macroprudential policy communication on the capital buffer, the quantile regression results suggest that regulatory capital measures indicating a reduction ($D\_LIB = 1$) or an increase ($D\_RES = 1$) in the regulatory capital requirement have an effect on lower quantiles of $BUFFER$. An explanation for this result is that the normative macroprudential policy communication is relevant for banks most prone to risk or likely to violate regulatory capital requirements. As a consequence, banks use the capital buffer to accommodate unexpected shocks to their capital ratio (Nier and Baumann, 2006).

Lastly, in most models, the coefficient signals estimated on ROE, D_GAP, $CRED\_GAP$, and LIQ corroborate the signals found in the OLS and GMM estimates. The $BUFFER$ response to ROE is symmetric, negative, and significant in all quantiles. The signal of GDP_GAP and $CRED\_GAP$ coefficients indicates that $BUFFER$ responds in higher magnitude in the low quantiles. This evidence suggests that the banks are more responsive to the macroeconomic cycles in riskier positions. When $BUFFER$ is high enough, the banks respond less to $CRED\_GAP$ and GDP_GAP.

3 Conclusion

This work has examined the effect of monetary policy and central bank communication on the financial stability of the Brazilian economy during the period from January 2006 to December 2016. This was done by using OLS, GMM, and QREG analyses. The capital buffer, defined as the excess capital held by banks in relation to the regulatory capital requirement in force in Brazil, was used as a proxy for financial stability. In particular, this work investigated how monetary policy changes and central bank communications about monetary policy and normative macroprudential policy affect the capital buffer.

The empirical evidence presented in this work suggests that banks behave procyclically in relation to monetary policy changes, increasing the capital buffer (risk aversion) to protect themselves against a possible scenario of economic deterioration and reducing the capital buffer (risk taking) in a scenario of economic boom.

Regarding central bank communication, the results showed that banks react in a forward-looking manner to central bank monetary policy communication, increasing (decreasing) the capital buffer when monetary policy communication signals an increase (reduction) in the interest rate. Finally, considering the central bank normative macroprudential policy communication, the analysis revealed an undesired behavior in macroprudential terms, as banks increase (decrease) the capital buffer when liberalizing (restrictive) capital measures are announced by the central bank. This result demonstrated that normative macroprudential policy communication did not contribute to increasing the soundness of the banking system, suggesting instead that the capital buffer is used by banks to accommodate regulatory capital shocks (new regulatory capital measures).

The response of the capital buffer to the CBB's communication suggests that the normative macroprudential policy communication should be improved because it is not able to anchor the behavior of banks to the objectives of macroprudential policy. If the normative macroprudential policy communication were conducted in the same way as the monetary policy communication, that is, a regular and systematic communication, it might be better able to anchor the behavior of the banks to meeting the objectives of the capital buffer to guarantee financial stability.

References

Altunbas, Y., Gambacorta, L., and Marques-Ibanez, D. (2009). Securitisation and the bank lending channel. *European Economic Review*, 53(8):996–1009.

Ayuso, J., Pérez, D., and Saurina, J. (2004). Are capital buffers pro-cyclical?: Evidence from Spanish panel data. *Journal of Financial Intermediation*, 13(2):249–264. Bank Capital Adequacy Regulation under the New Basel Accord.

Basel Committee on Banking Supervision (2010). Guidance for national authorities operating the countercyclical capital buffer. *Bank for International Settlements.*

Blinder, A. S., Ehrmann, M., Fratzscher, M., Haan, J. D., and Jansen, D.-J. (2008). Central Bank Communication and Monetary Policy: A Survey of Theory and Evidence. Working Paper 13932, National Bureau of Economic Research.

Borio, C. (2011). Rediscovering the Macroeconomic Roots of Financial Stability Policy: Journey, Challenges, and a Way Forward. *Annual Review of Financial Economics*, 3(1):87–117.

Borio, C. and Zhu, H. (2012). Capital regulation, risk-taking and monetary policy: A missing link in the transmission mechanism? *Journal of Financial Stability*, 8(4):236–251.

Born, B., Ehrmann, M., and Fratzscher, M. (2012). Communicating About Macro-prudential Supervision – A New Challenge for Central Banks. *International Finance*, 15(2):179–203.

Brooks, C. (2014). *Introductory Econometrics for Finance.* Cambridge University Press.

Carvallo, O., Kasman, A., and Kontbay-Busun, S. (2015). The Latin American bank capital buffers and business cycle: Are they pro-cyclical? *Journal of International Financial Markets, Institutions and Money*, 36(C):148–160.

de Moraes, C. O., Montes, G. C., and Antunes, J. A. P. (2016). How does capital regulation react to monetary policy? New evidence on the risk-taking channel. *Economic Modelling*, 56:177–186.

Durbin, J. (1954). Errors in Variables. *Review of the International Statistical Institute*, 22(1/3):23–32.

Fitzenberger, B. (1998). The moving blocks bootstrap and robust inference for linear least squares and quantile regressions. *Journal of Econometrics*, 82(2):235–287.

Galati, G. and Moessner, R. (2013). Macroprudential Policy – A Literature Review. *Journal of Economic Surveys*, 27(5):846–878.

Guidara, A., Lai, V. S., Soumaré, I., and Tchana, F. T. (2013). Banks' capital buffer, risk and performance in the Canadian banking system: Impact of business cycles and regulatory changes. *Journal of Banking and Finance*, 37(9):3373–3387.

Hansen, L. (1982). Large Sample Properties of Generalized Method of Moments Estimators. *Econometrica*, 50(4):1029–54.

Hausman, J. (1978). Specification Tests in Econometrics. *Econometrica*, 46(6):1251–71.

Johnston, J. (1984). *Econometric Methods*. McGraw-Hill economics series. McGraw-Hill.

Jokipii, T. and Milne, A. (2008). The cyclical behaviour of European bank capital buffers. *Journal of Banking and Finance*, 32(8):1440–1451.

Jokipii, T. and Milne, A. (2011). Bank capital buffer and risk adjustment decisions. *Journal of Financial Stability*, 7(3):165–178.

Koenker, R. W. and Bassett, G. (1978). Regression Quantiles. *Econometrica*, 46(1):33–50.

Konishi, M. and Yasuda, Y. (2004). Factors affecting bank risk taking: Evidence from Japan. *Journal of Banking and Finance*, 28(1):215–232.

Lindquist, K.-G. (2004). Banks' buffer capital: how important is risk. *Journal of International Money and Finance*, 23(3):493–513.

Milne, A. and Whalley, A. E. (2001). Bank capital regulation and incentives for risk-taking. *Cass Business School Research Paper*.

Montes, G. C. and Scarpari, A. (2015). Does central bank communication affect bank risk-taking? *Applied Economics Letters*, 22(9):751–758.

Nier, E. and Baumann, U. (2006). Market discipline, disclosure and moral hazard in banking. *Journal of Financial Intermediation*, 15(3):332–361.

Paoli, B. D. and Paustian, M. (2017). Coordinating Monetary and Macroprudential Policies. *Journal of Money, Credit and Banking*, 49(2–3):319–349.

Poloz, S. S. (2015). Integrating Financial Stability into Monetary Policy. *Business Economics*, 50(4):200–205.

Quint, D. and Rabanal, P. (2014). Monetary and Macroprudential Policy in an Estimated DSGE Model of the Euro Area. *International Journal of Central Banking*, 10(2):169–236.

Ramsey, J. B. (1969). Tests for Specification Errors in Classical Linear Least-Squares Regression Analysis. *Journal of the Royal Statistical Society. Series B (Methodological)*, 31(2):350–371.

Repullo, R. (2005). Liquidity, Risk Taking, and the Lender of Last Resort. *International Journal of Central Banking*, 1(2).

Rosa, C. and Verga, G. (2007). On the consistency and effectiveness of central bank communication: Evidence from the ECB. *European Journal of Political Economy*, 23(1):146–175.

Rubio, M. and Carrasco-Gallego, J. A. (2014). Macroprudential and monetary policies: Implications for financial stability and welfare. *Journal of Banking and Finance*, 49:326–336.

Shim, J. (2013). Bank capital buffer and portfolio risk: The influence of business cycle and revenue diversification. *Journal of Banking and Finance*, 37(3):761–772.

Stolz, S. and Wedow, M. (2011). Banks' regulatory capital buffer and the business cycle: Evidence for Germany. *Journal of Financial Stability*, 7(2):98–110.

Windmeijer, F. (2005). A finite sample correction for the variance of linear efficient two-step GMM estimators. *Journal of Econometrics*, 126(1):25–51.

Woodford, M. (2010). Financial Intermediation and Macroeconomic Analysis. *Journal of Economic Perspectives*, 24(4):21–44.

Wooldridge, J. M. (2001). Applications of Generalized Method of Moments Estimation. *Journal of Economic Perspectives*, 15(4):87–100.

Wooldridge, J. M. (2009). *Introductory Econometrics: A Modern Approach.* ISE - International Student Edition. South-Western.

Wu, D.-M. (1974). Alternative Tests of Independence between Stochastic Regressors and Disturbances: Finite Sample Results. *Econometrica*, 42(3):529–546.

Table 1: Regression results on $BUFFER$ – OLS and GMM

	OLS				
Regressors	**Eq(1)**	**Eq(2.1)**	**Eq(2.2)**	**Eq(3.1)**	**Eq(3.2)**
CONSTANT	**3.752****	**3.655****	**3.721****	**3.607****	**3.767****
	(1.680)	(1.615)	(1.745)	(1.663)	(1.668)
	[2.234]	[2.262]	[2.132]	[2.169]	[2.232]
ROE	**-0.103****	**-0.105****	**-0.105****	**-0.096****	**-0.103****
	(0.040)	(0.040)	(0.042)	(0.040)	(0.040)
	[-2.568]	[-2.614]	[-2.508]	[-2.372]	[-2.545]
GDP_GAP	**-1.8E-05*****	**-1.8E-05*****	**-1.8E-05*****	**-1.9E-05*****	**-1.8E-05*****
	(3.1E-06)	(2.9E-06)	(3.2E-06)	(3.0E-06)	(3.1E-06)
	[-5.919]	[-6.296]	[-5.678]	[-6.308]	[-5.898]
CRED_GAP	**-0.244*****	**-0.250*****	**-0.252****	**-0.239*****	**-0.242*****
	(0.088)	(0.088)	(0.099)	(0.086)	(0.088)
	[-2.783]	[-2.825]	[-2.553]	[-2.777]	[-2.763]
$\Delta(LIQ)$	**0.272**	**0.309**	**0.275**	**0.213**	**0.272**
	(0.343)	(0.348)	(0.342)	(0.340)	(0.342)
	[0.791]	[0.887]	[0.806]	[0.627]	[0.795]
IR	**1.488***	**1.527***	**1.514***	**1.496***	**1.485***
	(0.839)	(0.812)	(0.893)	(0.835)	(0.844)
	[1.774]	[1.880]	[1.696]	[1.792]	[1.760]
D_UP		**0.069**			
		(0.164)			
		[0.418]			
D_DOWN			**-0.027**		
			(0.181)		
			[-0.152]		
D_LIB				**0.530***	
				(0.274)	
				[1.937]	
D_RES					**-0.049**
					(0.127)
					[-0.388]
SUBPRIME CRISIS	**0.988*****	**1.016*****	**1.006*****	**0.944*****	**0.981*****
	(0.306)	(0.311)	(0.310)	(0.305)	(0.309)
	[3.222]	[3.271]	[3.244]	[3.101]	[3.178]
POLITICAL CRISIS	**-1.778*****	**-1.775*****	**-1.791*****	**-1.816*****	**-1.787*****
	(0.491)	(0.497)	(0.518)	(0.494)	(0.490)
	[-3.624]	[-3.575]	[-3.456]	[-3.677]	[-3.646]
Adjusted R^2	0.557	0.555	0.553	0.569	0.554
F-statistic	24.357	21.248	21.152	22.424	21.175
Prob. F-statistic	0.000	0.000	0.000	0.000	0.000
Ramsey RESET (1)	2.683	2.847	2.540	2.904	2.735
Prob. Ramsey RESET (1)	0.104	0.094	0.114	0.091	0.101
Rank					
J-statistic					
Prob. J-statistic					
Prob. Durbin-Wu-Hausman Test					

Continued on the next page

Table 1: Regression results on $BUFFER$ – OLS and GMM (Continued)

	GMM 1-STEP				
Regressors	**Eq(1)**	**Eq(2.1)**	**Eq(2.2)**	**Eq(3.1)**	**Eq(3.2)**
CONSTANT	**1.669**	**3.018*****	**2.856***	**2.217**	**2.814****
	(1.847)	(1.299)	(1.594)	(1.592)	(1.401)
	[0.903]	[2.323]	[1.791]	[1.393]	[2.008]
ROE	**-0.179*****	**-0.199*****	**-0.246*****	**-0.154*****	**-0.198*****
	(0.040)	(0.045)	(0.050)	(0.033)	(0.039)
	[-4.475]	[-4.432]	[-4.878]	[-4.643]	[-5.026]
GDP_GAP	**-2.5E-05*****	**-2.E-05*****	**-2.5E-05*****	**-2.4E-05*****	**-2.3E-05*****
	(3.7E-06)	(3.4E-06)	(4.15E-06)	(3.5E-06)	(2.7E-06)
	[-6.875]	[-7.230]	[-6.105]	[-6.958]	[-8.507]
CRED_GAP	**-0.326*****	**-0.364*****	**-0.523*****	**-0.276*****	**-0.329*****
	(0.117)	(0.120)	(0.145)	(0.100)	(0.101)
	[-2.793]	[-3.037]	[-3.617]	[-2.767]	[-3.273]
$\Delta(LIQ)$	**2.809****	**2.110****	**2.445****	**2.721*****	**-0.063**
	(1.202)	(0.883)	(1.206)	(0.704)	(0.731)
	[2.338]	[2.389]	[2.027]	[3.863]	[-0.087]
IR	**2.888*****	**2.264*****	**2.809*****	**2.485*****	**2.545*****
	(0.883)	(0.687)	(0.774)	(0.758)	(0.643)
	[3.272]	[3.294]	[3.627]	[3.279]	[3.956]
D_UP		**0.503*****			
		(0.175)			
		[2.867]			
D_DOWN			**-0.698*****		
			(0.241)		
			[-2.901]		
D_LIB				**0.751***	
				(0.442)	
				[1.697]	
D_RES					**-0.742***
					(0.404)
					[-1.834]
SUBPRIME CRISIS	**1.350*****	**1.985*****	**2.317*****	**1.259*****	**1.495*****
	(0.411)	(0.418)	(0.523)	(0.285)	(0.313)
	[3.288]	[4.746]	[4.433]	[4.423]	[4.775]
POLITICAL CRISIS	**-3.060*****	**-2.439*****	**-2.902*****	**-2.808*****	**-2.771*****
	(0.608)	(0.622)	(0.603)	(0.522)	(0.434)
	[-5.031]	[-3.918]	[-4.810]	[-5.380]	[-6.386]
Adjusted R^2	0.256	0.319	0.199	0.301	0.393
F-statistic					
Prob. F-statistic					
Ramsey RESET (1)					
Prob. Ramsey RESET (1)					
Rank	18	21	21	25	23
J-statistic	12.093	11.696	12.921	14.773	17.166
Prob. J-statistic	0.279	0.470	0.375	0.541	0.247
Prob. Durbin-Wu-Hausman Test	0.761	0.833	0.899	0.978	0.971

Continued on the next page

Table 1: Regression results on *BUFFER* – OLS and GMM (Continued)

	GMM 2-STEP				
Regressors	**Eq(1)**	**Eq(2.1)**	**Eq(2.2)**	**Eq(3.1)**	**Eq(3.2)**
CONSTANT	**1.123**	**2.652**	**2.001**	**0.046**	**2.320**
	(3.191)	(1.982)	(2.504)	(2.899)	(3.223)
	[0.352]	[1.338]	[0.779]	[0.016]	[0.720]
ROE	**-0.193*** **	**-0.195** **	**-0.193* **	**-0.132*** **	**-0.181** **
	(0.067)	(0.088)	(0.103)	(0.049)	(0.089)
	[-2.877]	[-2.209]	[-1.873]	[-2.716]	[-2.032]
GDP_GAP	**-2.8E-05*** **	**-2.7E-05*** **	**-2.5E-05*** **	**-2.7E-05*** **	**-2.5E-05*** **
	(6.7E-06)	(6.5E-06)	(7.5E-06)	(6.0E-06)	(6.0E-06)
	[-4.166]	[-4.093]	[-3.354]	[-4.480]	[-4.210]
CRED_GAP	**-0.320** **	**-0.357** **	**-0.433** **	**-0.275* **	**-0.392*** **
	(0.160)	(0.163)	(0.219)	(0.151)	(0.133)
	[-2.002]	[-2.188]	[-1.977]	[-1.824]	[-2.936]
$\Delta(LIQ)$	**3.097** **	**2.440** **	**3.185* **	**1.609* **	**0.934*** **
	(1.420)	(1.145)	(1.719)	(0.952)	(1.817)
	[2.180]	[2.130]	[1.853]	[1.689]	[0.514]
IR	**3.229** **	**2.390** **	**2.848** **	**3.281** **	**2.717* **
	(1.538)	(1.181)	(1.221)	(1.256)	(1.493)
	[2.099]	[2.023]	[2.332]	[2.612]	[1.819]
D_UP		**0.529** **			
		(0.249)			
		[2.125]			
D_DOWN			**-0.601** **		
			(0.294)		
			[-2.045]		
D_LIB				**1.639* **	
				(0.873)	
				[1.878]	
D_RES					**-1.183* **
					(0.696)
					[-1.700]
SUBPRIME CRISIS	**1.384** **	**1.985*** **	**1.794** **	**0.865* **	**1.221* **
	(0.683)	(0.730)	(0.901)	(0.522)	(0.714)
	[2.026]	[2.717]	[1.991]	[1.657]	[1.709]
POLITICAL CRISIS	**-3.360*** **	**-2.537*** **	**-2.881*** **	**-3.146*** **	**-3.199*** **
	(1.001)	(1.045)	(0.908)	(0.867)	(0.906)
	[-3.357]	[-2.428]	[-3.172]	[-3.627]	[-3.531]
Adjusted R^2	0.145	0.256	0.182	0.323	0.187
F-statistic					
Prob. F-statistic					
Ramsey RESET (1)					
Prob. Ramsey RESET (1)					
Rank	18	21	21	23	23
J-statistic	11.129	10.706	13.804	13.021	12.405
Prob. J-statistic	0.347	0.554	0.313	0.525	0.574
Prob. Durbin-Wu-Hausman Test	0.853	0.904	0.863	0.981	0.809

Note: Marginal significance levels: (***) denotes 0.01, (**) denotes 0.05, and (*) denotes 0.1. Standard errors between parentheses and t-statistics between square brackets.

Table 2: Regression results on $BUFFER$ - Quantile regression

	Quantiles				
	0.1	**0.2**	**0.3**	**0.4**	**0.5**
ROE	**-0.114*****	**-0.107*****	**-0.089*****	**-0.089*****	**-0.123*****
	(0.023)	(0.033)	(0.033)	(0.030)	(0.029)
GDP_ GAP	**-1.93E-05*****	**-2.07E-05*****	**-2.26E-05*****	**-2.32E-05*****	**-2.16E-05*****
	(2.22E-06)	(1.71E-06)	(1.82E-06)	(1.94E-06)	(1.95E-06)
CRED_ GAP	**-0.360*****	**-0.307*****	**-0.289*****	**-0.363*****	**-0.324*****
	(0.063)	(0.086)	(0.085)	(0.084)	(0.080)
$\Delta(LIQ)$	**-0.211**	**-0.487**	**-0.367**	**-0.009**	**0.173**
	(0.448)	(0.453)	(0.481)	(0.495)	(0.500)
IR	**0.682****	**1.307*****	**1.957*****	**2.204*****	**2.407*****
	(0.285)	(0.416)	(0.339)	(0.391)	(0.446)
ROE	**-0.123****	**-0.106*****	**-0.091*****	**-0.118*****	**-0.122*****
	(0.054)	(0.038)	(0.035)	(0.032)	(0.028)
GDP_ GAP	**-2.38E-05*****	**-2.11E-05*****	**-2.26E-05*****	**-2.31E-05*****	**-2.15E-05*****
	(3.68E-06)	(2.14E-06)	(1.94E-06)	(1.87E-06)	(1.90E-06)
CRED_ GAP	**-0.428*****	**-0.293*****	**-0.356*****	**-0.326*****	**-0.301*****
	(0.136)	(0.101)	(0.089)	(0.081)	(0.083)
$\Delta(LIQ)$	**-0.117**	**-0.231**	**-0.125**	**0.078**	**0.061**
	(0.698)	(0.470)	(0.488)	(0.429)	(0.442)
IR	**1.032***	**1.172*****	**1.864*****	**2.206*****	**2.400*****
	(0.534)	(0.439)	(0.429)	(0.412)	(0.431)
D_ UP	**0.349***	**0.185**	**0.145**	**2.205**	**0.170**
	(0.196)	(0.148)	(0.145)	(0.131)	(0.112)
ROE	**-0.113*****	**-0.105****	**-0.090*****	**-0.125*****	**-0.124*****
	(0.019)	(0.043)	(0.033)	(0.034)	(0.031)
GDP_ GAP	**-1.90E-05*****	**-2.05E-05*****	**-2.27E-05*****	**-2.21E-05*****	**-2.15E-05*****
	(2.18E-06)	(2.91E-06)	(1.86E-06)	(2.04E-06)	(2.02E-06)
CRED_ GAP	**-0.369*****	**-0.312****	**-0.286*****	**-0.367*****	**-0.337*****
	(0.070)	(0.136)	(0.098)	(0.098)	(0.094)
$\Delta(LIQ)$	**-0.170**	**-0.343**	**-0.327**	**0.027**	**0.284**
	(0.431)	(0.615)	(0.465)	(0.470)	(0.479)
IR	**0.635*****	**1.346****	**2.066*****	**2.473*****	**2.413*****
	(0.220)	(0.560)	(0.361)	(0.403)	(0.481)
D_ DOWN	**-0.031**	**-0.060**	**0.040**	**-0.132**	**-0.019**
	(0.081)	(0.144)	(0.123)	(0.138)	(0.142)

Continued on the next page

Table 2: Regression results on $BUFFER$ - Quantile regression (Continued)

	Quantiles			
	0.6	**0.7**	**0.8**	**0.9**
ROE	**-0.134*****	**-0.120*****	**-0.099****	**-0.100**
	(0.031)	(0.041)	(0.043)	(0.065)
GDP_ GAP	**-2.09E-05*****	**-1.76E-05*****	**-1.54E-05****	**-1.49E-05*****
	(2.03E-06)	(2.71E-06)	(3.06E-06)	(4.37E-06)
CRED_ GAP	**-0.266*****	**-0.189**	**-0.037**	**-0.074**
	(0.099)	(0.120)	(0.127)	(0.187)
$\Delta(LIQ)$	**0.163**	**0.129**	**-0.073**	**0.205**
	(0.473)	(0.500)	(0.461)	(0.657)
IR	**2.415*****	**2.435*****	**1.736***	**1.603**
	(0.588)	(0.873)	(1.010)	(1.383)
ROE	**-0.126*****	**-0.151*****	**-0.097****	**-0.107***
	(0.030)	(0.036)	(0.038)	(0.060)
GDP_ GAP	**-2.09E-05*****	**-1.84E-05*****	**-1.50E-05****	**-1.49E-05*****
	(2.02E-06)	(2.47E-06)	(2.54E-06)	(4.23E-06)
CRED_ GAP	**-0.261*****	**-0.215***	**-0.059**	**-0.067**
	(0.098)	(0.126)	(0.112)	(0.158)
$\Delta(LIQ)$	**0.072**	**0.103**	**-0.011**	**0.160**
	(0.440)	(0.435)	(0.431)	(0.589)
IR	**2.381*****	**2.834*****	**1.628****	**1.571**
	(0.518)	(0.741)	(0.797)	(1.340)
D_ UP	**0.142**	**0.223**	**0.072**	**-0.036**
	(0.129)	(0.176)	(0.200)	(0.209)
ROE	**-0.142*****	**-0.158*****	**-0.114****	**-0.101**
	(0.036)	(0.047)	(0.054)	(0.078)
GDP_ GAP	**-2.09E-05*****	**-1.92E-05*****	**-1.63E-05****	**-1.50E-05*****
	(2.32E-06)	(3.09E-06)	(3.54E-06)	(4.90E-06)
CRED_ GAP	**-0.251****	**-0.304****	**-0.041**	**-0.077**
	(0.112)	(0.142)	(0.136)	(0.193)
$\Delta(LIQ)$	**0.087**	**0.211**	**-0.087**	**0.195**
	(0.496)	(0.517)	(0.492)	(0.766)
IR	**2.548*****	**2.942*****	**2.068***	**1.657**
	(0.688)	(0.913)	(1.104)	(1.473)
D_ DOWN	**-0.110**	**-0.277**	**-0.126**	**-0.013**
	(0.160)	(0.240)	(0.302)	(0.381)

Continued on the next page

Table 2: Regression results on *BUFFER* - Quantile regression (Continued)

	Quantiles				
	0.1	**0.2**	**0.3**	**0.4**	**0.5**
ROE	**-0.102*****	**-0.107****	**-0.089*****	**-0.121*****	**-0.123*****
	(0.018)	(0.033)	(0.035)	(0.035)	(0.030)
GDP_ GAP	**-2.10E-05*****	**-2.07E-05*****	**-2.26E-05*****	**-2.18E-05*****	**-2.18E-05*****
	(1.60E-06)	(1.90E-06)	(1.76E-06)	(2.14E-06)	(1.91E-06)
CRED_ GAP	**-0.364*****	**-0.307****	**-0.288*****	**-0.277*****	**-0.304*****
	(0.045)	(0.090)	(0.086)	(0.090)	(0.084)
$\Delta(LIQ)$	**-0.154**	**-0.487**	**-0.367**	**-0.183**	**0.056**
	(0.310)	(0.449)	(0.492)	(0.488)	(0.431)
IR	**0.725*****	**1.307****	**1.925*****	**2.362*****	**2.430*****
	(0.236)	(0.384)	(0.327)	(0.391)	(0.445)
D_ LIB	**0.510*****	**0.365**	**0.447**	**0.384**	**0.442**
	(0.176)	(0.495)	(0.424)	(0.658)	(0.530)
ROE	**-0.131*****	**-0.107****	**-0.095*****	**-0.133*****	**-0.122*****
	(0.023)	(0.035)	(0.035)	(0.031)	(0.030)
GDP_ GAP	**-2.07E-05*****	**-2.07E-05*****	**-2.26E-05*****	**-2.20E-05*****	**-2.15E-05*****
	(2.19E-06)	(2.03E-06)	(1.92E-06)	(2.03E-06)	(1.94E-06)
CRED_ GAP	**-0.367*****	**-0.307*****	**-0.283*****	**-0.312*****	**-0.332*****
	(0.071)	(0.094)	(0.090)	(0.090)	(0.083)
$\Delta(LIQ)$	**-0.614**	**-0.487**	**-0.177**	**-0.284**	**0.297**
	(0.444)	(0.569)	(0.464)	(0.498)	(0.507)
IR	**1.333*****	**1.307****	**2.023*****	**2.443*****	**2.395*****
	(0.330)	(0.430)	(0.383)	(0.402)	(0.462)
D_ RES	**-0.339***	**-0.065**	**-0.097**	**-0.084**	**0.021**
	(0.200)	(0.219)	(0.207)	(0.203)	(0.176)

Continued on the next page

Table 2: Regression results on *BUFFER* - Quantile regression (Continued)

	Quantiles			
	0.6	**0.7**	**0.8**	**0.9**
ROE	**-0.136*****	**-0.116*****	**-0.098****	**-0.099**
	(0.031)	(0.043)	(0.047)	(0.081)
GDP_ GAP	**-2.08E-05*****	**-1.82E-05*****	**-1.66E-05****	**-1.49E-05*****
	(2.09E-06)	(2.93E-06)	(3.19E-06)	(5.04E-06)
CRED_ GAP	**-0.248****	**-0.191**	**-0.094**	**-0.075**
	(0.089)	(0.126)	(0.129)	(0.211)
$\Delta(LIQ)$	**0.009**	**0.101**	**0.107**	**0.196**
	(0.448)	(0.546)	(0.479)	(0.766)
IR	**2.423*****	**2.112****	**1.715***	**1.615**
	(0.583)	(0.891)	(1.035)	(1.540)
D_ LIB	**0.264**	**0.403**	**0.686**	**0.507**
	(0.568)	(0.727)	(0.686)	(2.422)
ROE	**-0.134*****	**-0.122*****	**-0.099****	**-0.100**
	(0.033)	(0.042)	(0.033)	(0.069)
GDP_ GAP	**-2.08E-05*****	**-1.71E-05*****	**-1.54E-05****	**-1.49E-05*****
	(1.99E-06)	(2.63E-06)	(2.45E-06)	(4.53E-06)
CRED_ GAP	**-0.264****	**-0.188**	**-0.037**	**-0.074**
	(0.096)	(0.120)	(0.108)	(0.208)
$\Delta(LIQ)$	**0.155**	**0.147**	**-0.073**	**0.204**
	(0.476)	(0.520)	(0.341)	(0.723)
IR	**2.411*****	**2.274****	**1.736****	**1.611**
	(0.632)	(0.903)	(0.804)	(1.437)
D_ RES	**-0.004**	**-0.120**	**-0.080**	**-0.001**
	(0.186)	(0.226)	(0.178)	(0.459)

Note: Marginal significance levels: (***) denotes 0.01, (**) denotes 0.05, and (*) denotes 0.1. Standard errors are between parentheses

A Appendix

Table A.1: Descriptive Statistics

Variables	Mean	Median	Maximum	Minimum	Stand.Dev.
BUFFER	5.744	5.640	7.650	3.960	0.807
CRED_GAP	-5.8E-12	-0.003	1.771	-1.962	0.668
D_DOWN	0.326	0.000	1.000	0.000	0.470
D_LIB	0.038	0.000	1.000	0.000	0.192
D_RES	0.136	0.000	1.000	0.000	0.344
D_UP	0.409	0.000	1.000	0.000	0.493
GDP_GAP	-5.1E-07	-463.766	70955.55	-107446.1	39840.61
LIQ	2.004	1.900	2.800	1.400	0.352
IR	2.417	2.424	2.871	1.961	0.214
ROE	17.011	15.860	25.160	11.260	4.198

Note: Authors' elaboration

Table A.2: Classification of key words and expressions from COPOM minutes

Dummy variable	key words and expressions from COPOM minutes
D_UP	- The monetary policy should remain especially vigilant. - Maintenance of the interest rate represents a nonnegligible risk for meeting the target (projected inflation above target). - Potential inflationary impacts of supply shocks yet to materialize. - Monetary policy should remain vigilant in order to avoid the propagation of shocks and exchange rate depreciation. - Monetary policy firmly committed to meeting the inflation targets. - Inflation remains high/monetary policy should be firm. - The monetary authority will be ready to adopt an active posture if projected inflation diverges from the target. - Inflation trend incompatible with the target. - COPOM will need to be less tolerant if shocks threaten to raise inflation above the target. - The Central Bank will not allow supply shocks to lead to an increase in the inflation rate. - The Committee understands that it is appropriate to continue the adjustment pace of the monetary conditions underway. - The monetary authority must remain vigilant so that short-term pressures do not contaminate longer time horizon. - The monetary authority should be ready to adjust the pace and magnitude of the interest rate adjustment process to the circumstances.
D_DOWN	- COPOM decided to continue the process of monetary easing. - Expected inflation below target/expectations consistent with the inflation risks/targets are less significant. - Consolidation of favourable perspectives for inflation in the medium term/COPOM considers that there is still room for. further cuts in the selic rate in the future. - Benign scenario for the evolution of inflation (with reduction of uncertainties/favourable external scenario). - Economic activity consistent with supply conditions, with low probability of inflation pressures. - The gradual easing of the monetary stance will not compromise the important achievements made in lowering inflation.

Note: Authors' elaboration

Table A.3: Classification of capital regulatory measures

Date	Restrictive regulation	Date	Liberalizing regulation
Feb/2007	Resolution CMN 3,444	Dec/2008	Resolution CMN 3,674 and Circular BCB 3,425
Aug/2007	Resolution CMN 3,490	Jul/2014	Circular BCB 3,711
Jan/2008	Resolution CMN 3,535	Aug/2014	Circular BCB 3,714
Dec/2008	Resolution CMN 3,655	Nov/2014	Circular BCB 3,730
Oct/2009	Circular BCB 3,471	Aug/2016	Circular BCB 3,809
Dec/2009	Resolution CMN 3,825 and Circular BCB 3,476		
Jun/2010	Circular BCB 3,498		
Dec/2010	Circular BCB 3,515		
Nov/2011	Circular BCB 3,563		
Dec/2011	Circular BCB 3,568		
Aug/2012	Circular BCB 3,608		
Aug/2012	Circular BCB 3,608		
Mar/2013	Resolution CMN 4,192; 4,193 and 4,195		
Jul/2013	Law 12,838		
Sep/2013	Resolution CMN 4,271		
Oct/2013	Resolution CMN 4,277 and 4,279; Circular BCB 3,674; 3,676; 3,677 and 3,679		
Jan/2014	Circular BCB 3,696		
Dec/2014	Circular BCB 3,741		
Feb/2015	Circular BCB 3,748		
Oct/2015	Circular BCB 3,768; 3,769 and 3,770		

Note: Authors' elaboration

Table A.4: Unit Root Test

				Critical values		
Variables	**I/T**	**Lag**	**Test**	**1%**	**5%**	**10%**
			ADF			
BUFFER	1	0	-2.917	-3.481	-2.884	-2.579
ROE		12	-1.854	-2.584	-1.943	-1.615
GDP_GAP		3	-4.182	-2.583	-1.943	-1.615
CRED_GDP		12	-4.280	-2.584	-1.943	-1.615
LIQ		0	-0.200	-2.583	-1.943	-1.615
$\Delta(LIQ)$		0	-12.609	-2.583	-1.943	-1.615
IR	I	2	-3.130	-3.482	-2.884	-2.579
			PP			
BUFFER	I	0.852	-2.917	-3.481	-2.884	-2.579
ROE		1.4	-1.730	-2.583	-1.943	-1.615
GDP_GAP		7.64	-2.644	-2.583	-1.943	-1.615
CRED_GDP		3	-2.076	-2.583	-1.943	-1.615
LIQ		1.52	-0.178	-2.583	-1.943	-1.615
$\Delta(LIQ)$		0.132	-12.609	-2.583	-1.943	-1.615
IR	T/I	16.1	-1.998	-4.030	-3.444	-3.147
$\Delta(IR)$		2.49	-3.367	-2.583	-1.943	-1.615
			KPSS			
BUFFER	T/I	18.8	0.063	0.119	0.146	0.216
ROE	T/I	50.7	0.153	0.119	0.146	0.216
GDP_GAP	I	59.1	0.156	0.347	0.463	0.739
CRED_GDP	I	33.5	0.097	0.347	0.463	0.739
LIQ	T/I	33.1	0.147	0.119	0.146	0.216
IR	I	70.9	0.194	0.347	0.463	0.739

Note: ADF test based on Schwarz criterion. PP and KPSS test bandwidth is Andrews using Bartlett kernel. Based on Schwarz criterion, intercept (I) or time trend (T/I) was applied.

Table A.5: Residual diagnostic tests

	Eq(1)	Eq(2.1)	Eq(2.2)	Eq(3.1)	Eq(3.2)
LM Test (1)	65.528	63.605	64.035	60.197	64.665
Prob. LM Test (1)	0.000	0.000	0.000	0.000	0.000
LM Test (2)	33.023	32.219	32.264	30.581	32.849
Prob. LM Test (2)	0.000	0.000	0.000	0.000	0.000
ARCH (1)	19.182	18.318	19.716	17.331	18.432
Prob. ARCH (1))	0.000	0.000	0.000	0.000	0.000
Jarque-Bera	0.377	0.269	0.346	0.698	0.464
Prob. Jarque-Bera	0.828	0.874	0.841	0.705	0.793

Note: Authors' elaboration

5

Revisiting Herding Investment Behavior on the Zagreb Stock Exchange: A Quantile Regression Approach

Tihana Škrinjarić[*♣]

[♣]Faculty od Economics and Business, University of Zagreb

ABSTRACT: Herding investment behavior on stock markets has consequences for practitioners, theorists, and policy makers. Thus, empirical research on this topic in the last couple of years has grown exponentially. However, there exist only a few papers dealing with herding behavior that consider the Croatian stock market. This study employs the quantile regression approach of estimating several herding investor behavior models of this market for the first time in the literature. Based upon daily data for the 37 most liquid stocks in the Zagreb Stock Exchange (ZSE) for the period September 22, 2014 to May 8, 2018, several model specifications are determined using quantile regression. Because the quantile regression approach deals with specific characteristics of financial data (stylized facts) better than the OLS method, more robust results can be achieved for evaluating if herding behavior is present in the Croatian market. The results indicate very weak to almost nonexistent evidence of herding behavior in the ZSE. Moreover, market volatility does not have any effect on herding behavior. Finally, the economic and political crisis (regarding concern Agrokor) in 2017 was controlled for in the model and the crisis was found insignificant. It seems that herding behavior does not need to be taken into account when tailoring investment strategies on the ZSE.

Keywords: herding investor behavior, quantile regression, Agrokor concern crisis, stock market

[*]Corresponding Author. Email: tskrinjar@net.efzg.hr

Introduction

In the past 20 years, the research on herding investment behavior has grown exponentially. The studies of Christie and Huang (1995) and Chang et al. (2000) are probably among the most cited papers with empirical research measuring herding behavior as well as estimating its variability under different stock market conditions. The most common approach to empirically evaluating herding behavior in a stock market is ordinary least squares (OLS) estimation using one of several popular models. Newey and West (1987) corrections of the estimated variance-covariance matrix are sometimes made if autocorrelation and/or heteroskedasticity are present in the data. However, OLS estimation, in general, focuses on the expected mean of a dependent variable. On the other hand, characteristics of financial data and financial markets (known as stylized facts) are different from other economic variables (Franses and Dijk, 2000; Guidolin and Pedio, 2018). Thus, OLS estimation is not always the best method of estimating a financial model due to the strong variable distribution assumptions that OLS requires, and because OLS focuses only on the conditional mean. A natural extension to OLS estimation is quantile regression (QR), a semi-parametric method of estimation which evaluates the whole distribution of the dependent variable (not only the mean). QR is robust to outliers in data and asymmetries as well as to non-normality, and it deals with heteroskedasticity in data very well (for a detailed discussion, see Koenker (2005), Davino et al. (2013)). Thus, its popularity has increased for finance applications in the last couple of years because it deals efficiently with characteristics of financial data.

Because herding investment behavior is mostly linked to extreme market movements (detailed results and an overview will be given in the next section), QR can be employed to successfully evaluate the nature of herding behavior in the lower and upper tails of distributions of the dependent variable in the model (see also Lobäo and Serra, 2002; Voronkova and Bohl, 2005; Tan et al., 2008). In this way, detailed insights into investors' behavior can be provided. This is relevant for individual investors and investment funds in order to exploit possible profitable investment strategies, for academic theoreticians and their developments of asset pricing theories, as well as for economic policy makers who try to stabilize the development of financial and stock markets in particular. Existing research on developing stock markets, as well as on Central and Eastern European (CEE) markets, is scarce. The majority of the studies in the literature use OLS in order to estimate simpler forms of the herding behavior model. Only a few exist which apply QR to explore such investment behavior on different markets, and this is especially true for the CEE markets and, in particular, the Croatian market. However, to the best of this author's knowledge, the augmented model of Chiang et al. (2013) has not yet been applied to the Croatian market.[1]

[1]The relevance of this model can be seen in the methodology part of the paper.

Another contribution of this study is the comparison of the QR estimates of the coefficients and their confidence bands across quantiles with the OLS estimates. This has rarely been done in the existing literature, and provides immediate insight into whether there are differences between these estimation methods.

Finally, another gap in the literature is the lack of reports of the effect of the Agrokor crisis in Croatia since 2017 on investor herding behavior. Agrokor is one of the biggest concerns in Croatia and South-East Europe. It consists mostly of large retailers, newsstands, meat producers, and agricultural-industrial companies in Croatia. Thus, controversies around this concern, which are still ongoing, have surely affected the Croatian stock market due to several listed Agrokor stocks.[2] Some of these were suspended from trading in March 2017 due to a sharp decline in their prices as a result of political events at the beginning of that year.

Thus, the purposes of this paper are to empirically evaluate the herding behavior of investors in Croatia, to test for asymmetries in such behavior, and to see if the Agrokor crisis has affected this behavior. The paper is structured as follows. Section 1 reviews previous relevant literature on herding behavior; three subsections explore the theory and its empirical applications in mature and developing markets. Section 2 describes the methodology used in this study. Results of the empirical research are given in Section 3. The last section concludes the paper with recommendations for future research.

1 Previous Research

1.1 Theory of Herding Behavior

An enormous amount of literature has dealt with the theoretical reasoning behind herding behavior. The most cited research includes studies by Scharfstein and Stein (1990), Devenow and Welch (1996), Cote and Sanders (1997), Bikhchandani et al. (1998), Christie and Huang (1995), Hirshleifer and Teoh (2001), Rook (2006), and Tan et al. (2008). Herding behavior "arises when investors decide to imitate the observed decisions of others or movements in the market rather than follow their own beliefs and information" (Hwang and Salmon, 2004). Some other definitions include "doing what everyone else is doing, even when one's private information suggests doing something else", the obvious intentions of investors to copy the behavior of others, suppressing one's own beliefs and basing investment decisions upon collective actions of the market (Banerjee, 1992; Christie and Huang, 1995). Explicit explanation of herding behavior dates from the works of behavioral economists such as Kahneman, Tversky, and others, but the idea dates back as early as Keynes (1936) who theoretically posited

[2]The stocks refer to the companies which Agrokor acquired over the several decades. More details are given in the empirical part of the paper.

that investors would follow others solely because of their fear that contrarian behavior on the market would damage their reputation. However, explanations of this behavior have become more promoted in the late 1990s and early 2000s.[3]

The explanations can be divided into two main groups: institutional versus individual investor herding behavior and rational versus non-rational explanations. Institutional investor herding is explained in depth in studies by Shiller and Pound (1989) and Lakonishok et al. (1991, 1992), where it is explained that such investors have more information about each others' trading activities. Moreover, because investment managers are evaluated against one another when decisions are made about their compensations, those managers do not want to be singled out for not having portfolios similar to those of others. Individual herding is explored in Merli and Roger (2013), Barber et al. (2009), and Venezia et al. (2011), where it is noted that herding among individuals is stronger compared to that among institutions as well as being more persistent and highly correlated to market volatility.

However, the vast majority of published studies concern the rational versus non-rational group of explanations. Rational explanations include information-, reputation-, and compensation-based herding. Information-based herding is based on a relative lack or excess of information compared to other market participants (imperfect information) and, basically, that information cascades occur on the market itself (Bikhchandani and Sharma, 2001).[4] Often, one group starts to follow another group, despite having information which could indicate different outcomes. However, new information shocks can disrupt those cascades. Sometimes, this type of herding is called cascade herding (Devenow and Welch, 1996). In these situations, investors often ignore their own beliefs about future movements of the market.

Reputation-based herding (or principal agent theory-based herding) is based on managers 'staying in the herd' and having similar performance to others because they want to hedge themselves against bad performances on the market. However, by doing so, they also lose above average gain potential (Scharfstein and Stein, 1990). If an individual investor/manager makes a bad investment decision, he/she loses some of his reputation. On the other hand, if a group of investors all make the same bad investment decision, no one is singled out and individual managers are not held responsible. This was discussed by Keynes (1936), who noted that it may be better for one's reputation to fail in a conventional way rather than succeed unconventionally.

Compensation-based herding also refers mostly to managers. Trueman (1994) explains that analysts make similar forecasts to each other based upon already published ones. In

[3]See Tversky and Kahneman (1974) for the psychological explanations of herding behavior, where cognitive biases lead to herding behavior because individuals follow ill-judged decisions of a group. See Baddeley (2010) for a detailed review and approach to psychological explanations.

[4]Informed traders actually reveal inside information which others follow (Shleifer and Summers, 1990; Calvo and Mendoza, 2000).

that way, those who have lower abilities just mimic the actions of others in order to get the same results and thus, compensation. Differently said, a manager's performance is measured compared to other professionals in the market. Thus, they are motivated to mimic others in the market in order to receive adequate compensation (Bikhchandani and Sharma, 2001).

Non-rational explanations are often based on psychology. Devenow and Welch (1996) state that investors feel more secure by blindly following others; Lux (1995) uses the expression "contagion of feelings" to explain conformity; Hatfield et al. (1993) and Barsade (2001) found evidence that emotions are contagious and this affects behavior. Some investors follow others and "hide in the herd" due to having a sense of security if they follow the majority (Goldbaum, 2008). Irrational herding is also linked to the theory of noise trading (see DeLong (1990); DeLong et al. (1991)). For further discussion of this topic, see Cote and Sanders (1997), Rook (2006), and Spyrou (2013).

1.2 Empirical Research Overview: Mature and Developed Markets

In examining the literature, we see that the early papers empirically evaluated more developed markets such as those in the United States, the United Kingdom, Germany, etc.[5] A review of this early work can be found in Lobäo and Serra (2007). In the last several years, emerging and frontier markets have been explored as well. Empirical results are divided based on the level of development of the markets examined in the studies. Most of the research uses daily data and the OLS method of estimation (with standard error corrections). Recently, some studies have used methodologies other than the OLS, but not QR approach as well (e.g., Markov switching in Bohl et al. (2013), threshold regression in Saumitra (2012)). The research approaches have included dividing the whole sample into subsections related to the events such as a financial crisis. Moreover, some of the research uses individual investor portfolios and individual stock level data, another part observes sector index data, and still another part uses portfolio and/or investment fund level data. Which type is used depends upon not only data availability, but on the researcher's specific questions as well. Summarized results are given in Table 1, where we see that the original model (defined in formula 3) has been tested in the majority of cases. Depending on the time span used, researchers have found different results and reached conclusions for the same market. However, when herding behavior is found, it is often in more extreme market movements (especially when markets go up).

[5]The distinction between developed, developing, and frontier markets has been made based upon suggestions in Chen (2013) and MSCI (Morgan Stanley Capital International) market classification.

1.3 Empirical Research Overview: Developing and Frontier Markets

This section will give an overview of recent papers relevant to this study, specifically studies examining CEE and other markets with similar characteristics to the Croatian market. The literature on herding investor behavior today is very large, so the focus here is on that research which is most closely linked to the Croatian market and the application of QR. In recent years, research on developing and emerging markets has grown rapidly. Much research has been focused on Asian markets, due to the Asian financial crisis in the late 1990s. A good overview of the Asian and Latin American markets is given in Chiang and Zheng (2010); on Pacific Basin markets in Chiang et al. (2013); and on different markets around the world in Garg and Gulati (2013) and Chen et al. (2017). Moreover, the theoretical models of Christie and Huang (1995) and Chang et al. (2000) have been extended in recent years: Chiang et al. (2013) add conditional return volatility to the original herding model of Christie and Huang (1995); Yao et al. (2014) modified that original model from 1995 to reduce multicollinearity and heteroskedasticity. New measures of herding behavior have also been developed (Hwang and Salmon, 2004, 2007). The majority of empirical studies have used daily data. Other frequencies are used less often. In some cases, when researchers have included other frequencies, the results indicate herding behavior only in the daily data. See Caporale et al. (2008), for an explanation of these results as a short-term phenomenon.

If we focus on markets similar to Croatia (small, problems with liquidity, emerging CEE markets) and research which employs QR methodology in observing herding behavior, a few conclusions can be drawn. The main findings are summarized in Table 2. We see that the QR method of estimation has emerged only in the last couple of years. The majority of the findings indicate that herding is present in stock markets, especially when the market goes up. However, when comparing estimated parameters across quantiles, herding is found to be an exception, not the rule. This means that the OLS estimation of herding behavior could lead potentially to spurious conclusions across the whole distribution of the herding variable. The Croatian stock market was examined by Pochea et al. (2017) using the QR method and by Škrinjarić and Šego (2018) using maximum likelihood general autoregressive conditional heteroskedasticity (ML-GARCH). The study of Pochea et al. (2017) found that herding in the Croatian market is an isolated phenomenon at the 25% quantile, with some asymmetries regarding effects of trading volume and volatility on herding behavior. The research of Škrinjarić and Šego (2018) focused only on the Croatian market, implemented 26 different specifications of the model, and confirmed the previous results. However, these two existing studies did not employ some of the models which will be used in this study, nor was there any assessment of the Agrokor crisis.

2 Methodology

Christie and Huang (1995) defined investor herding as the observed cross-sectional dispersion on the stock market as given by:

$$CSSD_t = \sqrt{\frac{1}{n-1}\sum_{j=1}^{n}(r_{j,t} - r_{m,t})^2} \quad (1)$$

where $CSSD_t$ denotes the cross-sectional standard deviation at time t, $r_{j,t}$ the return on stock j at time t, and $r_{m,t}$ the market return at time $t, j \in \{1, 2, ..., n\}$. The rationale is in the definition of investor herding: investors observe the actions of others and follow them despite their own beliefs. Thus, the dispersion around the market return is small and the measure given in (1) is smaller with greater herding. Chang et al. (2000) redefine the herding measure using the cross-sectional absolute deviation, $CSAD_t$:

$$CSAD_t = \frac{1}{n}\sum_{j=1}^{n}|r_{j,t} - r_{m,t}|. \quad (2)$$

Most of the recent literature uses the measure given in (2), due to it being more robust to outliers in the data.[6]

The original model of herding behavior is as follows:

$$CSAD_t = \beta_0 + \beta_1|r_{m,t}| + \beta_2 r_{m,t}^2 + \varepsilon_t \quad (3)$$

where it is assumed that in a rational asset pricing model, a linear relationship between market return and $CSAD$ exists (positive value of parameter β_1). Moreover, if herding occurs during extreme market movements (denoted with the squared market return), then the value of parameter β_2 should be negative. The variable ε_t is the error term; when estimating model (3) using the OLS method, it is assumed that $\varepsilon_t \sim N(0, \sigma^2)$. Because return series are used in the empirical research, this assumption is usually violated. Thus Newey and West (1987) corrections of the variance-covariance matrix of error terms are made, or the GARCH specification is added to the model as well.

Chiang et al. (2013) extended model (3) to the following specification:

$$CSAD_t = \beta_0 + \beta_1|r_{m,t}| + \beta_2 r_{m,t}^2 + \beta_3 r_{m,t}^3 + \beta_4 r_{m,t}^2 \sigma_t^2 + \varepsilon_t \quad (4)$$

[6]The authors based this measure on the conditional CAPM model of Black (1972). Thus, the measure in (2) is the approximation of the expected cross-sectional absolute deviation of the market. As Spyrou (2013) states: "The notion behind this approach is that if herding is present during periods of extreme market conditions, then there should be a less than proportional increase (or even decrease) in the CSAD measure."

where the cubed market returns term, $\beta_3 r_{m,t}^3$, represents the product of the $r_{m,t}^2$ and $r_{m,t}$ terms, interpreted as the interaction of herding behavior with the market return. This is based on evidence of and arguments regarding prevailing market returns (DeLong, 1990; DeLong et al., 1991; Sentana and Wadhwani, 1992): positive feedback traders will sell (buy) stocks in a falling (rising) market and the opposite is true for negative feedback traders. This was also observed by Friedman (1953), and other research finds this to be true (Goodfellow et al., 2009; Holmes et al., 2013; Gavriilidis et al., 2013).

The interaction of the squared return and conditional volatility (σ_t^2) is based upon arguments in Butler and Joaquin (2002) and Forbes and Rigobon (2002): the herding (i.e., cross-market correlations) is smaller when market volatility is small. This was observed empirically, such as in Economoua et al. (2010) and Holmes et al. (2013).

Conditional volatility is estimated in the first step with the GARCH model specification and used in the second step to estimate model (4). If the value of β_3 is positive, then herding is smaller in a downward market; a negative value means that herding is smaller in an upward market. A similar result is interpreted for the value of β_4 (a positive value means that herding decreases as volatility rises and vice versa). Model (4) has not yet been examined on CEE markets, especially Croatian, even without the inclusion of QR methodology.

Yao et al. (2014) defined the following model:

$$CSAD_t = \beta_0 + \beta_1 |r_{m,t}| + \gamma_1 \left(r_{m,t} - \overline{r_m}\right)^2 + \gamma_2 CSAD_{t-1} + \varepsilon_t \tag{5}$$

to reduce multicollinearity and autocorrelation, where $\overline{r_m}$ is the expected market return.

Binary variables are often added in various specifications of herding models in order to measure asymmetries in bull and bear markets, and to include effects of some shocks such as the global financial crisis of 2007/2008 or some local crisis (such as Agrokor in Croatia). That is why models (4) and (5) will be extended as:

$$CSAD_t = \beta_0 + \beta_1 |r_{m,t}| + \beta_2 r_{m,t}^2 + \beta_3 r_{m,t}^3 + \beta_4 r_{m,t}^2 \sigma_t^2 + \beta_5 D_{1,t} + \varepsilon_t \tag{6}$$

where

$$D_{1,t} = \begin{cases} 1 & \text{for period March-April 2017,} \\ 0 & \text{otherwise.} \end{cases}$$

The inclusion of the binary variable for up and down markets is not needed in this specification of the model due to the inclusion of the cubed value of market returns and the volatility interaction. However, model (5) needs the inclusion of the second binary variable as well:

$$\begin{aligned} CSAD_t &= \beta_0 + \beta_1|r_{m,t}| + |D_{2,t} + \phi_1|r_{m,t}|(1 - D_{2,t}) \\ &+ \gamma_1 \left(r_{m,t} - \overline{r_m}\right)^2 D_{2,t} + \phi_2(r_{m,t} - \overline{r_m})^2(1 - D_{2,t}) \\ &+ \gamma_2 CSAD_{t-1} D_{2,t} + \phi_3 CSAD_{t-1}(1 - D_{2,t}) + \beta_5 D_{1,t} + \varepsilon_t \end{aligned} \tag{7}$$

where

$$D_{2,t} = \begin{cases} 1 & r_{m,t} > 0, \\ 0 & \text{otherwise.} \end{cases}$$

Now, in models (3)–(7), a quantile regression specification is added. Quantile regression has advantages over the least squares method because QR can deal with different types of variable distributions; it does not focus only on the conditional mean of the dependent variable; different effects of variables in the model can be extracted which cannot be done when using OLS; QR is more robust to outliers in data; and, if the data is non-normal, then QR estimates are more precise compared to OLS estimates. We follow Koenker and Bassett (1978), Koenker (2005), and Davino et al. (2013) in describing the methodology. A linear quantile regression model is given by the following:

$$y_i = \beta_\theta + \sum_{k=1}^{K} x_i \beta_k(\theta) + \varepsilon_i \tag{8}$$

where $\beta_k(\theta)$ is the k-th unknown parameter at the θ-th quantile, $k \in \{0, 1, ..., K\}$. Model (8) is estimated at the θ-th quantile, $Q_\theta(y|X)$, $0 < \theta < 1$, via the minimization problem given as:

$$\underset{\beta_k(\theta)}{\arg\max} \left[\sum_{i:y_i<\widehat{y}_1} (1-\theta) \left| y_i - \beta_0(\theta) - \sum_{k=1}^{K} x_i \beta_k(\theta) \right| \sum_{i:y_i \geq \widehat{y}_i} \theta \left| y_i - \beta_0(\theta) - \sum_{k=1}^{K} x_i \beta_k(\theta) \right| \right]. \tag{9}$$

We observe that the optimization problem in (9) is a weighted sum of absolute deviations of estimated values from the real ones. The usual procedure to minimize the expression in (9) is by using a linear programming model. The goodness of fit of the model is measured at each quantile with pseudo-R squared, calculated as the difference between the residual and total absolute sum of weighted deviations:

$$R_\theta^2 = 1 - \frac{\sum_{i:y_i \geq \widehat{y}_i} \widehat{\theta}|y_i - \widehat{y}_i| + \sum_{i:y_i < \widehat{y}_i} (1-\widehat{\theta})|y_i - \widehat{y}_i|}{\sum_{i:y_i \geq \widehat{\theta}} \widehat{\theta}|y_i - \widehat{\theta}| + \sum_{i:y_i < \widehat{\theta}} (1-\widehat{\theta})|y_i - \widehat{\theta}|}. \tag{10}$$

Of course, the pseudo-R squared cannot be compared to the regular coefficient of determination because the pseudo-R squared measures goodness of fit only at the θ-th quantile. Because this method is semi-parametric, statistical inference based on estimated values of parameters in the model can be made after a bootstrapping procedure us used to estimate the standard errors of the beta parameters. Two of the most commonly used bootstrapping procedures are the *xy-pair* method and the MCMB (Markov chain marginal bootstrap). The usual Wald test can be conducted to test for any linear hypothesis in the model, including the test for asymmetries across quantiles. Thus, all the herding models described above will be estimated using the QR approach at the following quantiles: 0.01, 0.05, 0.1, 0.25, 0.5, 0.75, 0.90, 0.95, and 0.99. The extreme quantiles are included in order to observe herding behavior in the tails of the herding variable distribution. Because Christie and Huang (1995) state that herding is more prominent during extreme market movements, extreme quantiles are observed to get more insights about these situations. The results are given in the next section.

3 Empirical Results

3.1 Croatian Stock Market Characteristics

The Croatian stock market is a relatively young market, having started in 1997. Detailed analysis of the legislation and its effects on the Zagreb Stock Exchange (ZSE) is given in Šeba (2017). This research concludes that the legislation did not serve to develop this market and, today, the ZSE is mostly a platform for institutional investors. The value of the official stock market index CROBEX, the total capitalization, and the number of transactions were stagnating until 2003. Afterward, all the series showed an increased growth until the last financial crisis in 2007–2008 (Figures 1 and 2). A mild recovery of the ZSE in 2010 ended the next year, and it has stagnated ever since. Before the financial crisis, the Croatian stock market was bigger than the Romanian and Baltic markets combined (considering market capitalization). This was due to initial public offerings (IPOs) of some of the biggest companies in Croatia (HT, Atlantic Group, Ingra, Magma and Optima; Zagreb Stock Exchange, 2006, 2007, 2008).

Škrinjarić and Besek (2014) analyzed the stock market capitalization within the total capitalization.[7] The results showed that investors' euphoria and IPOs contributed to the development of the market before the crisis. The stock capitalization showed a negative trend after 2008 and Škrinjarić and Besek (2014) concluded that this was a result of the introduction of new structured securities and investors' prudence (investing more into bonds).

[7]Total capitalization includes stock market, bond market and other financial instruments capitalization on ZSE.

Jošić (2006) adds that the beginning of the negotiations with the European Union in the early 2000s have positively affected the development of the market as well. The Croatian market today is shallow. For example, in 2013, the most liquid stocks have constituted almost 60% of the total market capitalization (the clustering of liquidity is seen only in big company stocks, such as the above mentioned HT and Atlantic group, as well as the IGH institute and Dalekovod).

Another problem is the illiquidity of the market. This is especially true for the period after the crisis. In the last year (2017), the total number of traded securities on the ZSE (including bonds and other types of investments) was 184, with many companies withdrawn from the stock market itself. Vidović (2013) examined whether investors are rewarded for the illiquidity premium on the ZSE. The results of the analysis indicated a negative answer.

3.2 Data Description

For the purpose of empirical study of the Croatian market, daily data on prices of 37 stocks and the value of the stock market index, CROBEX, were collected from the Zagreb Stock Exchange (2018) for the period September 22, 2014 through May 8, 2018. The sample is restricted due to using liquid stocks (illiquid stocks are a problem prominent on the Croatian stock market). Because there are not many stocks to choose from on the ZSE, stocks which were traded at least 30% of the time in the observed period (at least 272 days in total) are used in the sample. If this criterion was higher, e.g., 60%, then only 25 stocks would have been left in the analysis. For the value of 75% only 17 stocks would be used, and there would be only 9 stocks that were traded at least 90% of the time. Thus, when the ZSE is being empirically evaluated (regardless of the area which is being researched), the usual practice is to pick the liquid stocks which have been most frequently traded. The stock market return is constructed based on stocks which constituted the index CROBEX in each official revision. This means that not all the 37 stocks constituting this index are in the whole sample. Returns for each stock price were calculated as continuous returns. The $CSAD_t$ value was calculated as defined in formula (2). The augmented Dickey-Fuller (ADF) and Zivot-Andrews structural unit root tests were performed for the deviation variable and market return series. All the tests (also controlling for the drift, and for the drift and trend) reject the hypothesis of unit root (with a structural break in the case of the Zivot-Andrews test).[8] The conditional variance of the market returns was estimated using a GARCH (1,1) process with the assumption of Student's distribution and an ARMA(1,1) process of market return series.[9] A binary variable was constructed in order to control for the Agrokor crisis,

---

[8]Detailed results are available upon request.

[9]The specification of ARMA(1,1)–GARCH(1,1) was chosen based upon the diagnostics of the model. Detailed results are available upon request.

which became publicly prominent at the beginning of March 2017. Agrokor's stocks were delisted from the Zagreb Stock Exchange at the end of April 2017. Thus, the first binary variable is equal to 1 for the period from March 1, 2017 to April 30, 2017 and 0 otherwise. The second binary variable was constructed to control for the market going up or down, with the variable being equal to 1 if the market return is greater than 0 on day t and 0 otherwise.

Descriptive statistics were determined for the $CSAD$ variable in the observed period to additionally confirm the need for using the QR method. Skewness of the $CSAD$ variable is equal to 18.24 and the Jarque-Bera test rejects the normality hypothesis at the usual levels of significance (test statistic value is equal to 10019.16). The coefficient of autocorrelation for the $CSAD$ variable is equal to 0.58 at lag 1, and is statistically significant at the usual levels (test value in Ljung-Box test is equal to 313.83). This justifies including the lagged value of the dependent variable, as is done in model (5). Moreover, the QQ-plot of the herding variable and its comparison to the normal distribution confirms the results of the Jarque-Bera test (Figure 3). Additionally, the asymmetry compared to the median value of the $CSAD$ is examined in Figure 4, where it can be seen that major discrepancies exist when comparing the upper and lower tails of the distribution. This justifies the use of QR methodology to explore herding behavior on the Croatian market.

3.3 The Agrokor Crisis Explained

Inclusion of the binary variable for the Agrokor crisis is due to the size of this concern and the current political events and problems surrounding it. At the end of 2016, Agrokor employed more than 58,000 people in the Balkan area, with a significant drop to 52,500 people in 2017 (Agrokor 2016, 2018). The spread of Agrokor to other countries in the 2000s was significant, based on acquisitions in Serbia, Bosnia and Herzegovina, Hungary, and leading up to the final bigger acquisition in Slovenia at the beginning of the 2010s.

Controversy among investors arose due to Agrokor's high indebtedness when Slovenia's Mercator was bought in 2014. Through the 2010s, Agrokor's growth and operating profit growth rates were lower than the borrowing rate. The increasing market shares of Lidl and Kaufland (small retailers) were also affecting the total business of this concern. And moreover, the economic crisis lasted in Croatia from 2008 until 2014, which affected the revenues of Agrokor as well (Klepo et al., 2017). At the end of 2016, due to Agrokor's inability to pay back debts, the Croatian Bank for Reconstruction and Development granted it new loans. The public was more concerned at the beginning of 2017, when the credit agency Moody's lowered the rating of Agrokor from B2 to B3 (this was a first major negative news about Agrokor which got public). In February 2017, the rating was lowered once again.

Chain events were triggered afterward, mostly political. These included the appointment of a new extraordinary commissioner for the concern, and new legislation, called *lex Agrokor*.

In March 2017, the Croatian government and Agrokor's representatives met regarding the problems. The Speaker of the Croatian Parliament, Božo Petrov, resigned from his position due to his disagreements with the rest of the Parliament and Petrov submitted criminal charges against the Agrokor Management Board. Newspapers got hold of e-mail communications between some members of the Croatian government and Agrokor's top people which exposed that some people in the Government knew what was going on. Since then, more data and information has become available, including that Agrokor used shadow banking (using unsecured bills of exchange; see Klepo et al. (2017)). The Agrokor companies with stocks on the ZSE saw their prices drop significantly in March and April of 2017.

The uncertainty regarding the Agrokor situation spilled over into the ZSE, with the food sector index dropping in value by 45.1% in 2017 (ZSE, 2018). Some of the greatest decreases in Agrokor stock prices in 2017 were: Ledo (-97.31%), Jamnica (-97.23%), Zvijezda (-97.02%), Pik (-96.3%), Vupik (-90.89%), and Tisak (-88.39%). The transaction volume rose greatly on the ZSE in March due to selling of those stocks: the total volume increased by 41%, and offering volume increased by 37% because investors wanted to get rid of the stocks. The total market index, CROBEX, dropped in value by 10% and the revision of the food sector index excluded all of the Agrokor's stocks.

Because of all these problems, Agrokor's stocks were withdrawn from the ZSE at the end of April 2017. Moreover, Hanfa (the Croatian financial services supervisory agency) surveyed what was going on at the ZSE and demanded that trading of those stocks be stopped due to the total macroeconomic effects of Agrokor's crisis (Hanfa, 2017) and the visible effects on factoring companies as well (there was a decrease of 56.5% in the value of their assets).

Analysis by the Croatian National Bank reveals that the country experienced a slowdown in economic growth in the second quarter of 2017, due to uncertainties around the Agrokor concern, as well as a decrease in consumer confidence in April of that year. The crisis due to the problems surrounding this concern affected the dispersion around the market return, increasing it in March and April 2017. As a result of investors getting rid of Agrokor's stocks and some speculative attacks made on the ZSE, some sectors experienced a significant drop in index values (e.g., food) and some experienced great growth (e.g., tourism).

This research assumes that the Agrokor crisis had a significant impact on the $CSAD$ variable, as well as on herding. This is based on Devenow and Welch (1996) who proposed that herding can be irrational at a single point in time, such as when a large decline in stock prices causes investors to instantly sell stocks in order to avoid great portfolio losses and without having done any analysis of the situation.

3.4 Estimated Models Results

The original model given in equation 3 with the binary variable $D_{1,t}$ was estimated using both OLS and QR methods to obtain initial insights into the relationship between market returns and dispersion. Detailed results are given in Table 8. It can be seen that the linear relationship exists in lower quantiles (up to the median) and, afterward, the coefficient β_1 becomes statistically insignificant. Thus, the *CAPM* assumption of the linear relationship between risk and return is questionable on the Croatian market. The value of $\widehat{\beta}_1$ differs across quantiles: it ranges from 10.327 to -44.239. However, none of the estimated parameters on different quantiles are significant, meaning that very weak evidence on nonlinearities exist if we observe this model. Finally, the effects of the Agrokor crisis are present only in quantiles from 50% to 90% with positive estimated parameters (contributing to greater dispersion around the market return).

A graphical comparison of estimated values of the parameters of model (3) is shown in Figure 4. The 99% quantile was excluded because it is significantly different from the other quantiles and it disables the clear visualization of the other quantiles. The full representation of Figure 3 with the 99% quantile included is given in the appendix in Figures 5 and 6. Red lines denote the OLS estimation (solid line) with its 95% confidence bands (dashed lines), and black lines denote the estimates using the QR method. It seems there are no differences between the estimations with OLS and QR on any quantile with the exception of the 95% and 99% quantiles. Initially, it could be concluded that there do not exist significant differences between the two methods of estimation for the majority of the quantiles for both variables in the model. However, this original model ignores the effects of different market conditions (bull vs. bear markets), possible autocorrelation, effects of volatility, etc. That is why the QR specifications in equations (6) and (7) of the herding model have been estimated. The results are shown in Table 3, while graphical representations of the parameters are given in the appendix in Figures 7–16.

By observing Table 3, top panel, regarding model (6), we see that in the OLS specification only the variable *cubed market returns* was significant (at the 10% level of significance, indicating borderline significance). Thus, the validity of this model could be questionable from the OLS viewpoint. By adding a richer structure using the QR methodology, several conclusions can be drawn. First, the same variable-the cubed value of market returns, is insignificant for all quantiles. This means that the sign of the market return did not affect herding in the observed period on the ZSE. Parameter $\widehat{\beta}_3$ is negative only in the highest quantiles (95% and 99%), meaning that at the highest quantiles, the herding behavior is somewhat greater in an upward market (showing a bit more consensus in the market). This is in line with previous results regarding Croatia; however, here we do not find enough statistical evidence in favor of herding. Second, it is noticeable that the interaction effect between market return and volatility, $\widehat{\beta}_4$, is large for all quantiles, and $\widehat{\beta}_4$ has positive values for almost all. Although the sign is in line with previous research (such as Forbes and Rigobon (2002) and Venezia et al. (2011)), the values, once again, are not significant.

The mixed results for the quadratic term of market returns (parameter $\widehat{\beta}_2$) confirm previous conclusions in literature that this variable cannot by itself capture non-linearity in the model (Kabir, 2018). Finally, the Agrokor crisis has affected herding only at the 50% and 90% quantiles, with the effect being positive (values of $\widehat{\beta}_5$). This could be interpreted more as coincidence rather than actual effect. These results are in line with some previous findings which have also failed to detect herding (Chang et al. (2000) and Caparrelli et al. (2004); Pochea et al. (2017) for Croatia).

The results of the estimating model (7) are given in the lower panel of Table 3. Again, the linear part of the model and the squared term of market returns lead to similar conclusions; they are not significant in the model due to their inability to fully capture the herding behavior in the market (see columns for $\widehat{\beta}_1$, $\widehat{\phi}_1$, $\widehat{\gamma}_1$, and $\widehat{\phi}_2$). Only when the dispersion is quite low (from the 1% up to the 10% quantiles), the absolute value of the market return when the market goes down has somewhat (positive) effects on the dispersion. The lagged value of the dispersion variable is the only significant one for all quantiles, regardless of the market conditions (see columns for $\widehat{\gamma}_2$ and $\widehat{\phi}_3$). Although Pochea et al. (2017) estimated the model with the inclusion of the lagged value of the $CSAD$ variable, they did not separate the effects of up and down markets. The novelty in this study is distinguishing those effects when the market is bearish and bullish in order to test if differences exist. Although in the literature a lagged dependent variable is added to reduce autocorrelation in the data, the parameter of that variable can be interpreted as how persistent the behavior of that variable is through time. The column with the parameter $\widehat{\gamma}_2$) refers to bull markets; bear market conditions are captured in the column with parameter $\widehat{\phi}_3$.

Across all quantiles, both parameters are positive, which means a positive autocorrelation exists in herding behavior. Thus, when dispersion on day t is low, it is more likely to be low the next day. To see if the parameters for the bull and bear markets are equal (i.e., a symmetry test), a Wald test was performed for each quantile. The results are given in Table 4. We see that in extreme quantiles of the dispersion variable some persistence exists. Finally, the effect of the Agrokor crisis in such a setting is, again, not significant in the model. This is not unexpected; some research has found that in a crisis period when markets go down there is actually less herding, although this is contrary to many previous findings (see Choe et al. (1999) or Hwang and Salmon (2004)).

Additionally, models with the inclusion of the Agrokor binary variable in interaction with the squared market returns were estimated:

$$CSAD_t = \beta_0 + \beta_1 \left| r_{m,t} \right| + \beta_2 \, r_{m,t}^2 + \beta_5 \, D_{1,t} + \lambda \, D_{1,t} \, r_{m,t}^2 + \varepsilon_t, \tag{11}$$

in order to obtain more detailed insights into its effects on herding and the squared market return. The results are shown in Tables 5, 6, and 7. Again, if significant results are found, it is more often an isolated event rather than a rule. Thus, based on the results from models (11)–(13), it can be finally confirmed that herding on the ZSE is not prominent in the observed period after controlling for markets going up or down, the autocorrelation, volatility, and sign of the changes of the market return itself.

4 Conclusion

Herding investor behavior on stock markets has received more attention in the last 20 years, especially after financial crises, because it affects practitioners, policy makers, and academics. In order to enhance investment strategies to beat the market or to tailor suitable economic policies and theoretical models, studies into investor behavior on stock markets need to be done. The majority of the existing empirical literature focuses on more developed markets and uses simpler methodologies. However, investor behavior is not always simple or rational, and asymmetries in human behavior exist. As there is not much research on the Croatian stock market on this topic, the purpose of this paper was to fill some of the existing gaps in the literature. The main findings in this research include the following: Herding behavior on the Croatian market (as an example of a small, emerging, and illiquid market) is not observed with the models used in this study. It is slightly more visible when the market goes up, with the greatest effect being visible at extreme quantiles, especially at the right tail of the dispersion variable distribution. However, the results are insignificant; the signs of specific parameters change only when going from extremely low to extremely high quantiles.

Due to problems of illiquidity in this market, it is possible that herding is not a common phenomenon on the ZSE. This is in line with the explanations of Devenow and Welch (1996) and previous empirical literature which included Croatia in the analysis. The majority of the examined effects of different variables in the model are not significant, especially around the median and quantiles closer to it. Somewhat different behavior is detected sometimes in some extreme quantiles. However, this can be interpreted as due to chance alone. The only significant behavior was found in the persistence of $CSAD$ variable in markets going up or down. The Agrokor crisis was not found to be significant in affecting herding behavior. This could be because the stocks from that concern were withdrawn so quickly from trading that the effects were not severe.

Some of the shortfalls of this study include the following. A small sample of stocks was included in the study due to illiquidity problems on the ZSE. Only the Croatian market as a whole was observed. And small markets such as the Croatian one could be affected by other markets' movements such as those of the German and other CEE markets. Thus, future research should include spillover effects on herding behavior as well. Also, more insights can be obtained by observing institutional investors and the structures of their portfolios. Thus, more research is needed in that area in the future.

References

Ababio, K. A. and Mwamba, J. M. (2017). Test of herding behaviour in the Johannesburg stock exchange: application of quantile regression model. *Journal of Economic and Financial Sciences*, 10(3):457–474.

Al-Shboul, M. (2013). An Examination of Herd Behavior in the Jordanian Equity Market. *International Journal of Economics and Finance*, 5(1):234–249.

Arouri, M. E. H., Bellando, R., Ringuedé, S., and Vaubourg, A.-G. (2010). Herding by institutional investors: empirical evidence from French mutual funds. Working Papers hal-00507832, HAL.

Baddeley, M. (2010). Herding, social influence and economic decision-making: socio-psychological and neuroscientific analyses. *Philosophical Transactions of the Royal Society of London B: Biological Sciences*, 365(1538):281–290.

Banerjee, A. V. (1992). A Simple Model of Herd Behavior. *The Quarterly Journal of Economics*, 107(3):797–817.

Barber, B., Odean, T., and Zhu, N. (2009). Systematic noise. *Journal of Financial Markets*, 12(4):547–569.

Barsade, S. G. (2001). The Ripple Effect: Emotional Contagion In Groups. Yale school of management working papers, Yale School of Management.

Bikhchandani, S., Hirshleifer, D., and Welch, I. (1998). Learning from the Behavior of Others: Conformity, Fads, and Informational Cascades. *The Journal of Economic Perspectives*, 12(3):151–170.

Bikhchandani, S. and Sharma, S. (2001). Comportamiento gregario o de rebaño en los mercados financieros: una reseña. *Boletín*, 0(1):23–42.

Black, F. (1972). Capital Market Equilibrium with Restricted Borrowing. *The Journal of Business*, 45(3):444–55.

Blasco, N. and Ferreruela, S. (2008). Testing Intentional Herding in Familiar Stocks: An Experiment in an International Context. *Journal of Behavioral Finance*, 9(2):72–84.

Bohl, M. T., Klein, A. C., and Siklos, P. L. (2013). A Markov switching approach to herding. Working paper, Centre for International Governance Innovation.

Butler, K. C. and Joaquin, D. C. (2002). Are the gains from international portfolio diversification exaggerated? The influence of downside risk in bear markets. *Journal of International Money and Finance*, 21(7):981–1011.

Calvo, G. A. and Mendoza, E. G. (2000). Rational contagion and the globalization of securities markets. *Journal of International Economics*, 51(1):79 – 113.

Caparrelli, F., D'Arcangelis, A. M., and Cassuto, A. (2004). Herding in the Italian Stock Market: A Case of Behavioral Finance. *Journal of Behavioral Finance*, 5(4):222–230.

Caporale, G. M., Philippas, N., and Economou, F. (2008). Herding behaviour in extreme market conditions: the case of the Athens Stock Exchange. *Economics Bulletin*, 7(17):1–13.

Chang, E. C., Cheng, J. W., and Khorana, A. (2000). An examination of herd behavior in equity markets: An international perspective. *Journal of Banking and Finance*, 24(10):1651–1679.

Chen, T. (2013). Do Investors Herd in Global Stock Markets? *Journal of Behavioral Finance*, 14(3):230–239.

Chen, Y.-C., Wu, H.-C., and Huang, J.-J. (2017). Herd Behavior and Rational Expectations: A Test of China's Market Using Quantile Regression. *International Journal of Economics and Financial Issues*, 7(2):649–663.

Chiang, T., Tan, L., Li, J., and Nelling, E. (2013). Dynamic Herding Behavior in Pacific-Basin Markets: Evidence and Implications. *Multinational Finance Journal*, 17(3-4):165–200.

Chiang, T. C. and Zheng, D. (2010). An empirical analysis of herd behavior in global stock markets. *Journal of Banking and Finance*, 34(8):1911–1921.

Choe, H., Kho, B.-C., and Stulz, R. M. (1999). Do foreign investors destabilize stock markets? The Korean experience in 1997. *Journal of Financial Economics*, 54(2):227–264.

Chong, T. T.-L., Liu, X., and Zhu, C. (2017). What Explains Herd Behavior in the Chinese Stock Market? *Journal of Behavioral Finance*, 18(4):448–456.

Christie, W. G. and Huang, R. D. (1995). Following the Pied Piper: Do Individual Returns Herd around the Market? *Financial Analysts Journal*, 51(4):31–37.

Cote, J. and Sanders, D. (1997). Herding Behavior: Explanations and Implications. *Behavioral Research in Accounting*, 19:20–45.

Davino, C., Furno, M., and Vistocco, D. (2013). *Quantile regression: theory and applications.* John Wiley & Sons.

DeLong, J Bradford, e. a. (1990). Positive Feedback Investment Strategies and Destabilizing Rational Speculation. *Journal of Finance*, 45(2):379–395.

DeLong, J. B., Shleifer, A., Summers, L. H., and Waldmann, R. J. (1991). The Survival of Noise Traders in Financial Markets. *The Journal of Business*, 64(1):1–19.

Devenow, A. and Welch, I. (1996). Rational herding in financial economics. *European Economic Review*, 40(3-5):603–615.

Economoua, F., Kostakis, A., and Philippas, N. (2010). An Examination of Herd Behaviour in Four Mediterranean Stock Markets. In *Proceedings at the European Economics and Finance Society's 9th Annual Conference, 3-6 June 2010.* Global Imbalances, Financial Institutions, and Reforms in the Post-crisis Era, Athens, Greece.

Filip, A., Pochea, M., and Pece, A. (2015a). The Herding Behaviour of Investors in the CEE Stocks Markets. *Procedia Economics and Finance*, 32:307–315.

Filip, A.-M., Pece, A. M., and Pochea, M. M. (2015b). An Empirical Investigation of Herding Behavior in CEE Stock Markets under the Global Financial Crisis. *Procedia Economics and Finance*, 25:354 – 361.

Forbes, K. J. and Rigobon, R. (2002). No Contagion, Only Interdependence: Measuring Stock Market Comovements. *Journal of Finance*, 57(5):2223–2261.

Franses, P. H. and Dijk, D. v. (2000). *Non-Linear Time Series Models in Empirical Finance.* Cambridge University Press.

Friedman, M. (1953). *The Case for Flexible Exchange Rates, in: Essays in Positive Economics,.* University of Chicago Press.

Garg, A. and Gulati, R. (2013). Do investors herd in Indian market. *DECISION*, 40(3):181–196.

Gavriilidis, K., Kallinterakis, V., and Ferreira, M. P. L. (2013). Institutional industry herding: Intentional or spurious? *Journal of International Financial Markets, Institutions and Money*, 26(C):192–214.

Goldbaum, D. (2008). Coordinated investing with feedback and learning. *Journal of Economic Behavior and Organization*, 65(2):202–223.

Goodfellow, C., Bohl, M. T., and Gebka, B. (2009). Together we invest? Individual and institutional investors' trading behaviour in Poland. *International Review of Financial Analysis*, 18(4):212–221.

Guidolin, M. and Pedio, M. (2018). *Essentials of Time Series for Financial Applications.* Academic Press.

Hatfield, E., Cacioppo, J. T., and Rapson, R. L. (1993). Emotional Contagion. *Current Directions in Psychological Science*, 2(3):96–100.

Hirshleifer, D. and Teoh, S. H. (2001). Herd Behavior and Cascading in Capital Markets: A Review and Synthesis. MPRA Paper 5186, University Library of Munich, Germany.

Holmes, P., Kallinterakis, V., and Ferreira, M. P. L. (2013). Herding in a Concentrated Market: a Question of Intent. *European Financial Management*, 19(3):497–520.

Hwang, S. and Salmon, M. (2004). Market stress and herding. *Journal of Empirical Finance*, 11(4):585 – 616.

Hwang, S. and Salmon, M. (2007). Sentiment and Beta Herding. University of warwick, University of Warwick Working Paper.

Jošić, M. (2006). Utjecaj procesa pregovora Hrvatske s Europskom komisijom na razvoj tržišta dionica u Hrvatskoj (Impact of the Coatia's EU accession on the development of capital market in Croatia). *Zbornik Ekonomskog fakulteta u Zagrebu (Proceedings of the Faculty of Economics and Business in Zagreb)*, Vol. 4, No. 1:131–144.

Kabir, M. H. (2018). Did Investors Herd during the Financial Crisis? Evidence from the US Financial Industry. *International Review of Finance*, 18(1):59–90.

Kallinterakis, V. and Lodetti, M. (2009). Nonlinearities, Herd Behaviour and Market Illiquidity: Evidence from Montenegro? *Economic Analysis*, 42(3-4):7–17.

Keynes, J. M. (1936). *The general theory of employment, interest and money.* London : Macmillan, 1936.

Khan, H., Hassairi, S., and Viviani, J.-L. (2011). Herd behavior and market stress: The case of four European countries. *International Business Research*, 4(3):53–67.

Klepo, M., Bićanić, I., and Ivanković, v. (2017). Slučaj Agrokor: Kriza najveće hrvatske kompanije. Friedrich ebert stiftung analysis, Friedrich Ebert Stiftung.

Koenker, R. (2005). *Quantile Regression.* Cambridge University Press.

Koenker, R. W. and Bassett, G. (1978). Regression Quantiles. *Econometrica*, 46(1):33–50.

Kremer, S. and Nautz, D. (2011). Short-Term Herding of Institutional Traders: New Evidence from the German Stock Market. Discussion Paper 2011-015, Sonderforschungsbereich 649, Humboldt University, Berlin, Germany.

Lakonishok, J., Shleifer, A., and Vishny, R. W. (1991). Do Institutional Investors Destabilize Stock Prices? Evidence on Herding and Feedback Trading. Working Paper 3846, National Bureau of Economic Research.

Lakonishok, J., Shleifer, A., and Vishny, R. W. (1992). The impact of institutional trading on stock prices. *Journal of Financial Economics*, 32(1):23 – 43.

Lobäo, J. and Serra, A. (2007). *Diversification and Portfolio Management of Mutual Funds. Finance and Capital Markets Series.*, chapter Herding Behavior: Evidence from Portuguese Mutual Funds, pages 167–197. Palgrave Macmillan, London.

Lobäo, J. and Serra, A. P. (2002). Herding behavior: Evidence from Portuguese mutual funds. Working paper. In *Proceedings of the Second Conference of the Portuguese Finance Network.*

Lux, T. (1995). Herd Behaviour, Bubbles and Crashes. *Economic Journal*, 105(431):881–96.

Merli, M. and Roger, T. (2013). What drives the herding behavior of individual investors? *Finance*, 34(3):67–104.

Mobarek, A., Mollah, S., and Keasey, K. (2014). A cross-country analysis of herd behavior in Europe. *Journal of International Financial Markets, Institutions and Money*, 32(C):107–127.

Newey, W. and West, K. (1987). A Simple, Positive Semi-definite, Heteroskedasticity and Autocorrelation Consistent Covariance Matrix. *Econometrica*, 55(3):703–08.

Ouarda, M., Bouri, A. E., and Bernard, O. (2013). Herding Behavior under Markets Condition: Empirical Evidence on the European Financial Markets. *International Journal of Economics and Financial Issues*, 3(1):214–228.

Pochea, M.-M., Filip, A.-M., and Pece, A.-M. (2017). Herding Behavior in CEE Stock Markets Under Asymmetric Conditions: A Quantile Regression Analysis. *Journal of Behavioral Finance*, 18(4):400–416.

Pop, R. E. (2012). Herd behavior towards the market index: evidence from Romanian stock exchange. MPRA Paper 51595, University Library of Munich, Germany.

Rook, L. (2006). An Economic Psychological Approach to Herd Behavior. *Journal of Economic Issues*, 40(1):75–95.

Saastamoinen, J. (2008). Quantile Regression Analysis of Dispersion of Stock ReturnsEvidence of Herd behavior. Discussion Paper 57, University of Joensuu.

Saumitra, B. (2012). A note on the empirical test of herding: a threshold regression approach. MPRA Paper 38037, University Library of Munich, Germany.

Scharfstein, D. and Stein, J. (1990). Herd Behavior and Investment. *American Economic Review*, 80(3):465–79.

Šeba, M. G. (2017). 20 Years of the Croatian Capital Market. *Zagreb International Review of Economics and Business*, 20(s1):41–58.

Sentana, E. and Wadhwani, S. B. (1992). Feedback Traders and Stock Return Autocorrelations: Evidence from a Century of Daily Data. *Economic Journal*, 102(411):415–425.

Shiller, R. and Pound, J. (1989). Survey evidence on diffusion of interest and information among investors. *Journal of Economic Behavior and Organization*, 12(1):47–66.

Shleifer, A. and Summers, L. H. (1990). The Noise Trader Approach to Finance. *Journal of Economic Perspectives*, 4(2):19–33.

Škrinjarić, T. and Besek, B. (2014). Pre and post crisis performance measurement of Croatian stock market. *Zagreb International Review of Economics and Business*, 17(2):97–116.

Škrinjarić, T. and Šego, B. (2018). Exploring herding investment behaviour on Zagreb Stock Exchange. In *Proceedings of the ISCCRO - International Statistical Conference in Croatia*, pages 146–153.

Spyrou, S. (2013). Herding in financial markets: a review of the literature. *Review of Behavioral Finance*, 5(2):175–194.

Tan, L., Chiang, T., Mason, J. R., and Nelling, E. (2008). Herding behavior in Chinese stock markets: An examination of A and B shares. *Pacific-Basin Finance Journal*, 16(1-2):61–77.

Tessaromatis, N. and Thomas, V. (2009). Herding behavior in the Athens Stock Exchange. *Investment Management and Financial Innovations*, 6(3 (cont)):156–164.

Trenca, I., Petria, I., and Pece, A. M. (2015). Empirical inquiry of gregarious behavior: evidence from European emerging markets. *Revista Economică*, 67(2):143–160.

Trenca, I., Petria, N., and Pece, A. M. (2014). The Herding Behavior on Small Capital Markets: Evidence From Romania. *Analele Universitatii din Oradea. Stiinte Economice*, 23:795–801.

Trueman, B. (1994). Analyst Forecasts and Herding Behavior. *Review of Financial Studies*, 7(1):97–124.

Tversky, A. and Kahneman, D. (1974). Judgment under Uncertainty: Heuristics and Biases. *Science*, 185(4157):1124–1131.

Venezia, I., Nashikkar, A., and Shapira, Z. (2011). Firm specific and macro herding by professional and amateur investors and their effects on market volatility. Discussion Paper Series dp586, The Federmann Center for the Study of Rationality, the Hebrew University, Jerusalem.

Vidović, J. (2013). Investigation of Stock Illiquidity on Central and South East European markets in Naïve Portfolio Framework. *Economic Thought and Practice*, 22(2):537–550.

Voronkova, S. and Bohl, M. T. (2005). Institutional Traders' Behavior in an Emerging Stock Market: Empirical Evidence on Polish Pension Fund Investors. *Journal of Business Finance and Accounting*, 32(7-8):1537–1560.

Yao, J., Ma, C., and He, W. P. (2014). Investor herding behaviour of Chinese stock market. *International Review of Economics and Finance*, 29:12 – 29.

Zagreb Stock Exchange (2006–2017). Yearly and quarterly reports. available at http://www.zse.hr [accessed on october 2, 2018], Zagreb Stock Exchange.

Zhou, J. and Anderson, R. (2013). An Empirical Investigation of Herding Behavior in the U.S. REIT Market. *The Journal of Real Estate Finance and Economics*, 47(1):83–108.

Figure 1: Value of Market Index CROBEX on the ZSE

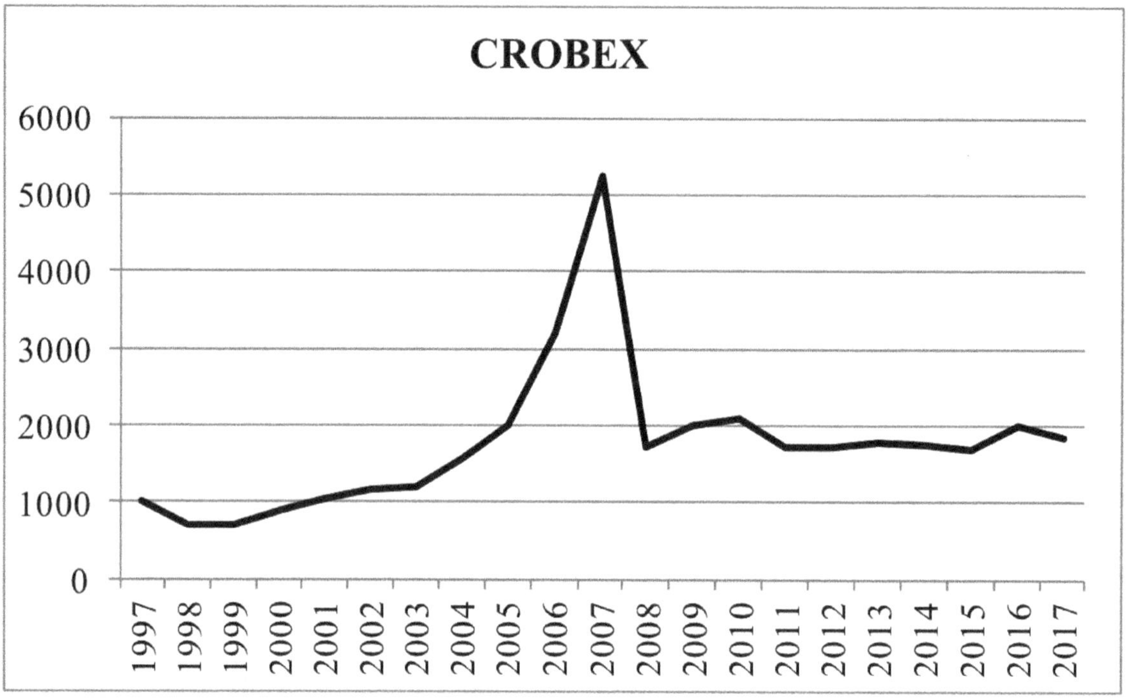

Figure 2: Total Market Capitalization and Number of Transactions on the ZSE

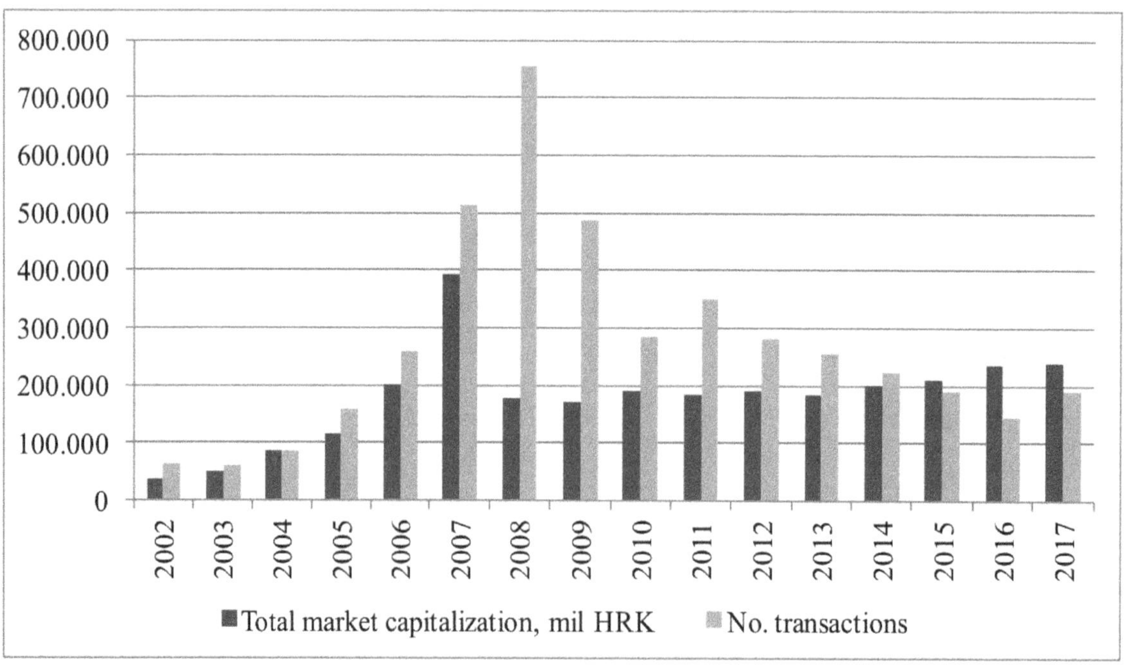

Figure 3: QQ plot of the CSAD, compared to the normal distribution (3a, left); QQ plot of CSAD, asymmetry compared to median (3b, right)

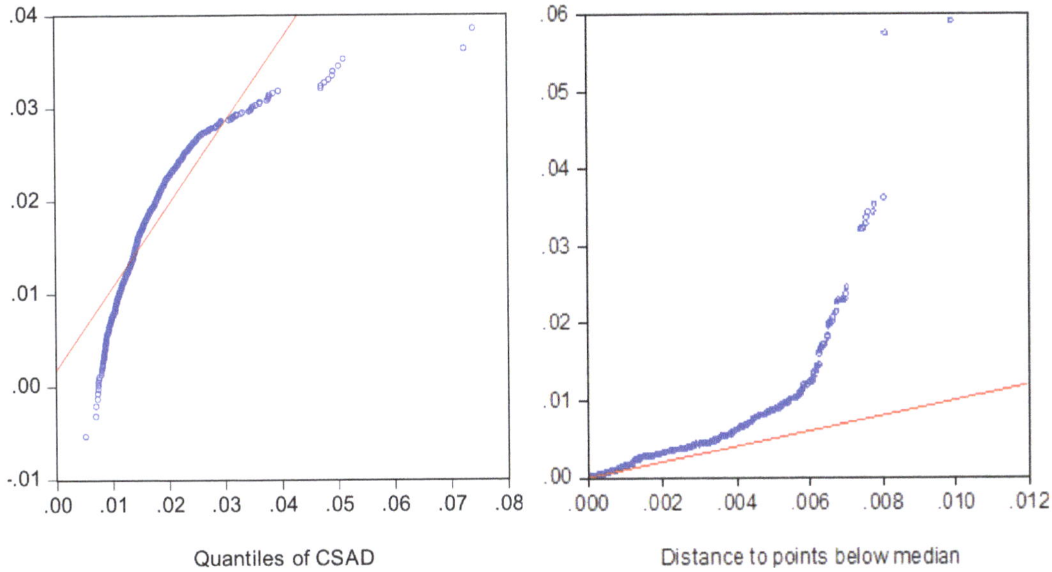

Figure 4: Comparison of estimated values of parameters from model, OLS vs. QR method, parameter $\hat{\beta}_1$ in left panel, parameter $\hat{\beta}_2$ in right panel

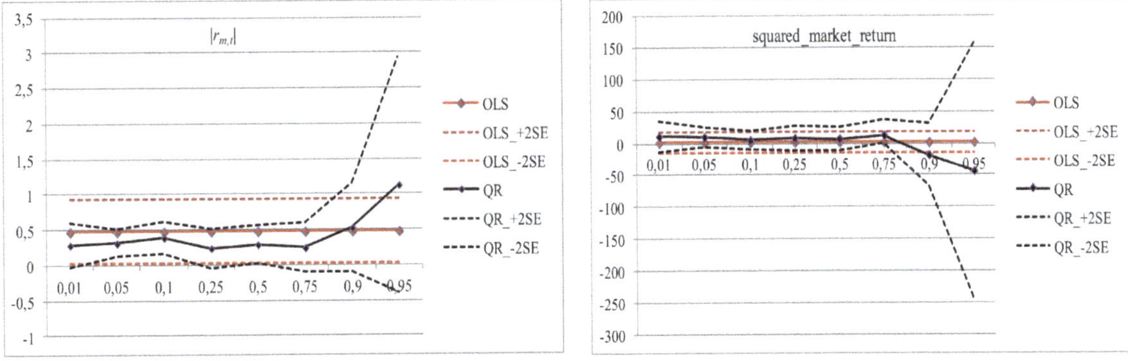

Figure 5: Comparison of estimated values of parameter $\hat{\beta}_1$ from model (3), OLS vs. QR method

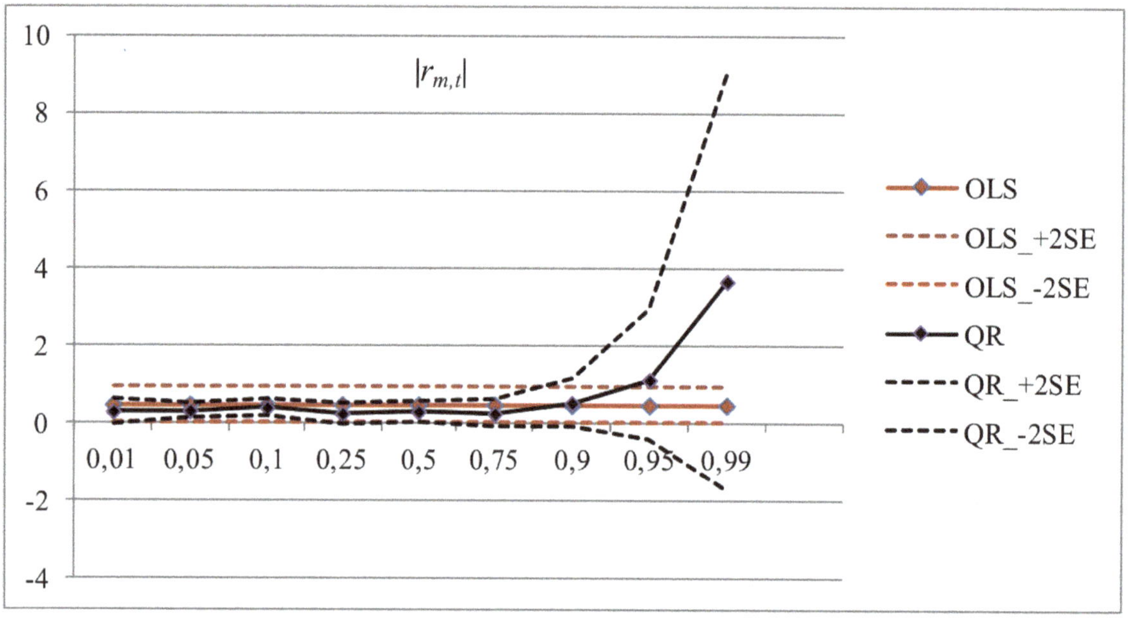

Figure 6: Comparison of estimated values of parameter $\hat{\beta}_2$ from model (3), OLS vs. QR method

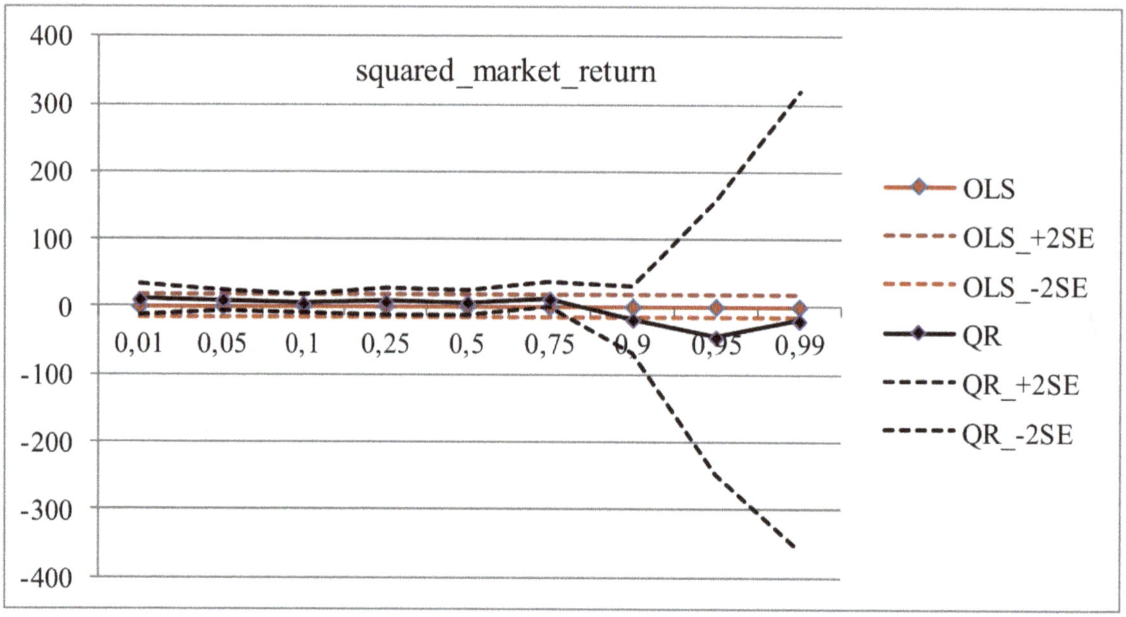

Figure 7: Comparisons of estimated values of parameter $\hat{\beta}_1$ from model (6), OLS vs. QR method

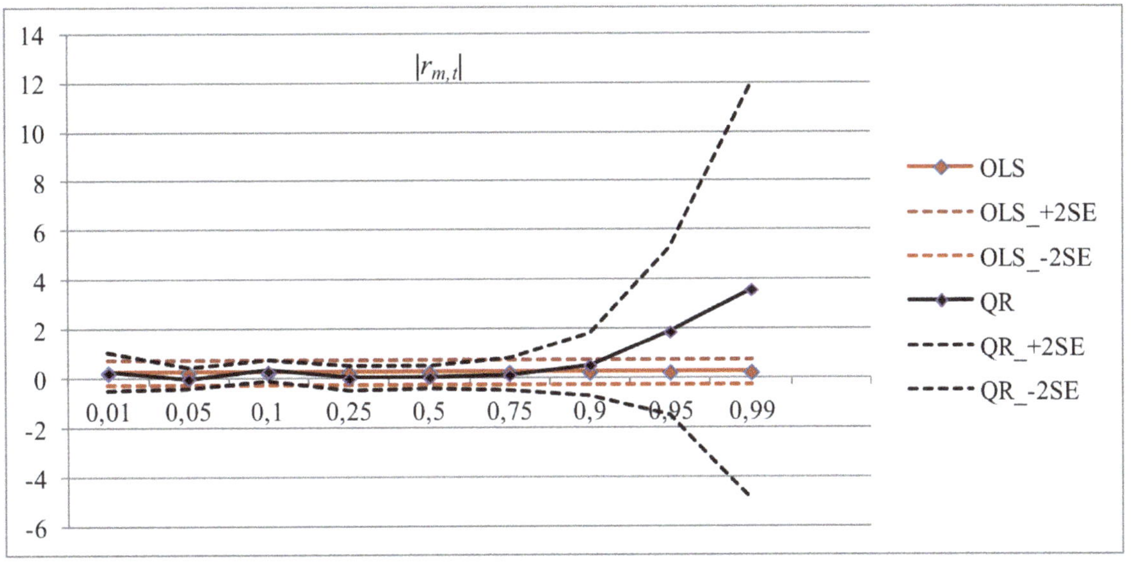

Figure 8: Comparison of estimated values of parameter $\hat{\beta}_2$ from model (6), OLS vs. QR method

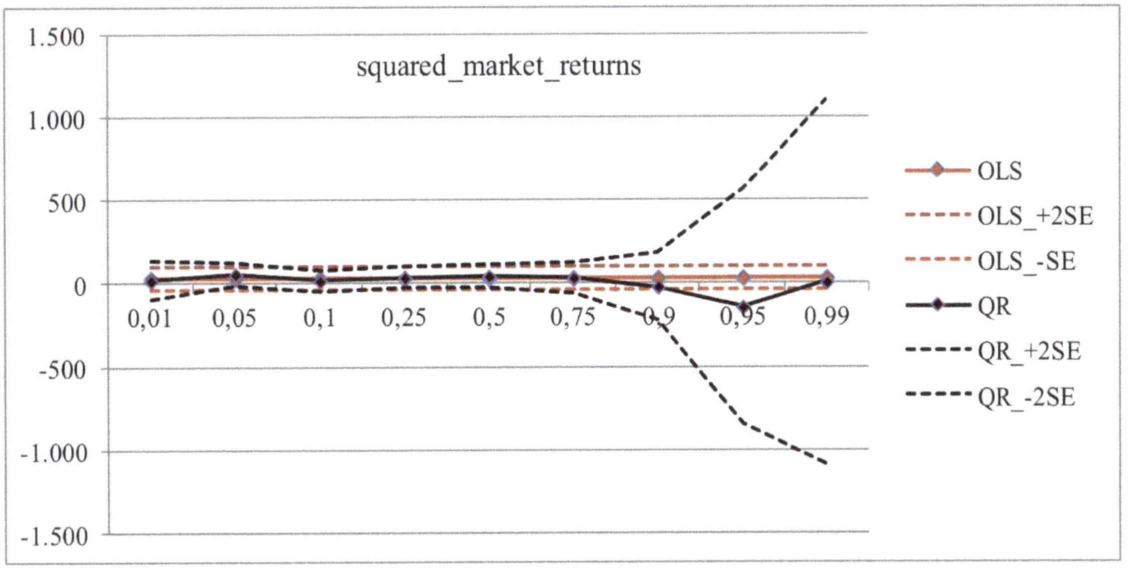

Figure 9: Comparison of estimated values of parameter $\hat{\beta}_3$ from model (6), OLS vs. QR method

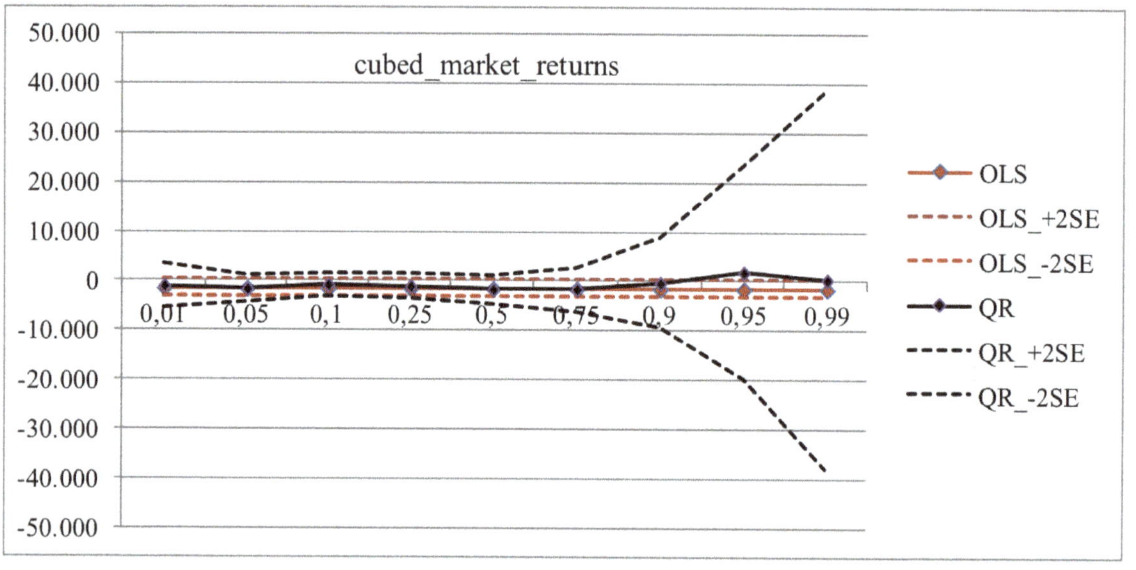

Figure 10: Comparison of estimated values of parameter $\hat{\beta}_4$ from model (6), OLS vs. QR method

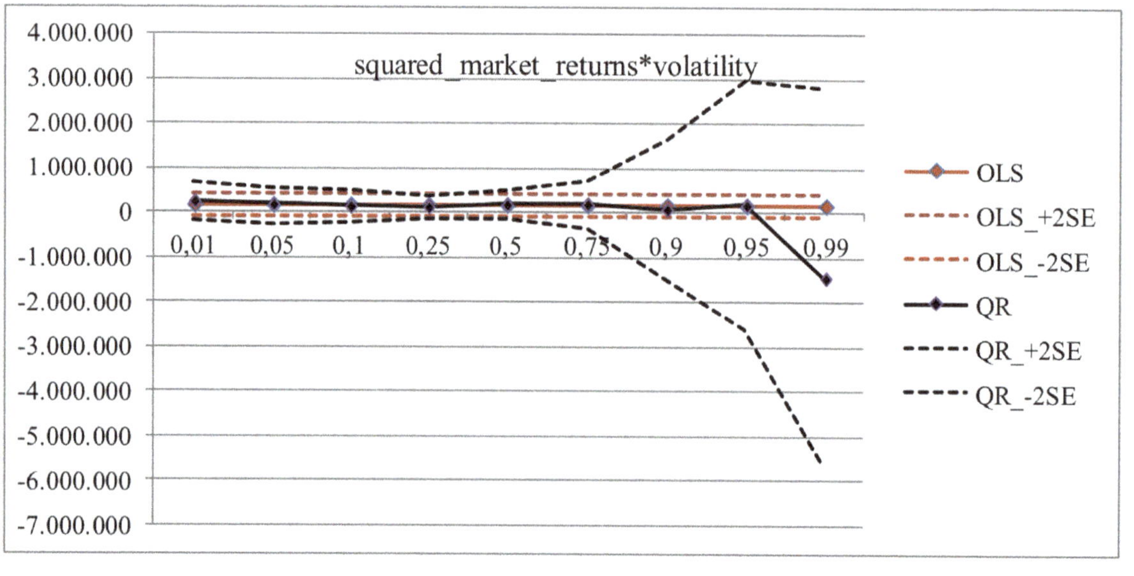

Figure 11: Comparison of estimated values of parameter $\hat{\beta}_1$ from model (7), OLS vs. QR method

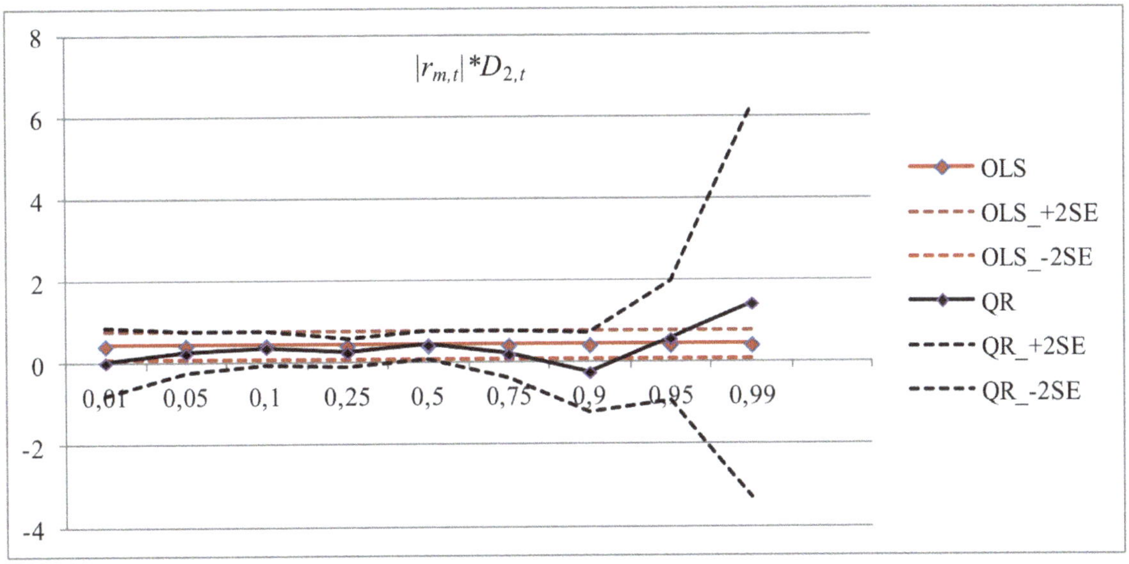

Figure 12: Comparison of estimated values of parameter $\hat{\phi}_1$ from model (7), OLS vs. QR method

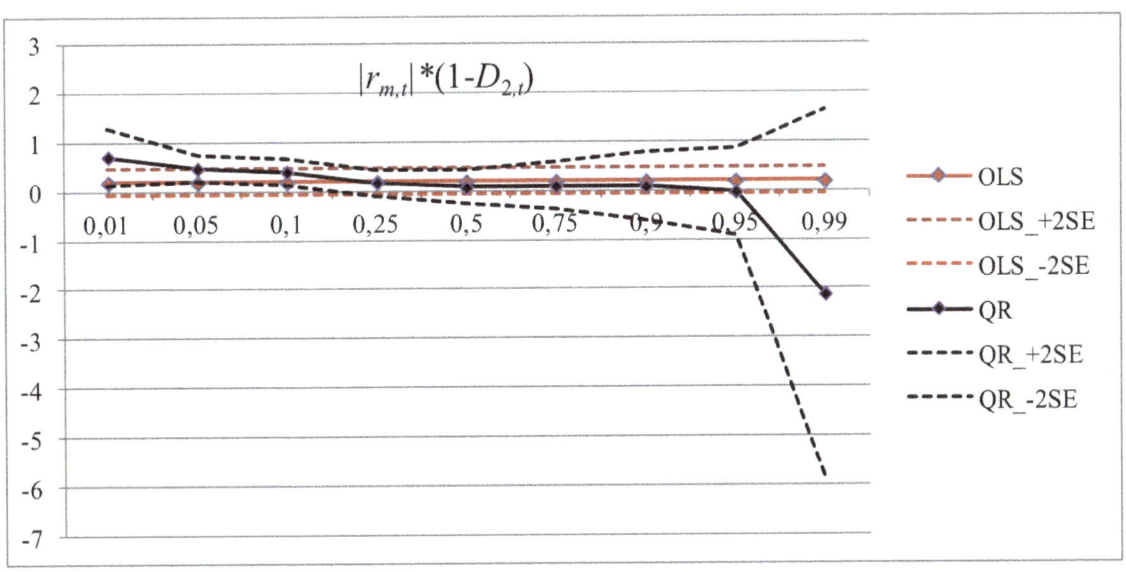

Figure 13: Comparison of estimated values of parameter $\hat{\gamma}_1$ from model (7), OLS vs. QR method

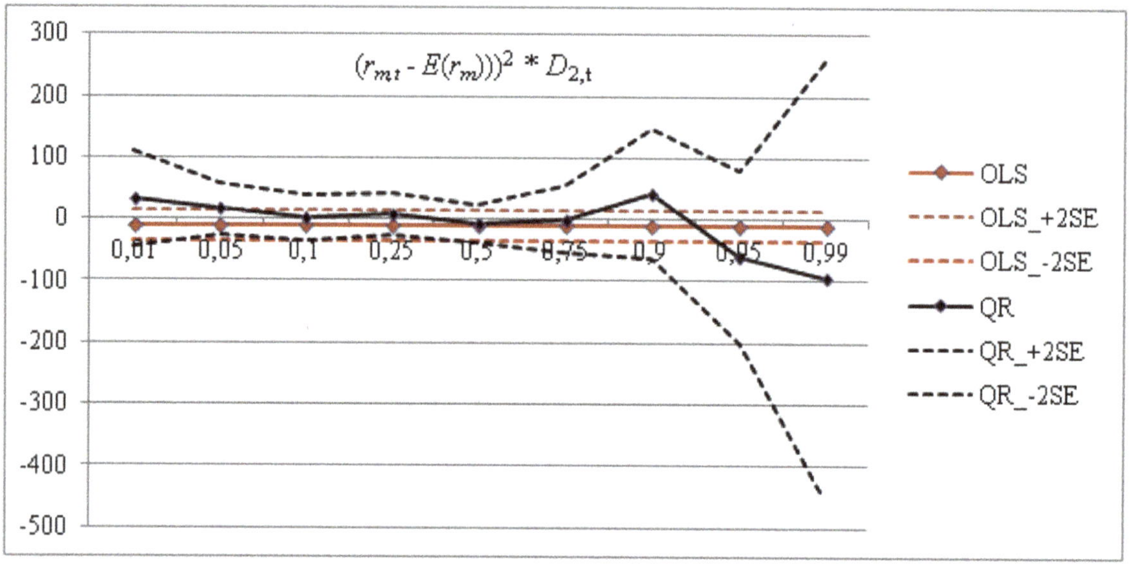

Figure 14: Comparison of estimated values of parameter $\hat{\phi}_2$ from model (7), OLS vs. QR method

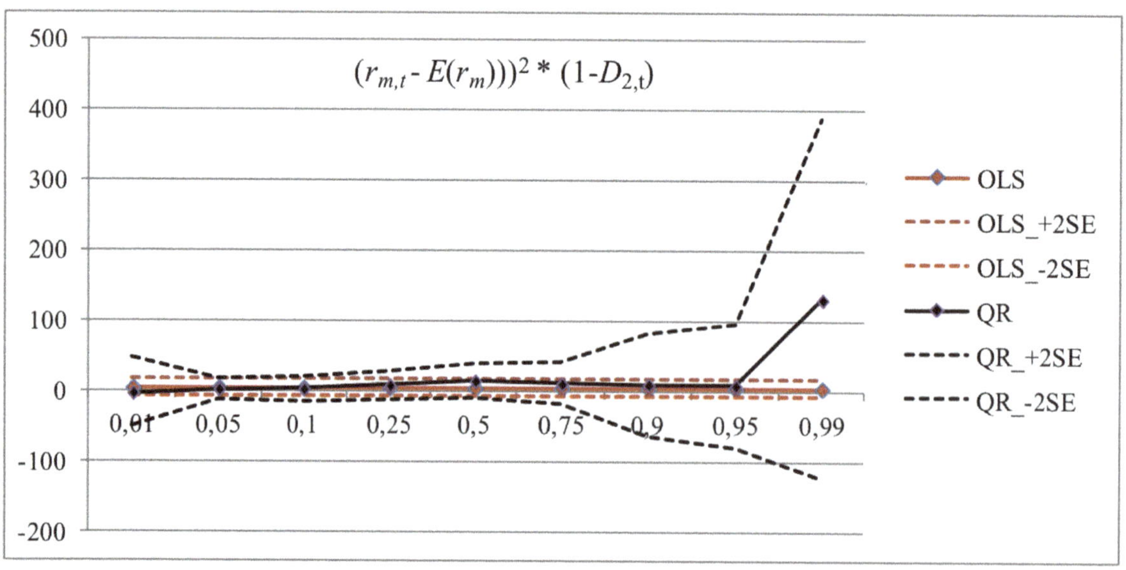

Figure 15: Comparison of estimated values of parameter $\hat{\gamma}_2$ from model (7), OLS vs. QR method

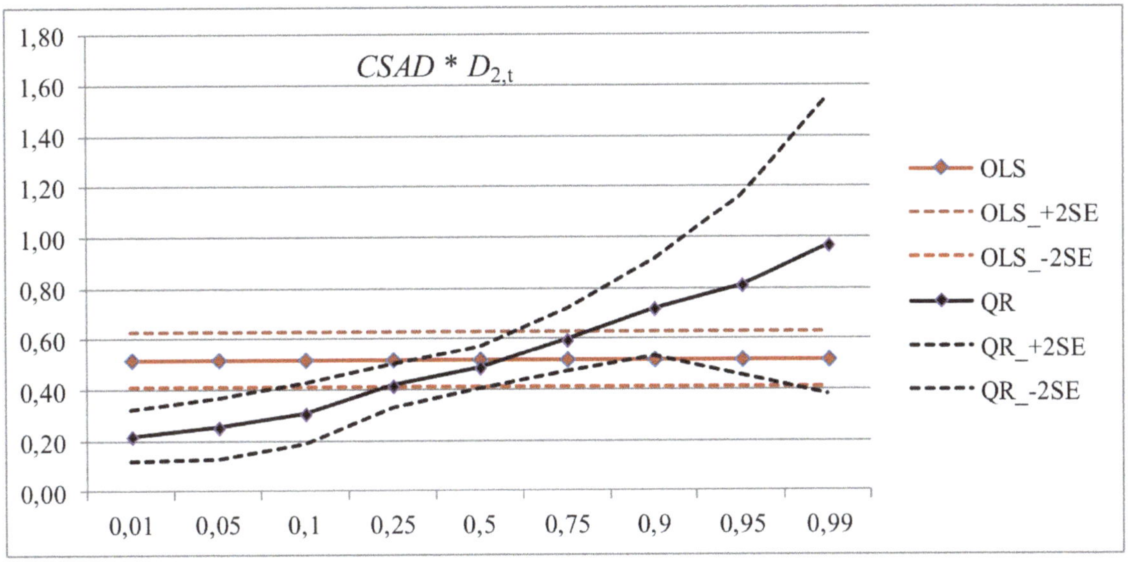

Figure 16: Comparison of estimated values of parameter $\hat{\phi}_3$ from model (7), OLS vs. QR method

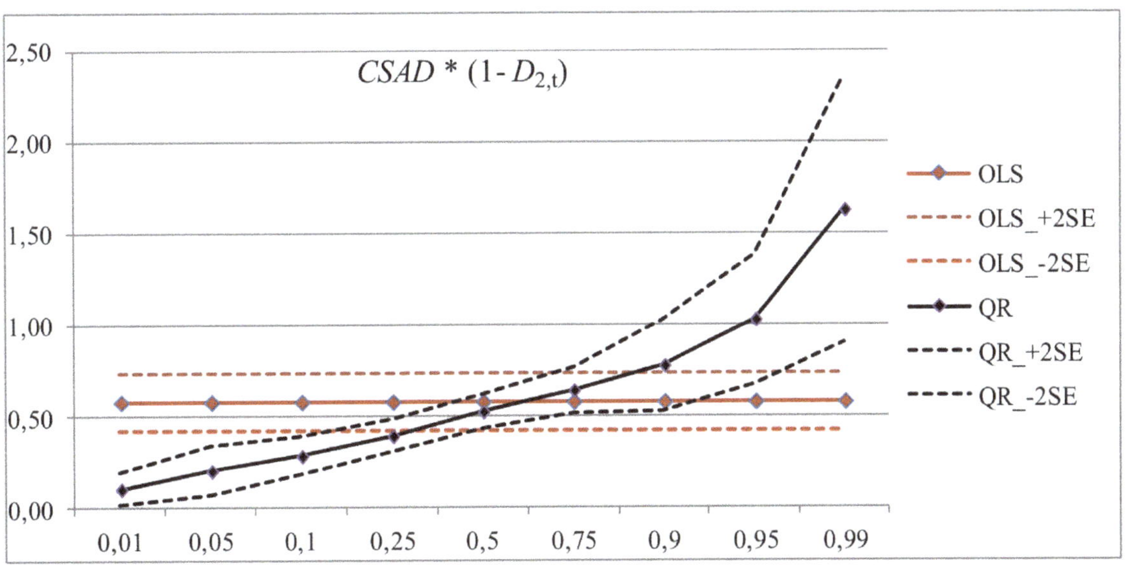

Table 1: Summary of Results from Previous Research: Mature Markets

Author(s)	Market(s)	Period	Methodology	Results
Caparrelli et al. (2004)	Italy	September 1, 1988 - January 8, 2001	OLS, original and augmented model; individual stock levels; size ranked portfolio levels.	Herding present in extreme market conditions.
Saastamoinen (2008)	Finland	June 28, 2002 - May 31, 2007	QR, basic model; individual stock level.	Nonlinear decrease of herding behavior as quantiles rise (partial evidence in favor of herding).
Blasco and Ferreruela (2008)	Germany United Kingdom United States Mexico, Japan Spain, France	January 1998 - April 2004	Original model, Z-test; stock level data.	Herding found only in Spain.
Tessaromatis and Thomas (2009)	Greece	January 1985 - June 2004	Original model; binary variables for up/down market; sub-periods observed (based upon development of Athens market); stock level data.	Herding was not a dominant behavior in the whole sample. Herding was found in the period 1998-2004.
Economoua et al. (2010)	Greece, Italy Spain, Portugal	1998-2008	OLS, original model; binary variables for up/down market.	Herding is stronger during periods of rising markets in Italy and Greece; in Portugal, herding is prominent in down markets; in Spain, there is no herding.

Continued on the next page

Table 1: Summary of Results from Previous Research: Mature Markets (Continued)

Author(s)	Market(s)	Period	Methodology	Results
Arouri et al. (2010)	France	1st Q 1999 - 3rd Q 2005	LSV measure; FHW indicator.	Herding is stronger in small capitalization companies; institutional herding in equity funds amounts to 6.5%.
Khan et al. (2011)	Germany, France UK, Italy	2003-2008	Factor model base; portfolio level data.	Presence of herding behavior in all countries, excluding periods of market turmoil and crisis.
Kremer and Nautz (2011)	Germany	July 1, 2006 - August 8, 2007	LSV measure; Sias (2004) measure.	Only 1.44% of institutions herd; a bit more herding in large stocks, not small, as theory suggests.
Zhou and Anderson (2013)	United States	January 1980 - December 2010	OLS and QR, original model; binary variables for up/down markets, binary variable for the financial crisis; equity Real estate investment trust data.	Herding behavior is present in high quantiles; herding is more prominent in turbulent market conditions and in bear markets-asymmetries exist.

Continued on the next page

Table 1: Summary of Results from Previous Research: Mature Markets (Continued)

Author(s)	Market(s)	Period	Methodology	Results
Merli and Roger (2013)	France	1999-2006	IHM measure, individual investors observed.	High level of herding and a significant persistence of this behavior; poor past performance increases probability of herding in the future.
Chen (2013)	23 developed markets	January 2004 - December 2009	Original models, OLS; state space models.	Evidence in favor of herding on all markets; both up and down markets. More prominent in down markets.
Ouarda et al. (2013)	EuroStoxx600 (more than 170 stocks included)	January 1998 - December 2010	OLS, original model, binary variable for up/down markets, high/low volatility; stock level data and sector level.	Majority of sectors: existence of herding; more herding when volatility higher; asymmetric behavior.
Mobarek et al. (2014)	Germany, France Portugal, Italy Ireland, Greece Spain, Sweden Finland, Denmark Norway	2001-2012	Original model, binary variable for up/down markets, high/low volatility, crisis binary variable; stock level data.	Herding is not significant during normal times; significant during crises and in regimes of different extreme market conditions.

Table 2: Summary of Results from Previous Related Research: Developing Markets

Author(s)	Market(s)	Period	Methodology	Results
Voronkova and Bohl (2005)	Poland	1999-2001	LSV measure; pension funds data; sector data.	Herding exists in small size stocks and stocks of particular industries.
Goodfellow et al. (2009)	Poland	July 9, 1996 - November 16, 2000	OLS; individual stock level; original model, nonlinear model, divided sample into market going up/down.	Individual investors: herding during market downswings; institutional investors do not herd.
Kallinterakis and Lodetti (2009)	Montenegro	March 2003 - May 2008	Original model, up/down markets model, portfolio-based data.	Herding is non-existent, irrespective of thin trading.
Pop (2012)	Romania	January 2003 - March 2012	MGARCH, stochastic volatility, Kalman filter; individual stock level.	Herding is persistent; crisis of 2007/2008 reduced herding. CAPM betas observed instead of CSSD or CSAD measures.
Al-Shboul (2013)	Jordan	2003-2010	QR, basic model, binary variable for up/down market; binary variable for crisis period; individual stock level.	No evidence of herding; linear relationship found both in up and down markets. In extreme movements, herding decreases even more.

Continued on the next page

Table 2: Summary of Results from Previous Related Research: Developing Markets (Continued)

Author(s)	**Market(s)**	**Period**	**Methodology**	**Results**
Trenca et al. (2014)	Romania	2003-2013	OLS, original, Yao et al. (2014) model; volatility and trading volume included; individual stock and institutional investors level.	No herding of individual investors; institutional investors: bear market: no herding, bull market: herding, asymmetries in behavior exist; high liquidity connected to greater herding.
Chen (2013)	20 emerging markets and 26 frontier markets	Time span varies; earliest is January 2004; latest is December 2009.	Original model, OLS, state space models.	Evidence in favor of herding on all markets; both up and down markets. More prominent in down markets.
Filip et al. (2015a)	Bulgaria Czech Republic Hungary Poland, Romania	January 2003 - December 2010	OLS, basic model, model for up/down markets, crisis 2007/2008 binary variable; sector level.	Evidence of herding behavior in all countries except Poland. Herding reduced in the crisis.
Filip et al. (2015b)	Bulgaria, Croatia Czech Republic Estonia, Hungary Latvia, Lithuania Poland, Romania Slovenia	January 2, 2003 - December 31, 2013	OLS and QR, basic model with binary variable for 2007/2008 crisis included; size ranked portfolio level.	Existence of herding behavior, even in crisis. However, herding present in some of the quantiles. Croatia: only on fifth quantile significant herding.

Continued on the next page

Table 2: Summary of Results from Previous Related Research: Developing Markets (Continued)

Author(s)	**Market(s)**	**Period**	**Methodology**	**Results**
Trenca et al. (2015)	Romania Bulgaria Croatia	January 2006 - December 2013	QR model, basic model, sample divided into pre-, crisis. and post-crisis.	Croatia: herding occurs only for pre-crisis period; Bulgaria: prevails during crisis period; Romania: exists especially during post-crisis period.
Ababio and Mwamba (2017)	South African Republic	January 2010 - September 2015	QR, original model; individual stock level for sector analysis.	Herding behavior exists in banking and real estate sectors; asymmetries exist in bull/bear markets (herding mostly when market goes up).
Pochea et al. (2017)	Bulgaria, Croatia Czech Republic Estonia, Hungary Latvia, Lithuania Poland, Romania Slovenia	January 2, 2003 - December 31, 2013	OLS and QR, basic and extended models, binary variables included, volatility and trading volume included; individual stock level.	Evidence of herding behavior in all countries except Poland and Romania. Croatia: herding is an isolated phenomenon at 25% quantile; asymmetries exist regarding trade volume and volatility.
Škrinjarić and Šego (2018)	Croatia	January 2, 2012 - October 31, 2017	ML-GARCH, basic and extended models, volatility and trading volume included; sector level.	Weak evidence of herding behavior in bull markets; no herding in bear markets. Higher volatility and trade volume linked to greater herding.

Continued on the next page

Table 2: Summary of Results from Previous Related Research: Developing Markets (Continued)

Author(s)	**Market(s)**	**Period**	**Methodology**	**Results**
Ababio and Mwamba (2017)	South African Republic	January 2010 - September 2015	QR, original model; individual stock level for sector analysis.	Herding behavior exists in banking and real estate sectors; asymmetries exist in bull/bear markets (herding mostly when market goes up).
Chen et al. (2017)	China	January 2, 2008 - November 27, 2015	QR; basic model and binary variable for crisis; individual stock level.	Herding behavior is more prominent in rising markets; greater herding in crisis period.
Chong et al. (2017)	China	January 2000 - December 2011	Basic and quadratic model; binary variable for up/down markets; manually divide 4 quantiles; OLS.	Found presence of herding, especially in extreme movements of financial crisis.

Table 3: Results of Estimation OLS and QR Specifications of Models (6) and (7)

Quantile	Model/ Parameters						
	Model (6)						
	$\hat{\beta}_0$	$\hat{\beta}_1$	$\hat{\beta}_2$	$\hat{\beta}_3$	$\hat{\beta}_4$	$\hat{\beta}_5$	$R^2/pseudoR^2$
OLS	0.015 (0.000)***	0.248 (0.344)	35.639 (0.300)	-1519.98 (0.090)*	169116 (0.203)	0.003 (0.265)	0.088
0.01	0.007 (0.000)***	0.572 (0.053)*	-14.445 (0.641)	348.658 (0.520)*	298023.1 (0.224)	0.001 (0.241)	0.084
0.05	0.009 (0.000)***	0.250 (0.113)	14.541 (0.467)	446.691 (0.230)	125892.3 (0.521)	-0.0002 (0.871)	0.064
0.10	0.009 (0.000)***	0.490 (0.002)***	-8.832 (0.593)	328.430 (0.334)	223834.6 (0.136)	0.002 (0.156)	0.058
0.25	0.012 (0.000)***	0.143 (0.509)	18.863 (0.386)	413.016 (0.370)	57601 (0.639)	0.001 (0.302)	0.045
0.50	0.014 (0.000)***	0.264 (0.148)	8.655 (0.651)	320.914 (0.502)	50403.40 (0.735)	0.003 (0.019)**	0.050
0.75	0.018 (0.000)***	0.375 (0.138)	-2.443 (0.926)	83.181 (0.904)	103840 (0.640)	0.004 (0.106)	0.055
0.90	0.021 (0.000)***	0.545 (0.336)	-21.579 (0.805)	158.133 (0.903)	62637.55 (928)	0.012 (0.047)**	0.058
0.95	0.023 (0.000)***	1.734 (0.129)	-107.252 (0.553)	-330.224 (0.930)	400984.6 (0.812)	0.011 (0.122)**	0.072
0.99	0.027 (0.002)***	3.588 (0.276)	7.192 (0.981)	-345.763 (0.944)	1423923 (0.581)	0.012 (0.110)**	0.126

Continued on the next page

Table 3: Results of Estimation OLS and QR Specifications of Models (6) and (7) (Continued)

Quantile	Model/ Parameters								
	Model (7)								
	$\hat{\beta}_0$	$\hat{\beta}_1$	$\hat{\phi}_1$	$\hat{\gamma}_1$	$\hat{\phi}_2$	$\hat{\gamma}_2$	$\hat{\phi}_3$	$\hat{\beta}_5$	$R^2/pseudoR^2$
OLS	0.006 (0.000)***	0.433 (0.020)**	0.189 (0.165)	-10.190 (0.411)	4.794 (0.460)	0.523 (0.000)***	0.577 (0.000)***	0.001 (0.472)	0.371
O.01	0.005 (0.000)***	0.031 (0.938)	0.721 (0.012)**	33.195 (0.384)	-2.988 (0.905)	0.218 (0.000)***	0.100 (0.035)**	0.002 (0.016)	0.119
0.05	0.005 (0.000)***	0.255 (0.317)	0.478 (0.001)***	16.640 (0.454)	2.177 (0.763)	0.253 (0.000)***	0.200 (0.003)***	0.002 (0.206)	0.124
0.10	0.005 (0.000)***	0.382 (0.090)*	0.408 (0.005)***	0.968 (0.961)	2.753 (0.735)	0.307 (0.000)***	0.281 (0.000)***	0.004 (0.582)	0.137
0.25	0.006 (0.000)***	0.264 (0.193)	0.179 (0.238)	7.240 (0.698)	8.027 (0.469)	0.415 (0.000)***	0.390 (0.000)***	0.0001 (0.902)	0.154
0.50	0.007 (0.000)***	0.445 (0.012)**	0.072 (0.719)***	-7.153 (0.667)	14.435 (0.253)	0.487 (0.000)***	0.522 (0.000)***	-0.0003 (0.867)	0.177
0.75	0.008 (0.000)***	0.213 (0.514)	0.093 (0.704)	-0.526 (0.989)	10.767 (0.493)	0.595 (0.000)***	0.638 (0.000)***	0.002 (0.160)	0.219
0.90	0.010 (0.000)***	-0.233 (0.618)	0.085 (0.857)	41.298 (0.398)	9.990 (0.806)	0.719 (0.000)***	0.774 (0.000)***	-0.001 (0.867)	0.265
0.95	0.010 (0.000)***	0.587 (0.359)	-0.035 (0.951)	-59.858 (0.307)	8.569 (0.871)	0.812 (0.000)	1.025 (0.000)***	0.007 (0.127)	0.319
0.99	0.013 (0.043)**	1.441 (0.546)	-2.117 (0.349)	-95.046 (0.585)	131.260 (0.386)	0.969 (0.001)***	1.623 (0.000)***	-0.004 (0.371)	0.391

Table 4: Wald Test Results for Equality of Parameters of the Lagged Value of CSAD Variable in Model (7)

Quantile	**Test value (p-value)**
0.01	5.96 (0.015)**
0.05	1.09 (0.296)
0.10	0.41 (0.523)
0.25	0.67 (0.413)
0.50	1.11 (0.293)
0.75	0.72 (0.396)
0.90	0.31 (0.579)
0.95	3.04 (0.081)*
0.99	3.65 (0.056)**

Table 5: Results of Estimation OLS and QR Specifications of Model (11)

	$\hat{\beta}_0$	$\hat{\beta}_1$	$\hat{\beta}_2$	$\hat{\beta}_5$	$\hat{\lambda}_4$	$R^2/pseudoR^2$
OLS	0.015 (0.000)***	0.300 (0.153)	23.078 (0.418)	0.004 (0.128)	-17.541 (0.487)	0.082
0.01	0.006 (0.000)***	0.758 (0.007)	-31.431 (0.266)	0.001 (0.450)	29.164 (0.103)	0.080
0.05	0.008 (0.000)***	0.424 (0.038)	-5.195 (0.833)	-0.0003 (0.844)	12.295 (0.493)	0.053
0.10	0.009 (0.000)***	0.527 (0.005)***	-6.823 (0.738)	0.001 (0.637)	9.213 (0.551)	0.051
0.25	0.012 (0.000)***	0.281 (0.216)	3.515 (0.870)	0.001 (0.461)	3.499 (0.818)	0.036
0.50	0.014 (0.000)***	0.209 (0.238)	16.005 (0.350)	0.003 (0.026)	-6.390 (0.627)	0.042
0.75	0.017 (0.000)***	0.343 (0.184)	2.842 (0.910)	0.003 (0.285)	6.460 (0.746)	0.047
0.90	0.021 (0.000)***	0.504 (0.568)	-15.250 (0.920	0.012 (0.086)	-2.330 (0.985)	0.054
0.95	0.024 (0.000)***	-0.159 (0.877)	288.288 (0.112)	0.017 (0.037)**	-290.938 (0.060)*	0.085
0.99	0.030 (0.000)***	2.463 (0.474)	57.111 (0.845)	0.003 (0.285)	6.460 (0.746)	0.047

Table 6: Results of Estimation OLS and QR Specifications of Model (12)

	$\hat{\beta}_0$	$\hat{\beta}_1$	$\hat{\beta}_2$	$\hat{\beta}_3$	$\hat{\beta}_4$	$\hat{\beta}_5$	λ	$R^2/pseudoR^2$
OLS	0.015 (0.000)***	0.304 (0.171)	20.613 (0.444)	189.565 (0.322)	189808.7 (0.054)**	0.004 (0.099)*	-28.753 (0.312)	0.083
0.01	0.006 (0.000)***	0.755 (0.015)**	-28.148 (0.394)	371.381 (0.569)	78554.63 (0.758)	0.001 (0.421)	30.488 (0.278)	0.082
0.05	0.008 (0.000)***	0.348 (0.085)*	3.751 (0.882)	466.490 (0.353)	-23530.57 (0.896)**	-0.0003 (0.830)	23.087 (0.326)	0.056
0.10	0.009 (0.000)***	0.535 (0.005)	-12.362 (0.555)	359.069 (0.453)	10666.6 (0.756)	0.002 (0.366)	15.475 (0.278)	0.054
0.25	0.012 (0.000)***	0.247 (0.348)	8.393 (0.764)	388.482 (0.443)	83995.07 (0.537)	0.001 (0.484)	4.165 (0.833)	0.038
0.50	0.009 (0.000)***	0.535 (0.005)***	12.362 (0.555)	359.069 (0.453)	10666.6 (0.756)	0.002 (0.366)	15.475 (0.278)	0.054
0.75	0.017 (0.000)***	0.350 (0.200)	-0.619 (0.984)	97.955 (0.900)	178601.6 (0.625)	0.004 (0.257)	-9.763 (0.761)	0.048
0.90	0.021 (0.000)***	0.458 (0.604)	-16.002 (0.915)	21.850 (0.989)	82859.76 (0.921)	0.012 (0.098)*	-9.513 (0.401)	0.052
0.95	0.024 (0.000)***	-0.257 (0.844)	300.202 (0.144)	385.910 (0.893)	34005.76 (0.986)	0.014 (0.055)*	-290.641 (0.058)	0.084
0.99	0.027 (0.003)***	3.741 (0.313)	-90.462 (0.799)	-2144.11 (0.614)	2109908 (0.453)	0.011 (0.146)	-255.903 (0.105)	0.138

Table 7: Results of Estimation OLS and QR Specifications of Model (13)

	$\hat{\beta}_0$	$\hat{\beta}_1$	$\hat{\phi}_1$	$\hat{\gamma}_1$	$\hat{\phi}_2$	$\hat{\gamma}_2$	$\hat{\phi}_3$	$\hat{\beta}_5$	λ	$R^2/pseudoR^2$
	0.007	0.175	-0.088	21.760	38.727	0.527	0.580	0.002	-27.186	
OLS	(0.000)***	(0.409)	(0.672)	(0.270)	(0.083)*	(0.000)***	(0.000)***	(0.176)	(0.128)	0.370
	0.005	0.434	1.070	-20.884	-59.767	0.197	0.093	0.001	38.629	
0.01	(0.000)***	(0.310)	(0.001)***	(0.643)	(0.099)*	(0.000)***	(0.027)**	(0.283)	(0.115)	0.122
	0.005	0.429	0.674	-6.575	-24.506	0.252	0.198	0.001	21.009	
0.05	(0.000)***	(0.106)	(0.003)***	(0.785)	(0.357)	(0.000)***	(0.006)***	(0.329)	(0.271)	0.118
	0.005	0.249	0.492	-2.623	-14.372	0.282	0.259	0.002	14.990	
0.10	(0.000)***	(0.103)	(0.024)**	(0.912)	(0.579)	(0.000)***	(0.000)***	(0.827)	(0.434)	0.130
	0.007	0.340	0.153	9.337	10.749	0.417	0.391	0.002	-1.594	
0.25	(0.000)***	(0.324)	(0.472)	(0.702)	(0.629)	(0.000)***	(0.000)***	(0.908)	(0.916)	0.146
	0.007	0.009	-0.087	10.033	33.522	0.463	0.495	0.001	-13.078	
0.50	(0.000)***	(0.110)	(0.703)	(0.656)	(0.093)	(0.000)***	(0.000)***	(0.777)	(0.389)	0.170
	0.008	-0.051	-0.163	24.962	34.027	0.589	0.630	0.003	-24.967	
0.75	(0.000)***	(0.976)	(0.553)	(0.436)	(0.178)	(0.000)***	(0.000)***	(0.064)*	(0.159)	0.216
	0.010	0.346	-0.210	20.760	48.127	0.696	0.779	0.012	-51.611	
0.90	(0.000)***	(0.926)	(0.752)	(0.756)	(0.514)	(0.000)***	(0.000)***	(0.053)*	(0.348)	0.260
	0.010	1.715	-0.450	-9.505	49.078	0.809	1.045	0.008	-41.395	
0.95	(0.000)***	(0.664)	(0.500)	(0.916)	(0.521)	(0.000)***	(0.000)***	(0.118)	(0.482)	0.317
	0.013	0.434	-1.390	-138.838	51.958	0.968	1.650	-0.006	35.895	
0.99	(0.051)*	(0.502)	(0.562)	(0.521)	(0.751)	(0.001)***	(0.000)***	(0.392)	(0.701)	0.386

Table 8: Results of Estimation of OLS and QR Specification of Model

Quantile	$\hat{\beta}_0$	$\hat{\beta}_1$	$\hat{\beta}_2$	$\hat{\beta}_5$	$R^2/pseudoR^2$
	0.0149	0.4757	1.3994	0.0032	
OLS	(0.000)***	(0.040)**	(0.867)	(0.191)	0.0844
	0.0071	0.2909	11.241	0.0009	
0.01	(0.000)***	(0.136)	(0.434)	(0.298)	0.0804
	0.0084	0.3133	10.327	-0.0002	
0.05	(0.000)***	(0.010)**	(0.290)	(0.882)	0.0560
	0.0091	0.3915	5.1215	0.0021	
0.10	(0.000)***	(0.004)***	(0.585)	(0.150)	0.0545
	0.0116	0.2409	7.9924	0.0015	
0.25	(0.000)***	(0.082)	(0.403)	(0.224)	0.0403
	0.0142	0.2919	7.0272	0.0033	
0.50	(0.000)***	(0.046)**	(0.488)	(0.020)**	0.0456
	0.0175	0.2441	12.449	0.0039	
0.75	(0.000)***	(0.227)	(0.315)	(0.099)*	0.0511
	0.0214	0.5265	-18.449	0.0122	
0.90	(0.000)***	(0.087)*	(0.427	(0.026)**	0.0577
	0.0237	1.2682	-44.239	0.0113	
0.95	(0.000)***	(0.134)	(0.653)	(0.119)	0.0701
	0.0274	3.6763	-19.985	0.0105	
0.99	(0.000)***	(0.191)	(0.912)	(0.141)	0.1149

6

Financial Instability and Inequality Dynamics in the WAEMU

Thierno Thioune *♣

♣Faculty of Economic and Management Sciences, Cheikh Anta Diop University of Dakar

---

ABSTRACT: This article assesses the effect of financial instability on income inequality and vice versa. The methodology used in this article is based on two approaches: the construction of the synthetic index of financial instability (SIFI) and the panel vector autoregressive (PVAR) approach. The results obtained help to explain that the disparity of income in a West African Economic and Monetary Union (WAEMU) country in each year negatively influences the stability of the financial sector the following year. Functions of impulse responses show that a shock to financial stability has a negative effect on itself and leads to a stable situation after seven periods. A rise in income inequality in WAEMU countries tends to mitigate financial instability at first, before boosting a higher level of instability. Following this increase, inequality will decline, but at a very slow pace.

Keywords: Financial instability, inequality, SIFI, PVAR, impulse response function, WAEMU

*Corresponding Author. Email: thierno.thioune@ucad.edu.sn

Introduction

The 2008 financial crisis - also referred to here as the Great Recession - continues to have a major effect on the global economy. Economic factors, such as the increase in inequality that has weakened effective consumption demand and spending, are believed to be the cause (Sheng, 2014). Many analysts have wondered whether inequality was partly responsible for the financial crisis. Among the most influential authors, Rajan (2010), followed by Kumhof and Ranciere (2011), suggested that an increase in inequality directly contributed to the credit boom in the 1930s and similarly in the first half of the year 2000. The analysis of disparities in the distribution of income and assets is essential to understanding the 2008 financial crisis and recovery (Raskin, 2013).

The question of the dynamics of inequality in this case is not foreign to the financial instability hypothesis. Minsky (1982) and the authors who expanded his thinking, including post-Keynesians Crotty (1993) and Keen (1995), had already suggested that the inequalities in distribution were likely to undermine financial stability and cause a reversal of the endogenous business cycles. Rajan (2010) was one of the first economists to attribute the 2008 financial crisis to the rise in income inequality, a thesis also shared by Krugman (2007) and Reich (2007).

It should be noted that the effects of the financial crisis are continuing to change on a day-by-day basis, so that the assessment of its consequences is still not easy. Furthermore, assessing the effects of the financial crisis on inequalities in West African Economic and Monetary Union (WAEMU) countries requires appropriate statistical approaches. The effort to understand the outcomes of the crisis requires constant observation and continuous adjustment of the analysis depending on the situation. The data that were available related to small chronological series that could be used for a panel data analysis, but did not allow for VAR or ECM modeling (based on temporal series). Therefore, to highlight the response functions for the different countries of the Union, data from the West African Central Bank (BCEAO) and the World Income Inequality Database (WIID) are used (Figure 1).

It has been shown that funding influences the distribution of income. However, little research has been devoted to examining the potential effect of financial policy on income inequality. This study analyzes the relationship between financial policies and income inequalities in WAEMU countries. Even if the financial system of the West African region is only weakly connected to the global financial system, the effects of the financial crisis were felt nonetheless. The narrowing of inequalities is a logical answer, but one that provokes questions about the relationship between the nature of the financial system and inequality in WAEMU countries, in particular, whether financial instability contributes to the widening of inequality in the Union. Through what mechanisms could the effects of the financial instability in the economies of WAEMU countries be transmitted to the inequalities within a Union country?

The general objective of this article is to assess the relevance of financial instability to income inequality in the WAEMU as well as the converse. It will specifically: Identify explanatory factors of financial instability in WAEMU; Assess the effect of financial instability on income inequality in the Union and, conversely, that of income inequality on financial stability.

1 Literature Review

1.1 Theoretical Review

From debt to the financial crisis and inequality

Theoretically, the role of debt abuse in the advent of financial instability and widening inequality has been established for a long time. According to Rajan (2010), the growth of inequality has resulted in political pressure for easy credit. Due to the concerns of the middle class, the authorities have preferred to support household consumption by facilitating access to credit rather than promoting income growth.

Bordo and Meissner (2012) asserted that the concentration of income has certainly tended to increase during the upswings of business cycles, but it does not play a significant role in the growth of credit. In other words, income inequality should not be significantly related to systemic banking crises. Such a link regarding the Great Depression is particularly questionable to them. Contrary to what Kumhof and Ranciere (2011) suggested, the increasing use of consumer credit does not appear to be a result of the desire of households to maintain their standard of living in the context of stagnant incomes; it rather responds to their desire to appropriate new sustainable consumer properties. However, if the Great Recession had been caused by the increasing concentration of income, it would be a historic singularity in relation to previous episodes of macroeconomic instability. In this sense, Bordo and Meissner (2012) link the emergence of macro financial instability in the 2000s to the dynamics of financial innovation in a context of low interest rates. Inequalities would, in their view, have a negligible role.

Inequalities often increase in the expansion phase of the economic cycle. For example, Roine et al. (2009) show that the incomes of upper credit tranches are correlated with periods of economic expansion. Bordo and Meissner (2012) therefore suggest that rising inequality is not the cause of credit booms (and the financial crises that follow), but rather a consequence thereof. Furthermore, the authors argue that the rich are better able to benefit from the credit boom than the poor, which would explain the increase in inequality during credit booms. Therefore, rising inequality may be coincidental, but is more likely a consequence of credit booms rather than the cause.

Wealth inequality and financial crisis

Growing inequality in wealth and its repercussions on the financial sphere are becoming increasingly important topics of public debate. Therefore, Raskin (2013) pointed out that the widening of income and wealth inequality is one of the most significant structural changes. Income inequality can hamper economic growth through its effects on consumption; the richest households tend to save more of their income, which depresses consumer spending, and hence aggregate demand. And wealth inequality may have even more profound macroeconomic implications, as the inequality is even greater than that of income.

On the one hand, poor families have fewer financial resources to protect themselves against shocks to their income, including problems of unemployment. On the other hand, most of their wealth is also real estate, what exposes more wealthy households to fluctuations in property prices.

Furthermore, Raskin (2013) argued that inequalities could also increase the effect of the financial crisis. The fall in property prices observed after 2006 reduced household wealth and restricted access to credit, which has led to reduced spending. This demand shock then led to a contraction in output. However, low - and middle - income households are also the main victims of the downturn in the labor market.

1.2 Empirical Review

Banking Sector and income inequality

The analysis of the consequences of the system of finance on income inequality has been the subject of several empirical developments. Kumhof and Ranciere (2011) provided new empirical elements and propose a general equilibrium model to reproduce the stylized facts that they update. According to them, the Great Depression and the Great Recession have two strong similarities: both follow a sharp increase in income inequality and an equally considerable rise in household leverage. The two authors believe that these developments are in close interaction with each other.

Recently, Sheng (2015), based on an extended post-Keynesian model, noted that the relationship between the savings rate and income inequality is negative if the savers' funds are borrowed for household spending and consumption, but positive if savings are channeled and used for investment in the production of enterprises. These results indicate that income inequality must be reduced to increase savings in deficit economies and reduce savings in surplus economies.

On the other hand, Johansson and Wang (2014) - using a modeling of the average method and generalized methods of moments (GMM) estimation - confirmed the positive relationship between financial repression and income inequality, that is, that financial repression tends to increase income inequality. They also noted that credit controls and barriers to entry in the banking sector are the two most important financial policies that affect inequality. These findings have important policy implications, not least for developing countries, where rising inequality is a major problem.

Seven and Coskun (2016) examined the contribution of banking development and the stock market to the reduction of income inequality and poverty in developing countries. Using a methodology of dynamic panel data for the period 1987 - 2011, the authors found that financial development promotes economic growth, but it does not necessarily benefit low incomes in emerging economies. For the link between finance and poverty, they found that neither the banks nor the stock markets play an important role in poverty reduction.

Finance, inequality and poverty

Gantman and Dabós (2012) showed that financial development has no statistically significant effect on economic growth. Rioja and Valev (2014) showed that in low-income countries, banks have a significant positive effect on capital accumulation. The stock market, however, did not contribute to capital accumulation or productivity growth in these countries.

By analyzing 47 developing economies from 1984 to 2008, Kpodar and Singh (2011) found that when institutions are weak, financial systems - specifically banks - are more likely to reduce poverty, but when institutions become more developed, financial systems based on the market become more effective at reducing poverty. Moreover, Kappel (2010) found that financial development can reduce poverty and income inequality. The effects of financial development on poverty are not only important in itself, it is also significantly greater than the effect on income inequality.

More recently, Uddin et al. (2014) studied the short- and long-term relationships between financial development, economic growth, and poverty reduction in Bangladesh, and showed the existence of a long-term relationship between these variables. Similarly, Abosedra et al. (2016) analyzed the relationship between financial development and poverty reduction in Egypt using data for the period 1975 to 2011. The authors found that financial development reduces poverty when domestic credit to the private sector is used as a proxy for financial development.

On the other hand, Jauch and Watzka (2016) analyzed the relationship between financial development and income inequality for developed countries and 138 developing countries between 1960 and 2008. The authors found that financial development increases income inequality after having controlled for fixed effects by country and possible endogeneity problems. Likewise, Sehrawat and Giri (2015) studied the link between finance and inequality in India for the period 1982 to 2012, suggesting that financial development exacerbates income inequality both in the long and short term. In turn, Rajan (2010) - based on a model of Kumhof and Ranciere (2011) - found that individuals with incomes in lower deciles borrow to increase their consumption more than do those with stagnant incomes. Kumhof and Ranciere (2011) model also worked with data from the Great Depression of the 1930s, prompting them to generalize that a rise in inequality can generate a credit boom which causes a financial crisis.

Bordo and Meissner (2012) provided further analysis of the phenomenon by including other variables in the model and increasing the sample to include data from 14 countries from 1920 to 2008 (rather than a single country for two periods as done by Kumhof and Ranciere (2011)). More recently, Seven and Yetkiner (2016), using panel data from 1991 to 2011, found that the development of the stock market has a positive effect on economic growth in high- and middle-income countries.

Monetary policy, credit expansion and financial crisis

Bordo and Meissner (2012) reported a strong relationship between credit growth and the emergence of a financial crisis. Moreover, their data showed that interest rate cuts (nominal and real) are also a significant determinant of credit growth, confirming the role of monetary policy in the formation of credit booms. Bordo and Meissner also discussed a study by Mendoza and Terrones (2008), which analyzed 49 credit booms in 48 countries between 1960 and 2006 and showed that financial crises usually follow an acceleration of credit growth. For their part, Schularick and Taylor (2012) found, using data from 1889 to the present, that the probability of a financial crisis occurring is related to credit growth.

Does an increase in inequality promote an acceleration of credit growth, thus increasing the risk that a financial crisis occurs? Bordo and Meissner (2012) answer was a definite no, either by isolating the 1%, with 0.01%, 5% and 10% richer.

Park and Shin (2015) examined the relationship between financial development and income inequality. Their findings suggested that financial development contributes to reducing inequality to some extent, but as additional financial products are developed, it eventually contributes to greater inequality.

2 Methodology. Theoretical framework

The methodology used in this article is based on two approaches:

- Construction of the Synthetic Index of Financial Instability (SIFI)

- Estimation of a PVAR model

2.1 Construction of the Synthetic Index of Financial Instability (SIFI)

Financial instability is the result of several phenomena from aggregate fluctuations describing the financial environment. Thus, it is important to capture financial instability using a synthetic index of financial instability (SIFI). To build a SIFI, it is necessary to rely on the elements of instability in the financial sphere. In the literature, there are different methods found for measuring the instability within an economic aggregate. One option is to use absolute values of the residuals of the regression of a variable considered on the long-term trend (Jeanneney and Kpodar, 2004). Another option is to extract the cyclical component of the variable source of instability because the cycle reflects all fluctuations around the trend component of a chronological series. It is this latter approach that is used in this work. Construction of the financial instability index is done in two steps:

Step 1: Analysis of Principal Components

Principal components analysis (PCA) brings out the similarities and differences between groups of individuals vis-à-vis the variables. The results of this analysis are used as the starting point of the development of the SIFI.

Step 2: Development of the SIFI

The level of instability of the financial system of a country was measured by the SIFI. This index is a combination of measures of instabilities related to the dimensions associated with this global instability, namely: the liquidity ratio, the domestic financing rate, the CFA Franc/U.S. Dollar exchange rate, and the interest rate. The coefficients used were determined using a factor analysis.[1] The SIFI used in this study was constructed from the factorial axes provided by the PCA. Based on the PCA results, the SIFI was developed through a combination of two axial indices. Each axial index was constructed using the variables correlated with that axis. For a country i and a set of variables correlated with a given axis j, the financial instability aspect associated with this axis is given by:

[1]Relevant only when the number of elements to be combined is not too small (i.e., at least four).

$$l_j(i) = \sum_{k=1}^{k} C_j^k \cdot V_k^i \tag{1}$$

where V_k^i is the value of the variable k for country i and C_j^k is the coordinate of the variable k on the axis j.

To make such a summation, we must ensure that the scale of measurement does not cause any variable to exceed another to the point that one cannot make a comparison between them. To solve this problem, all variables were normalized before they were included in the above formula. We used the z-transformation with the following formula:

$$V_k^\bullet = \frac{V_k - minV_k}{maxV_k - minV_k} \tag{2}$$

This formula has the disadvantage of being sensitive to extreme values to the introduction of a new value of the variable.

Once the axial indices were determined, the SIFI was calculated according to the following formula:

$$\left(\sum_{j=1}^{5} \lambda_j \cdot I_j(i)^{1/\alpha} \right)^{\alpha} \tag{3}$$

where λ_j is the weighting coefficient of axis j:

$$\lambda_j = \frac{\nu_j}{\sum_{j=1}^{5} \nu_j} \tag{4}$$

$I_j(i)$ is the contribution of the axis j with respect to the space formed by the five axes, in other words, it is the importance of inertia j in relation to the inertia of the five axes group, and α was set to equal 1.

2.2 Model to estimate: the PVAR model

This work aims to study the effect of changes in income inequality on the level of financial instability in the countries of the WAEMU. We used a vector autoregressive (VAR) model that highlights the relationships between a group of variables at one time, their lag values, and other variables considered as exogenous. Given the theoretical framework behind this investigation, and the panel data available for analysis, we used a panel vector autoregressive model (PVAR) of p - order with fixed effects, represented by the following linear system:

$$Y_{it} = Y_{i,t-1}\Lambda_1 + Y_{i,t-2}\Lambda_2 + \cdots + Y_{i,t-p+1}\Lambda_{p-1} + Y_{i,t-p}\Lambda_p + X_{i,t}B + u_i + e_{i,t} \quad (5)$$

where $i \in \{1, \ldots, N\}$, $t \in \{1, \ldots, T_i\}$; $Y_{i,t}$ is the vector of k endogenous variables; $X_{i,t}$ is a vector of exogenous l variables; and u_i are the fixed effects and e_{it} are the error terms. The parameters to be estimated are the components of matrices Λ_1, Λ_2, ..., Λ_{p-1}, Λ_p and B.[2] The hypotheses underlying the model are the following:

$$E[e_{i,t}] = 0, \qquad E[e_{i,t}{}'e_{i,t}] = \Sigma, \qquad E[e_{i,t}{}'e_{i,s}] = 0 \text{ for } t > s. \quad (6)$$

The estimate used for PVAR is made by GMM. This method makes it possible to consider a probable correlation in the errors (Hansen, 1982). The endogenous biases are corrected using instrumental variables. However, their use can reduce the degree of freedom in the model. To remedy this, Holtz-Eakin et al. (1988) proposed using variables of lagged observations (thus supposedly uncorrelated to error terms) as instrumental variables. Before estimating the system specified above, it is required to determine the optimal p delay delays and the optimal delays instruments. The first is that which minimizes the criterion of the moment and the model selection (MMSC) proposed by Andrews and Lu (2001), based on the j statistic of Hansen (1982), which is the analogue of the maximum-based likelihood criteria such as AIC (Akaike, 1969), the BIC (Akaike, 1977; Rissanen, 1978; Schwarz, 1978), and HQ (Hannan and Quinn, 1979). Following the estimates, to confirm the stability of the PVAR, we applied a stability test which ensures that the modules of the proper values are smaller than the unit. This helped highlight the impulse response functions and to factorize the variance of forecast error.

Brief description of the variables

To achieve the objective of this work, we have recourse to the variables below, based on better economic literature (Table 1):

- **The Gini index:** a classic indicator for measuring inequality of income distribution in an economy. The Gini index has an annual value. It is used in this study to illustrate income inequality in each of the eight WAEMU countries.

[2]Panel VARs have been used to address a variety of issues of interest to macroeconomists and policymakers. Panel VARs are built with the same logic of standard VARs but, by adding a cross sectional dimension, they are a much more powerful tool to address interesting policy

- **The SIFI:** this indicator, as mentioned above, is the variable set up to capture the financial instability for each country in the study. The calculation of the SIFI is presented in the paragraphs above.

- **The ratio of the budget deficit/GDP:** this is the main (and only) control variable in this study. It is calculated as the difference between public expenditure and state revenue, related to GDP.

The data used in this study are from the BCEAO and WIDD and were abstracted for the eight WAEMU[3] countries for the period 1996 - 2011 (Table 2).[4]

3 Empirical results

3.1 Statistic description. The SIFI

Note that the development of the index is based on the results of the PCA performed on the financial variables (i.e., the liquidity ratio, the internal financing rate, the exchange rate CFA Franc/U.S. Dollars and interest rate). From the analysis of the histogram of the values (see Figure 2), both are retained in the two first axes because it integrates more than 91% of the information. In addition, the axes with eigenvalues greater than 1 are the first two. The coefficients from the PCA are presented in Table 3.

3.2 Results

This section presents the estimation results and makes interpretations based on the elements. From the selection criteria proposed by Andrews and Lu (2001), in Table 4, the optimal delay in the PVAR is of order 1. Table 5 confirms the stability of the estimated model. In fact, the associated eigenvalues are modules below unity. The graphical representation of the eigenvalues shows the previous conclusion and therefore allows subsequent to the modeling to comment impulse responses of interest variables.

The PVAR estimate

The result of the estimation of the PVAR can be explained by a high degree of informality and a low degree of banking penetration in the countries concerned. In fact, the financial sector in the WAEMU is still very underdeveloped.

---

[3]Benin, Burkina-Faso, Côte d'Ivoire, Guinea Bissau, Mali, Niger, Senegal, Togo

[4]A function of the availability of data

An increase in the Gini index could mean that the richest increased their means of payment at the expense of the poorest. One should expect that this increase boosts savings enough that the supply of bank credit influences interest rates to the point of raising the level of financial instability. However, we do not observe this - economic agents in the sub - region do not show an increase in their income with increased savings. Similarly, the poor still earn less, and therefore high interest rates simply discourage them from borrowing from banks. The result is that the demand for bank credit will not explode and will instead sag, causing less fluctuation in financial aggregates.

Granger causality

The Granger causality analysis tests whether past values of a variable X influence the current value of another variable Y (so X is said to cause Y). In Table 6, we deduce that there exists a unidirectional causality. Indeed, income disparity in WAEMU countries in each year negatively influences the stability of the financial sector the following year. However, the levels of instability in the financial sector of a country do not affect the nature of income distribution.

Impulse response function and variance decomposition

Based on the variance decomposition of forecast errors, we noted that 43.16% of the variation of financial instability in WAEMU countries may be explained by the income inequalities inside them. On the other hand, the level of financial instability in these countries accounts for only 8% of variation in income inequality.

In terms of levels, Figure 3 shows that a shock on financial instability has a negative effect on itself and leads to a stable situation after seven times. On the other hand, an increase in income inequality in WAEMU countries tends to mitigate financial instability at first before boosting a higher level of instability. Following this increase, inequalities will decline but at a very slow pace.

4 Contribution of the finding

The analysis of the financial system and inequalities has occupied a prominent place in public debates both at times of crisis and at times of growth. Considering their supposedly close link could help to reduce inequalities in WAEMU countries. In this sense, the contribution of this research project will constitute an added value that will be shared by the research community, in that, the results that will be popularized may attract the interest of young researchers.

Also, the results will serve as a basis for advocacy at the level of public decision-makers in WAEMU countries for a more effective policy on fiscal inefficiency and reduction of inequality. Policy makers in WAEMU countries can be enlightened based on the results obtained, which may lead to a rethinking of current financial and anti - poverty policies.

Résumé

Cet article évalue la pertinence d'une instabilité financière par l'inégalité des revenus et inversement. La méthodologie utilisée dans cet article repose sur deux approches : la construction de l'Indice Synthétique d'Instabilité Financière (ISIF) et l'approche VAR considérée en panel faisant appel au PVAR. Les résultats obtenus permettent d'expliquer que la disparité des revenus dans un pays de l'UEMOA, une année donnée, influence négativement la volatilité du secteur financier l'année d'après. Des fonctions de réponses impulsionnelles montrent qu'un choc sur l'instabilité financière a un effet négatif sur lui-même et l'amène à une situation stable au bout de sept périodes. D'un autre côté, une hausse des inégalités de revenus dans les pays de l'UEMOA a tendance à atténuer l'instabilité financière dans un premier temps avant d'impulser une hausse du niveau d'instabilité. Par contre, suite à cette hausse, les inégalités vont baisser mais à un rythme très lent.

References

Abosedra, S., Shahbaz, M., and Nawaz, K. (2016). Modeling Causality Between Financial Deepening and Poverty Reduction in Egypt. *Social Indicators Research*, 126(3):955–969.

Akaike, H. (1969). Fitting autoregressive models for prediction. *Annals of the Institute of Statistical Mathematics*, 21(1):243–247.

Akaike, H. (1977). An objective use of Bayesian models. *Annals of the Institute of Statistical Mathematics*, 29(1):9–20.

Andrews, D. W. and Lu, B. (2001). Consistent model and moment selection procedures for {GMM} estimation with application to dynamic panel data models. *Journal of Econometrics*, 101(1):123–164.

Bordo, M. D. and Meissner, C. M. (2012). Does inequality lead to a financial crisis? *Journal of International Money and Finance*, 31(8):2147 – 2161.

Crotty, J. (1993). Rethinking Marxian Investment Theory: Keynes-Minsky Instability, Competitive Regime Shifts and Coerced Investment. *Review of Radical Political Economics*, 25(1):1–26.

Gantman, E. R. and Dabós, M. P. (2012). A Fragile Link? A New Empirical Analysis of the Relationship between Financial Development and Economic Growth. *Oxford Development Studies*, 40(4):517–532.

Hannan, E. J. and Quinn, B. G. (1979). The Determination of the Order of an Autoregression. *Journal of the Royal Statistical Society. Series B (Methodological)*, 41(2):190–195.

Hansen, L. P. (1982). Large Sample Properties of Generalized Method of Moments Estimators. *Econometrica*, 50(4):1029–1054.

Holtz-Eakin, D., Newey, W., and Rosen, H. S. (1988). Estimating Vector Autoregressions with Panel Data. *Econometrica*, 56(6):1371–1395.

Jauch, S. and Watzka, S. (2016). Financial development and income inequality: a panel data approach. *Empirical Economics*, 51(1):291–314.

Jeanneney, S. G. and Kpodar, K. (2004). Développement financier, instabilité financière, croissance et pauvreté. Macroeconomics, EconWPA.

Johansson, A. and Wang, X. (2014). Financial sector policies and income inequality. *China Economic Review*, 31(C):367–378.

Kappel, V. (2010). The Effects of Financial Development on Income Inequality and Poverty. CER-ETH Economics working paper series 10/127, CER-ETH - Center of Economic Research (CER-ETH) at ETH Zurich.

Keen, S. (1995). Finance and Economic Breakdown: Modeling Minsky's "Financial Instability Hypothesis". *Journal of Post Keynesian Economics*, 17(4):607–635.

Kpodar, K. and Singh, R. J. (2011). Does financial structure matter for poverty ? evidence from developing countries. Policy Research Working Paper Series 5915, The World Bank.

Krugman, P. (2007). *The Conscience of a Liberal.* New York: Norton & Norton.

Kumhof, M. and Ranciere, R. (2011). Inequality, Leverage and Crises. CEPR Discussion Papers 8179, C.E.P.R. Discussion Papers.

Mendoza, E. G. and Terrones, M. E. (2008). An Anatomy Of Credit Booms: Evidence From Macro Aggregates And Micro Data. NBER Working Papers 14049, National Bureau of Economic Research, Inc.

Minsky, H. P. (1982). *Can it happen again? Essay on instability and finance.* New York: ME Sharpe.

Park, D. and Shin, K. (2015). Economic Growth, Financial Development, and Income Inequality. ADB Economics Working Paper Series 441, Asian Development Bank.

Rajan, R. (2010). *Fault Lines: How Hidden Fractures Still Threaten the World Economy.* Princeton University Press, 1 edition.

Raskin, S. B. (2013). Aspects of inequality in the recent business cycle. Speech Delivered at the Building a Financial Structure for a More Stable and Equitable Economy, 22nd Annual Hyman P. Minsky Conference on the State of the U.S. and World Economies, New York, April 18. Retrieved April 15, 2017 (https://www.federalreserve.gov/newsevents/speech/raskin20130418a.htm).

Reich, R. (2007). *Supercapitalism.* Knopf Doubleday Publishing Group.

Rioja, F. and Valev, N. (2014). Stock markets, banks and the sources of economic growth in low and high income countries. *Journal of Economics and Finance*, 38(2):302–320.

Rissanen, J. (1978). Modeling by shortest data description. *Automatica*, 14(5):465 – 471.

Roine, J., Vlachos, J., and Waldenström, D. (2009). The long-run determinants of inequality: What can we learn from top income data? *Journal of Public Economics*, 93(7-8):974–988.

Schularick, M. and Taylor, A. M. (2012). Credit Booms Gone Bust: Monetary Policy, Leverage Cycles, and Financial Crises, 1870–2008. *The American Economic Review*, 102(2):1029–1061.

Schwarz, G. (1978). Estimating the Dimension of a Model. *The Annals of Statistics*, 6(2):461–464.

Sehrawat, M. and Giri, A. (2015). Financial development and income inequality in India: an application of ARDL approach. *International Journal of Social Economics*, 42(1):64–81.

Seven, U. and Coskun, Y. (2016). Does financial development reduce income inequality and poverty? Evidence from emerging countries. *Emerging Markets Review*, 26:34–63.

Seven, U. and Yetkiner, H. (2016). Financial intermediation and economic growth: Does income matter? *Economic Systems*, 40(1):39–58.

Sheng, L. (2014). Capital controls and international development: a theoretical reconsideration. *Global Policy*, 5(1):114–120.

Sheng, L. (2015). Theorizing income inequality in the face of financial globalization. *The Social Science Journal*, 52(3):415 – 424.

Uddin, G. S., Shahbaz, M., Arouri, M., and Teulon, F. (2014). Financial development and poverty reduction nexus: A cointegration and causality analysis in Bangladesh. *Economic Modelling*, 36:405–412.

Figure 1: Inequality and financial development

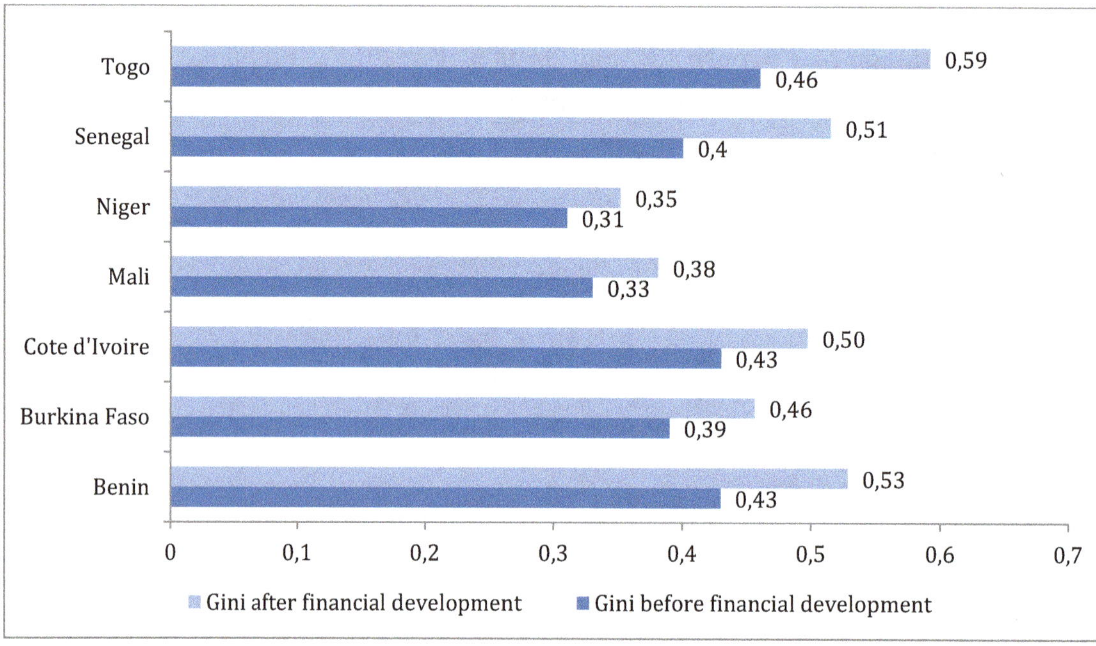

Note: Author's calculations, 2016, based on WIID data.

Figure 2: Histogram of eigenvalues

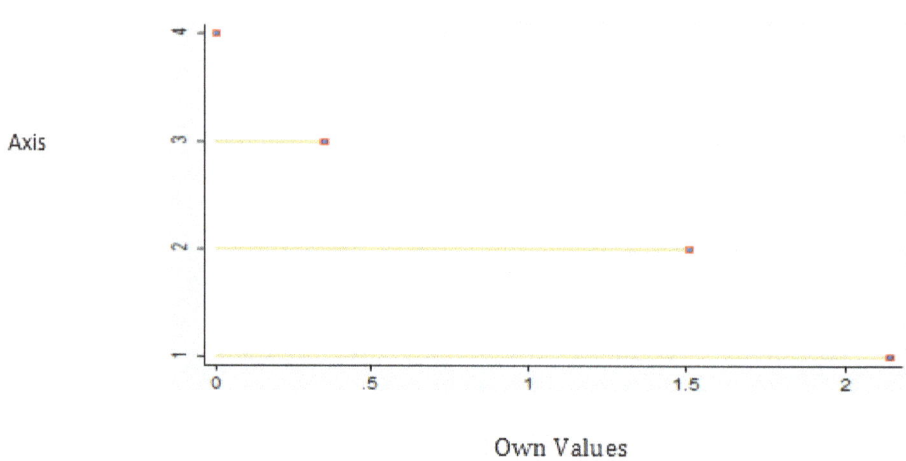

Figure 3: Impulse response functions

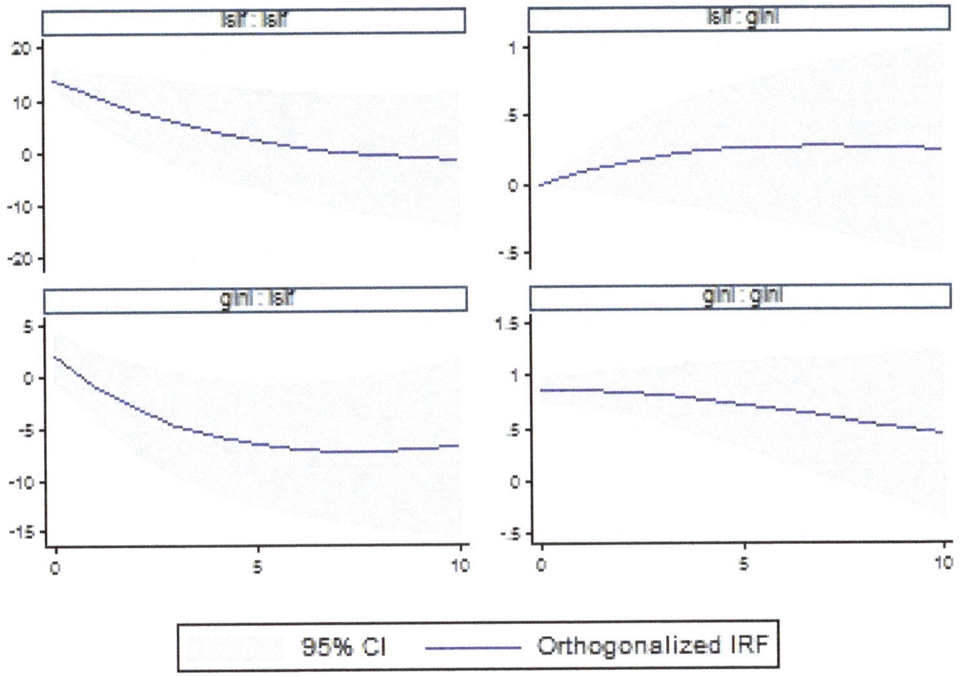

Table 1: Descriptive Statistics of Analyzed Variables

Variable	Description	Measure
SIFI	Synthetic index of financial instability	Index summarizing the fluctuations in descriptive variables of the financial sector
Gini	Gini index	Index measuring the inequality of income distribution in an economy
GOV_GDP	Budget balance rate	Overall budget balance (difference between public expenditure and state revenue) divided by GDP

Table 2: Statistic description

Synthetic index of financial instability in the WAEMU countries								
	Benin	**Burkina Faso**	**Ivory Coast**	**Guinea-Bissau**	**Mali**	**Niger**	**Senegal**	**Togo**
Average	48.335	48.335	48.335	48.335	48.335	48.335	48.335	48.335
Standard deviation	18.800	12.918	17.852	17.558	10.732	14.807	15.042	22.422
Min	24.279	27.165	26.911	20.188	31.154	30.152	28.397	21.839
Max	75.609	73.972	77.481	77.960	71.648	73.302	71.924	81.869
Gini index in the WAEMU countries								
	Benin	**Burkina Faso**	**Ivory Coast**	**Guinea-Bissau**	**Mali**	**Niger**	**Senegal**	**Togo**
Standard deviation	1.267	3.994	1.742	2.979	3.255	4.897	0.984	1.634
Min	34.076	38.146	38.445	34.980	31.122	29.962	36.761	33.450
Max	38.068	49.422	44.863	45.108	42.674	44.503	40.075	38.483

Table 3: Results of eigenvalues and weighting

Number of the axis	Eigen value of the axis	Weighting value
1	2.1441	0.5868
2	1.50999	0.4132

Table 4: Optimal delay

Delays	CD	J	J-*p-value*	MBIC	MAIC	MQIC
1	0,9851049	13,63348	0,3247234	-40,09457	-10,36652	-22,34321
2	0,9947965	6,567878	0,5838888	-29,25082	-9,432122	-17,41658
3	0,9751067	1,957026	0,7436629	-15,95232	-6,042974	-10,0352

Table 5: Stability of the model

eigenvalues		
Real	**imaginary**	**module**
0.8775852	0.0799631	0.8812207
0.8775852	-0.0799631	0.8812207

Table 6: PVAR Estimation Result

	gini	sifi
GINI(-1)	0.984*	-2.757*
	(2E -10)	(0.017)
SIFI(-1)	0.006	0.771*
	(0.204)	(3E -7)
GOV_GDP	0.001	0.000
	(0.498)	0.981)

Note: * statistically significant at 5% level
( ) p-value

Table 7: Granger Causality

Equation	Causes	Chi2	df	*p-value*
Gini				
	SIFI	1,614	1	0,204
	All	1,614	1	0,204
SIFI				
	Gini*	5,677	1	0,017
	All*	5,677	1	0,017

Note: * statistically significant at 5% level

7

On The Accuracy of GARCH Estimation in R Packages

Chelsey Hill[♣] and **B. D. McCullough**[*♣]

[♣]Department of Decision Sciences & MIS, Drexel University

ABSTRACT: The R software is commonly used in applied finance and generalized autoregressive conditionally heteroskedastic (GARCH) estimation is a staple of applied finance; many papers use R to compute GARCH estimates. While R offers three different packages that compute GARCH estimates, they are not equally accurate. We apply the FCP GARCH benchmark (Fiorentini, Calzolari and Panattoni 1996), proposed by McCullough and Renfro (1999), which uses the Bollerslev and Ghysels (1996) daily returns data, on three R packages: fGarch, rugarch, and tseries.

Keywords: algorithms, benchmark, software accuracy, GARCH

Introduction

Generalized autoregressive conditionally heteroskedastic (GARCH) models are especially popular models in the areas of economics and finance, although their application spans across many subject areas. In addition to their wide-ranging applications, their use in published research remains strong in recent years, as evidenced in Figure 1. Due to the complexity of GARCH, which involves non-linear estimation techniques, modeling is reliant on software implementation.

*Corresponding Author. Email: bdmccullough@drexel.edu

There are many commercial and open-source options for software programs that can estimate a GARCH model, including R, SAS, Matlab, Python and Stata. Due to the open-source nature of Python and R, there are 2 and 3 packages, respectively, that can fit a GARCH model. In this research, we specifically focus on the R software package, in which there are three distinct packages in which a univariate GARCH model can be fit: tseries, fGarch and rugarch.

Software choice can vary, but criteria often include popularity. To assess the popularity of the three packages, we consider formal citations, informal citations, download and dependencies. Based on citation data gathered in April 2019, the most frequently cited of the three packages is tseries. The tseries package documentation was published in 2007 and has a total of 211 citations, with 2018 producing the highest number of citations to date. The fGarch package, which also has package documentation citations beginning in 2007, has a total of 37 citations and the newest package, rugrach, has a total of 27 citations since its release in 2012.

Formal citations of software package documentation may be an unreliable measure of use, however, due in part to the consideration of software as technical, rather than scholarly contributions (Soito and Hwang, 2016). As a result, software packages are infrequently cited, if at all, in research. For this reason, a Google Scholar search from 2014-2018 of the package name keywords is depicted in Figure 2, which captures in-text references to the R packages. While fGarch displays largely stable citations over time, rugarch exhibits an increasing trend and tseries prevalence in the literature has also increased in recent years.

Considering the discrepancies between formal and informal citations of the packages in existing literature, we also evaluate the popularity of the packages using two measures based on the comprehensive R archive network: package downloads and dependencies. Using the dlstats package, monthly download metrics were collected for the three packages, as displayed in Figure 3. As shown, the monthly number of tseries downloads far outweighs the downloads of the other two packages. tseries demonstrates an increasing trend in user downloads, although the package reached its peak download numbers in the beginning of 2016. The other two packages have also seen increasing trends with respect to downloads, but have been comparatively stable over time.

Open source software packages do not exist in isolation, and instead have sometimes complex networks of reliance and dependencies within the larger R realm. Figure 4 depicts a comparison of the reverse dependencies, imports and suggestions for the three software packages. Consistent with the citation and download information, tseries is the most popular of the three, following by fGarch and rugarch, respectively.

Based on the prevalence of the tseries package with respect to formal citations, downloads and dependencies, it would appear that the tseries package should be preferred in GARCH modeling applications using R. Our findings, however, do not support this. While typical criteria for choosing software packages can include popularity, user-friendliness, computational efficiency and the range of features offered, these should be secondary considerations. Instead, accuracy must be the primary consideration. Our findings are consistent with previous research by McCullough and Renfro (2000), which found discrepancies across seven software packages with respect to the fitted GARCH parameters, suggesting that these issues continue to persist.

As discussed in McCullough and Vinod (2003a), in his "GARCH 101" tutorial, Engle (2001) simply ran the GARCH procedure with the options at default and in doing so failed to maximize the likelihood; thus he reported inaccurate GARCH coefficients. More specifically, McCullough and Vinod (2003a) document that Engle (2001) ran the EViews program at default and found a local maximum. Since accuracy was not a priority in Engle (2001), this should be unsurprising. Further details on the practicalities of using software to maximize likelihoods can be found in McCullough and Renfro (2000) and McCullough (2004), as well as McCullough and Vinod (2003b, 2004). To date, there is but one accuracy benchmark for GARCH models, proposed by McCullough and Renfro (1999), based on the work of Fiorentini, Calzolari and Panattoni (1996), which makes use of the Bollerslev and Ghysels (1996) data containing 1,974 observations on the daily percentage nominal returns for the Deutschemark/British pound exchange rate. We utilize this FCP GARCH Benchmark in this research to determine the accuracy of their estimates.

In this paper, we specifically evaluate the three packages with respect to optimization control and accuracy. Any GARCH procedure should have many user-controlled options, at least to control the nonlinear solver and a user should tune these options to obtain the best answer. In our research, we find that despite the **tseries** package's popularity, the **rugarch** package offers the greatest flexibility, range of options, consideration of benchmarking and consistency of the three packages, despite its seemingly underwhelming popularity in both citations and practice. Our findings also reinforce the importance of software documentation and benchmarking at the development-level and discernment and understanding at the user-level to promote reproducibility, accuracy, and interpretability of GARCH analysis results using the R software.

In Section 1, we describe the GARCH Model and introduce the R packages we consider, including a description of algorithms and options available to the user. In Section 2, we run them at default to produce some answer, then attempt to vary the options to establish that we have control over the package. Then, we introduce the FCP GARCH benchmark that is applied to the R packages and present our results. Section 3 presents the discussion and conclusions.

1 The GARCH Model and Estimation

The GARCH model is a popular extension of an ARCH model, in which an autoregressive moving average (ARMA) model, rather than autoregressive (AR), is used to model the variance of the time series (Engle, 1982; Bollerslev, 1986). Both ARCH and GARCH methods are commonly employed econometric techniques to handle the presence of volatility clustering. In this paper, we focus on the standard univariate GARCH model, which serves as the foundation for the family of GARCH models, which include the exponential GARCH, or eGARCH (Nelson, 1991), integrated GARCH, or iGARCH (Engle and Bollerslev, 1986), and GJR-GARCH (Glosten, Jaganathan and Runkle 1993) models.

Following McCullough and Renfro (1999), the basic GARCH(p, q) model, in which p is the lag parameter and q denotes the ARCH order, is given by

$$y_t = x_t'b + \epsilon_t \quad \epsilon_t|\Psi_{t-1} \sim N(0, h_t) \tag{1}$$

where y_t is the dependent variable, x_t is a vector of independent variables and b is a vector of parameters in a linear regression model. ϵ_t represents the stochastic process, ψ_t represents the information set through time t and h_t, the conditional variance is given by

$$h_t = \alpha_0 + \sum_{i=1}^{p} \alpha_i \epsilon_{t-1}^2 + \sum_{j=1}^{q} \beta_j h_{t-j} \tag{2}$$

where α_0, α_i and β_j are constants and $\alpha_0 > 0, \quad \alpha_i \geq 0, \quad i = 1, ..., p, \quad \beta_j \geq 0, \quad j = 1, ..., q$.

This gives rise to the conditional likelihood

$$L_t = \sum_{t=1}^{T} l_t(\theta) \tag{3}$$

$$l_t(\theta) = -\frac{1}{2}\ln h_t - \frac{1}{2}\frac{\epsilon_t^2}{h_t} \tag{4}$$

The mean is denoted μ. This model is only partially specified because starting values must be provided for μ, α_0, α_1, and β_1 and the initialization for h_t and ϵ_t^2 must be defined before the conditional likelihood can be maximized. This initialization is distinct from the starting values that are used to begin a nonlinear estimation and is an important facet of the estimation. A very common initialization is

$$h_t = \epsilon_t^2 = \frac{1}{T}\sum_{s=1}^{T} \epsilon_s^2 = \frac{SS}{T}, \quad t \leq 0 \tag{5}$$

where ϵ_s are estimated residuals from least squares regression. Since the initialized values of h_t and ϵ_t^2 are present in the likelihood function, the estimated model parameters will depend on the initial values, underscoring the importance of this initialization.

Once initialized, the log-likelihood can be maximized. The complexity of the GARCH estimation procedure stems in large part due to the non-linear estimation. Analytical and numerical methods can be used in the estimation, with varying degrees of precision. We define the gradient, $g(\theta)$, and the Hessian, $H(\theta)$, of the likelihood function and Q as the estimate of the covariance matrix.

Fiorentini et al. (1996) presented 5 estimates that can be used for the covariance matrix, which are used in the benchmarking procedures in McCullough and Renfro (1999). The first three methods are gradient methods and the latter two are maximum likelihood methods. Direct use of the Hessian involves setting $Q = -H^{-1}$. Alternatively, by setting $Q = g(\theta)g(\theta)'$, the outer product of the gradient (OPG) can be used to approximate the Hessian, as is typical in the BHHH algorithm. The estimated expected Hessian matrix, the information matrix, in which $Q = E[H^{-1}(\theta)]$, can also be used. The two maximum likelihood estimators are the quasi-maximum likelihood method (QMLE), in which $Q = H^{-1}(gg')H^{-1}$ and the Bollerslev and Wooldridge (BW 1992), where $Q = I^{-1}(gg')I^{-1}$.[1]

1.1 Estimation in R

First, we briefly describe the commands necessary to estimate a GARCH model in each package. Our goal is to get each package to produce a result by running it with the default options. After having produced an answer, we will make sure the options are subject to user control by limiting the number of iterations, which is perhaps the simplest option to demonstrate control. The three packages we consider are tseries (Trapletti and Hornik, 2018), fGarch (Wuertz and Chalabi, 2016), and rugarch (Ghalanos, 2017).

In addition to getting coefficient estimates, we also comment on the standard errors. There are many ways to get standard errors for nonlinear estimation (*e.g.*, BHHH, OPG, etc), and the output should clearly specify which type of standard error is reported. The user should not have to dig through the documentation to find out what kind of standard error is being used. Further, as a matter of usable software, the package should offer more than one method of computing the standard error. Except for rugarch, the documentation for these packages makes no mention of the accuracy of the GARCH estimates they produce.

[1] Since methods were introduced and demonstrated in FCP (1996), more than 20 years ago, we omit the rigorous derivations and direct the interested reader to this literature.

1.1.1 tseries

The tseries package is described as a package for "time series analysis and computational finance", with the ability to estimate both autoregressive moving average (ARMA) and GARCH models (Trapletti and Hornik, 2018). Package documentation indicates that the package is still being maintained by its authors, and was updated in 2018.

For tseries, the GARCH and control commands are as follows:

```
garch(x, order = c(1, 1), series = NULL, control = garch.
control(...), ...)

garch.control(maxiter = 200, trace = TRUE, start = NULL, grad =
c("analytical","numerical"), abstol = max(1e-20,.Machine$double.
eps^2), reltol = max(1e-10, .Machine$double.eps^(2/3)), xtol =
sqrt(.Machine$double.eps), falsetol = 1e2 * .Machine$double.
eps, ...)
```

The `garch` command is described as fitting the GARCH model by "computing the maximum likelihood estimates of the conditionally normal model". This is the only indication given that the sole conditional distribution that can be utilized is the normal distribution. The package offers either numerical or analytical gradient methods for optimization.

1.1.2 fGarch

The fGarch package is described as a "collection of functions to analyze and model heteroskedastic behavior in financial time series models" and is part of the larger Rmetrics offerings. Based on the change log on CRAN, the package has not been changed since 2013, although the published year on the documentation is listed as 2019.

The garch and control commands for the fGarch package are as follows:

```
garchFit(formula = ~ garch(1, 1), data = dem2gbp, init.rec =
c("mci", "uev"), delta = 2, skew = 1, shape = 4, cond.dist =
c("norm", "snorm", "ged", "sged", "std", "sstd", "snig", "QMLE"),
include.mean = TRUE, include.delta = NULL, include.skew = NULL,
include.shape = NULL, leverage = NULL, trace = TRUE, algorithm =
c("nlminb", "lbfgsb", "nlminb+nm", "lbfgsb+nm"), hessian =
c("ropt", "rcd"), control = list(), title = NULL, description
= NULL, ...)
```

```
garchFitControl(llh = c("filter", "internal", "testing"),
nlminb.eval.max = 2000, nlminb.iter.max = 1500, nlminb.abs.tol =
1.0e-20, nlminb.rel.tol = 1.0e-14, nlminb.x.tol = 1.0e-14,
nlminb.step.min = 2.2e-14, nlminb.scale = 1, nlminb.fscale =
FALSE, nlminb.xscale = FALSE, sqp.mit = 200, sqp.mfv = 500, sqp.met
= 2, sqp.mec = 2, sqp.mer = 1, sqp.mes = 4, sqp.xmax = 1.0e3,
sqp.tolx = 1.0e-16, sqp.tolc = 1.0e-6, sqp.tolg = 1.0e-6, sqp.told
= 1.0e-6, sqp.tols = 1.0e-4, sqp.rpf = 1.0e-4, lbfgsb.REPORT = 10,
lbfgsb.lmm = 20, lbfgsb.pgtol = 1e-14, lbfgsb.factr = 1,
lbfgsb.fnscale = FALSE, lbfgsb.parscale = FALSE, nm.ndeps = 1e-14,
nm.maxit = 10000, nm.abstol = 1e-14, nm.reltol = 1e-14, nm.alpha =
1.0, nm.beta = 0.5, nm.gamma = 2.0, nm.fnscale = FALSE,
nm.parscale = FALSE)
```

The fGarch package is plagued with many issues, one of which is sloppy documentation. For instance, the description of the `garchFit` command is: “Estimates the parameters of an univariate ARMA-GARCH/APARCH process.” While the documentation makes it clear that an APARCH model can be estimated using the function, the primary role of the `garchFit` function is clearly to estimate a GARCH model, and all examples in the documentation using this function are to fit a “pure” GARCH model of order (1,1). Meanwhile, the description of the `garchFitControl` command is: “Estimates the parameters of an univariate GARCH process.” The control command does not do this, nor is it likely that the control command was ever intended to do this. The purpose of this function is unclear in the documentation and no illustrative examples are provided. In fact, we will show that the control command does not even do what it is supposed to do.

Unlike the `garch` command in the tseries package, the `garchFit` command offers several options for specifying the conditional distribution and optimization method; however, the documentation does not clearly define what the abbreviations stand for.

1.1.3 rugarch

The rugarch package is the only package of the three considered which provides an instruction guide, known in R as a vignette (“Introduction to the rugarch Package”), in addition to the reference documentation. The documentation itself does address the issue of accuracy, though incompletely and incorrectly.

The rugarch package has a built-in function, `ugarchbench(benchmark = "published")`, which reports the rugarch-estimated parameters versus published benchmarks, which turns out to be the FCP GARCH Benchmark; however, it is up to the user to determine that the results are accurate. Further, the documentation for the command only cites Brooks (1997), which is a limited review of three software programs using simulated data and only using BHHH for the computation of standard errors. This does not appear to have anything to do with the benchmarking for accuracy; it does a simulation analysis and seems to look at the speed and cost, not accuracy. The documentation should reference the article by McCullough and Renfro (1999).

The `ugarchfit` command requires a specification of the garch model that is effected via the `spec` option with a call to `ugarchspec`. The pair of commands is given below.

```
ugarchfit(spec, data, out.sample = 0, solver = "solnp",
solver.control = list(), fit.control = list(stationarity = 1,
fixed.se = 0, scale = 0, rec.init = 'all'), numderiv.control =
list(grad.eps=1e-4, grad.d=0.0001, grad.zero.tol=
sqrt(.Machine$double.eps/7e-7), hess.eps=1e-4, hess.d=0.1,
hess.zero.tol=sqrt(.Machine$double.eps/7e-7), r=4, v=2),...)
```

```
ugarchspec(variance.model = list(model = "sGARCH", garchOrder =
c(1, 1), submodel = NULL, external.regressors = NULL,
variance.targeting = FALSE), mean.model = list(armaOrder = c(1, 1),
include.mean = TRUE, archm = FALSE, archpow = 1, arfima = FALSE,
external.regressors = NULL, archex = FALSE), distribution.model =
"norm", start.pars = list(), fixed.pars = list(), ...)
```

The `ugarchfit` command is described as a "method for fitting a variety of univariate GARCH models". The command offers six possible solvers, and defines each in the "Details" section of the manual. There are many options for specifying the conditional distribution, as outlined in the `ugarchspec` section of the manual. As in the fGarch package, rugarch estimates μ by default.

2 Analysis

Our methodology for evaluating the three available R packages for univariate GARCH modeling involves two major components: (1) examining the ability to control the optimization procedure and (2) assessing the performance against an established GARCH benchmark.

The data used in the analysis is the Bollerslev and Ghysels (1996) data containing 1,974 observations on the daily percentage nominal returns for the Deutschemark/British pound exchange rate. We use the FCP GARCH Benchmark to determine the accuracy of their estimates.

2.1 Optimization Control

2.1.1 tseries

When run at default, in particular executing the command `garch(x)`, trace is on and we can observe that the optimizer performed 27 iterations before declaring false convergence. The false convergence can be eliminated by providing decent starting values. By specifying starting values of 0.01, 0.1, and 0.8 for α_0, α_1 and β_1, respectively, or

```
garch(x, order=c(1,1), control=garch.control(start=c(0.01,0.1,0.8))),
```

relative convergence is indicated.

To demonstrate control over the optimization procedure, we limit the number of iterations by changing the command to

```
garch(x,control=garch.control(maxiter=5)).
```

This successfully limits the number of iterations to 5, so we believe we have control over the optimizer and have obtained a solution.

While we are able to demonstrate control over the optimizer, there are some shortcomings identified. Based on the output obtained when running the command, the results does not include an estimate of μ. The documentation does not describe what type of GARCH model is being fitted, and makes no mention of why no mean parameter is estimated (even though GARCH models typically are fitted with a mean). The estimated parameters exclude μ, and there is no mention in the documentation if it is being estimated and withheld or if there is an alternate assumption underlying the model.

2.1.2 fGarch

Running at default, `garchFit(~ garch(1,1),x)`, we find a solution in 19 iterations. The default algorithm is `nlminb` so it seems natural to limit the number of iterations as follows:

```
garchFit(formula = ~ garch(1, 1), data = x,
control=garchFitControl(nlminb.iter.max=5)),
```

but the number of iterations is still 19 *and* several warnings are issued, all of the variety:

```
In if (.params$control$llh == "internal") { ... : the condition has
length > 1 and only the first element will be used.
```

Adding the option `llh=''filter''` to `garchFitControl` removes the warnings, but as one can see, the default for `llh` *is* `filter`, so the source of the error is unclear. Further, the number of iterations is not limited to 5; again we get 19 iterations.

Running `garchFit( ~ garch(1,1),x)@fit\$params\$control` to view the control options and defaults, we see that the default maximum iterations is 5000. Running

```
garchFit(formula= ~ garch(1,1), data = x,
control=garchFitControl(nlminb.iter.max=5))@fit\$params\$control
```

shows not only

```
$nlminb.iter.max
[1] 5
```

but also

```
$MIT
[1] 2000
```

even though

```
garchFit(formula= ~ garch(1,1), data = x,
control=garchFitControl(nlminb.iter.max=5))
```

results in 19 iterations.

Thus, the value of 5 is passed to the function but it has no effect on the number of iterations, and there are also several control parameters, including `MIT`, that are not listed in the documentation! This certainly looks like "maximum iterations"; but setting "`MIT = 5`" still results in 19 iterations. It appears, then, that arguments passed from the function call to the optimizer do not have an effect on the modeling, even though the information passed is updated in the model output! Specifically, using the options to specify the maximum number of iterations *does not work*; at least we could not make it work in what we consider to be a reasonable amount of time. Furthermore, Nash (2014) suggests that the R optim port routines that the fGarch package utilizes should be deprecated.

As mentioned, the lack of examples provided in the documentation further contributes to the difficulty of understanding the specifications and gaining control over the function and estimation of the GARCH model, particularly with respect to the `garchControlFit` function. We conclude that without demonstrable control over the options for the optimizer, we will have to execute all runs at default settings for the fGarch package. We also note that the documentation is obviously wrong in many places, which suggests a sloppiness that may well pervade the underlying code, *e.g.*, the `MIT` option mentioned above. However, unlike the tseries package, the default command sets `include.mean=TRUE` and `garchFit` estimates μ by default.

2.1.3 rugarch

The most parsimonious command we could get to run is `ugarchfit(spec = ugarchspec(),x)` but it did not show the number of iterations. According to the manual for `solnp`, the default solver in `ugarchfit`, it should print the coefficients at each iteration, but somehow this feature is suppressed. To get the number of iterations we had to run `ugarchfit(spec = ugarchspec (), x, solver.control = list(trace=1))` from which we see convergence in two iterations. If we run `ugarchfit(spec = ugarchspec(), x, solver.control = list(trace=1, outer.iter=1))` we get a failure to converge message, and if we set `outer.iter=2` we get the same answer as the previous runs. We believe that we have control over the optimizer.

The `ugarchfit` function returns two sets of standard errors. The "robust" standard errors are vaguely described as "based on White (1982)" (Ghalanos, 2017, p. 27), which is hardly specific, since there are many robust methods "based on" White's article. With respect to the default standard errors estimated, the reference manual and vignette do not even hint at the method used to compute the default standard errors. We will have to see if we can deduce whether the default standard errors are based on the gradient, the Hessian or the Information Matrix.

2.2 Accuracy

Since this benchmark was published nearly 20 years ago and it is the only available GARCH benchmark, every package should permit this initialization if only for the purpose of benchmarking the package; any package that does not permit this initialization is not written by a person who wants to benchmark his package. Again, we emphasize that this initialization is distinct from the choice of starting values that are used for parameter estimation.

FCP estimated this model with analytic derivatives, which are more accurate than numerical derivatives and generally lead to more accurate parameter estimates. We cannot expect that packages using numerical derivatives can achieve more than a few digits of accuracy; certainly we do not expect packages with numerical derivatives to achieve full six-digit accuracy.

Table 1 will allow us to answer two questions: How accurate are the estimates? and, if necessary, What kind of standard errors does the package offer?

First and foremost, we have to ask, Can the benchmark model be estimated? This requires that the FCP initialization be used. If so, then two more questions follow: (1) how many accurate digits at default? and (2) how many accurate digits can we get if we tune the optimizer by carefully choosing the options?

To tune the optimizer, we do the following:

1. Select starting values rather than let the software choose them. We first tried using

the default results, but those produced false convergence. We settled on using the first significant digit of the default results: 0.01, 0.1, 0.8.

2. Analytic derivatives are the default, and they are generally better than numerical derivatives, so we kept analytic derivatives.

3. We varied some options, e.g., tolerances, but we did not conduct an exhaustive search to find the combination of options that produces the most accuracy.

2.2.1 tseries

The documentation makes no mention of accuracy and the output also does not identify the type of standard error reported. The garch function offers one solver, with only the vague description that it is a "Quasi-Newton optimizer", which uses a "Hessian approximation computed from the BFGS update". For this reason, especially poor approximations are likely to result in the event of early termination of the iterative estimation and the quasi-Newton approach lacks the safeguards against saddle points inherent in Newton-Raphson (McCullough and Renfro, 1999). Quasi-Newton methods are, however, less sensitive to the initial starting values.

In the documentation for the `summary.garch` command, we find that the covariance matrix is computed by the outer product of the gradient (OPG) method, which is the only method offered by the package. Unfortunately, this is an inferior method that only uses first derivative information, although it uses analytic derivatives. It offers only one type of standard error, and the type is not labeled in the output. Instead, the user has to search the documentation for it.

tseries makes no mention of an initialization. The actual initialization of h_t and ε_t is not discussed at all. Per the tseries documentation, "default initialization is to set the GARCH parameters to slightly positive values and to initialize the intercept such that the unconditional variance of the initial GARCH is equal to the variance of x" (page 10). This actually refers to starting values for parameter estimation, not the initialization for the recursion of the error term. Running at default, `summary(garch(x))` produces results for a three parameter model, although a "false convergence" message is produced.

Tuning the model involved altering the convergence tolerance and starting parameters for the parameter estimation. Tuning produced only a marginal improvement in accuracy, which is limited to 2-3 significant digits, as shown in Table 2. This is exceedingly poor performance for analytic derivatives. We conjecture that some initialization other than the benchmark initialization is being used.

The tuned estimates of the OPG standard errors are shown in Table 3. While the `garch` command in the tseries package has the benefit of producing analytical derivatives and we are able to prove that we have control over the optimizer, the performance compared to the FCP benchmark is poor. Despite attempts to obtain improvements in performance by tuning, the benefit of tuning was negligible in improving the accuracy of the estimates. In addition, we are forced to make comparisons based on a three parameter model instead of a four parameter model, as is the case of the FCP benchmark.

2.2.2 fGarch

The documentation makes no mention of accuracy. The package offers several solvers, but we cannot even limit the number of iterations for the default solver. The package offers two types of standard errors, one based on the Hessian and another based on QMLE, but the output and manual lack clarity. There are many options available in the package for estimation, but a combination of poor documentation and technical issues limits us to running the package with the default options.

fGarch has an option `init.rec` to specify "a character string indicating the method how to initialize the mean and variance recursion relation" which can take one of two arguments, "`mci`" and "`uev`". However, the documentation makes no mention of what "`mci`" and "`uev`" might mean. The "`mci`" option produces default results, which is to be expected, while the "`uev`" option produces an error message:

```
Error in .garchFit(formula.mean = args$formula.mean, formula.var =
 args$formula.var,  :   Algorithm only supported for mci Recursion
```

It is most unusual to release software with options that are not supported.

The default model using the fGarch package is estimated using the command:

```
summary(garchFit(~garch(1,1),x))
```

which includes the phrase "Std. Errors: based on Hessian". Yet the documentation ("Details" section of the command `garchFit`) discusses QMLE and refers the reader to Davidson and MacKinnon's 2004 text for a discussion of the robust covariance matrix. Via experimentation, we discovered that if we invoke the option to change the conditional distribution from normal to QMLE, then the output contains QMLE standard errors. This was not at all obvious, and should be spelled out clearly in the manual because QMLE standard errors are generally better for GARCH estimation.

We are unable to tune the procedure, since the options do not seem to change anything. We failed to limit the number of iterations already. Here we tried to change the default absolute, relative and x tolerance from their default values of 0, 1E-10, and 1.58E-10, respectively, to 1E-7 and observed no change in the solution. We do not have reason to believe that our changes in defaults have been made, given our lack of control over the optimizer.

As shown in Table 4, the coefficients are estimated with 4-6 digits of accuracy, and the Hessian standard errors are estimated with 2-4 digits of accuracy as shown in Table 5.

With some difficulty, we were able to identify the default standard errors as Hessian standard errors. If QMLE is specified as the conditional distribution instead of the default, the output produces QMLE standard errors, specifically the Eicker-White sandwich estimators. These details should be explicitly and clearly stated, not hidden. These estimates are accurate to 1 or two digits, as shown in Table 6. If we could tune the procedure, we might be able to obtain more accuracy.

```
summary(garchFit(~garch(1,1),x, cond.dist="QMLE"))
```

We are able to change the conditional distribution and thus estimate QMLE standard errors, as suggested in the documentation, rather than the default method, which provides standard errors based on the Hessian. The QMLE standard errors are estimated with 1-3 digits of accuracy.

The accuracy of the estimates found using the `garchFit` command in the fGarch package compared to the FCP benchmark is an improvement over those found using the tseries package. Additionally, all parameters are estimated, including μ. Unfortunately, without control over the optimizer we cannot tune the optimzer to obtain better results.

2.2.3 rugarch

The reference manual does mention accuracy, without asserting that it hits a benchmark, and cites the wrong article. The ugarchbench procedure documentation cites Brooks (1997), which is a review of software for GARCH models, and makes no mention of benchmarking. The package offers several optimization algorithms and two types of standard errors, but is missing more precise information regarding the latter. rugarch also has an option `init.rec`, and the documentation explains clearly that when this is set to "all" it is the FCP initialization. It also happens to be the default choice for this option. According to the rugarch manual, we are able to run the FCP GARCH benchmark on the BG data via its `ugarchbench` function.

The FCP Benchmark model with four parameters is specified and then estimated with the following commands:

```
model=ugarchspec(
  variance.model = list(model = "sGARCH", garchOrder = c(1, 1)),
  mean.model = list(armaOrder = c(0, 0), include.mean = TRUE),
  distribution.model = "norm")

 mygarch = ugarchfit(spec = model, data = x)
```

The above is the default model because we have not altered the algorithm or the tolerances, etc. Table 6 shows these default coefficients, which are accurate to 2 or 3 digits. The corresponding standard errors are given in Tables 7 (Hessian) and 8 (robust), which are accurate to 3 and zero digits, respectively. The poor accuracy of the robust standard error makes us suspect that rugarch uses some robust standard error other than QMLE. The author really should specify what method he uses.

Tuning does not lead to better performance and are omitted for this reason. We are surprised that we cannot squeeze an extra digit of accuracy by tuning, but maybe the defaults have been chosen for maximal accuracy.

In the "Details" section of `ugarchfit-methods` it states that "the GARCH optimization routine first calculates a set of feasible starting points which are used to initiate the GARCH recursion". From `ugarchfit-methods` section, we also find that the `rec.init` option determines the type of initialization for the variance recursion. "Valid options are 'all' which uses all the values for the unconditional variance calculation, an integer greater than or equal to 1, denoting the number of data points to use for the calculation, or a positive numeric value less than one, which determines the weighting for use in an exponential smoothing backcast". "all" is the default option, and appears to correspond to the initialization for the FCP benchmark, though it would be nice if this were more explicitly stated in the documentation.

The `ugarchfit` command in the rugarch package has many strengths with respect to the estimation, documentation and accuracy of GARCH models. We are able to demonstrate control over the solver. It seems that the defaults were chosen with the FCP benchmark in mind, resulting in optimal performance; if this is true it should be explicitly stated. However, the "robust" standard error is not the QMLE used by many other packages, and the documentation does not specifically state what type of robust standard error is used. There are some areas of documentation that are lacking, but overall the estimation of the parameters of the GARCH model have high accuracy and transparency with respect to their performance against the benchmark.

2.2.4 Comparing Coefficient Accuracy

Following McCullough and Renfro (1999), we present the log relative error (LRE), to compare the tuned coefficient and standard error estimates across the three packages. The log relative error is computed as

$$LRE = -log_{10}[\mid x - c \mid / \mid c \mid] \tag{6}$$

where x is the estimated value and c is the benchmark value. The LRE measures the number of accurate digits, where larger LRE values indicate a more accurate estimate.

Table 10 presents the LRE values for the coefficient estimates of the three packages. As shown, fGarch produces the most accurate coefficient estimates, followed by rugarch and tseries.

The LRE for the standard errors are presented in Table 11, organized by the estimate of the covariance matrix used. This table further highlights the poor performance of tseries with respect to accuracy. As shown and expected, the accuracy is highest when directly using the Hessian matrix, which fGarch and rugarch can do.

3 Discussion and Conclusion

Despite more than 20 years passing since the introduction of a benchmarking procedure for univariate GARCH methods, the persistence of the problems identified in McCullough and Renfro (1999) in our current estimation of GARCH models using 3 packages in the same software program emphasizes the non-triviality of the issue. Despite Fiorentini et al. (1996) presenting and examining closed-form options for maximizing the GARCH conditional likelihood, we find that the most popular package of the three considered, tseries, makes use of a method that they find to be inferior.

In this paper, we have examined the three R packages that offer GARCH estimation, tseries, fGarch and rugarch, and concluded that rugarch is the package we would use for GARCH estimation, although it is not without flaws. rugarch, while its documentation leaves something to be desired, offers several optimizers, two different types of standard errors, can hit the benchmark, offers forecasting capabilities and can be tuned. However, its "robust standard error" is of an unspecified variety, and does not hit any of the five benchmarked standard errors; we don't know what kind of robust standard error the package employs.

The second package that hits the benchmark, fGarch, has poor documentation, poor control of options and we cannot tune the optimizer to improve performance. While it offers two different types of standard errors and forecasting ability, these glaring deficiencies should warrant skepticism from users.

Most importantly, perhaps, we find that the most popular GARCH modeling package, tseries, has several weaknesses that make it a particularly poor choice for econometrics practitioners. tseries does not estimate a model with a mean, has only one optimizer, one type of standard error (based on the inferior OPG method that fails to make use of second derivative information), cannot produce out-sample forecasts and cannot hit the FCP GARCH benchmark.

References

Bollerslev, T. (1986). Generalized Autoregressive Conditional Heteroscedasticity. *Journal of Econometrics*, 31:307–327.

Bollerslev, T. and Ghysels, E. (1996). Periodic Autoregressive Conditional Heteroscedasticity. *Journal of Business and Economic Statistics*, 14:139–151.

Brooks, C. (1997). GARCH Modelling in Finance: A Review of the Software Options. *Economic Journal*, 107(443):1271–1276.

Engle, R. (1982). Autoregressive Conditional Heteroscedasticity with Estimates of the Variance of United Kingdom Inflation. *Econometrica*, 50(4):987–1008.

Engle, R. (2001). GARCH 101: The Use of ARCH/GARCH Models in Applied Econometrics. *Journal of Economic Perspectives*, 15(4):157–168.

Engle, R. and Bollerslev, T. (1986). Modelling the Persistence of Conditional Variances. *Econometric Reviews*, 5(1):1–50.

Fiorentini, G., Calzolari, G., and Panattoni, L. (1996). Analytic Derivatives and the Computation of GARCH Estimates. *Journal of Applied Econometrics*, 11:399–417.

Ghalanos, A. (2017). Introduction to the rugarch package. (Version 1.3-8). https://cran.r-project.org/web/packages/rugarch/.

Glosten, L. R., Jagannathan, R., and Runkle, D. E. (1993). On the Relation between the Expected Value and the Volatility of the Nominal Excess Return on Stocks. *Journal of Finance*, 48(5):1779–1801.

McCullough, B. D. (2004). Some Details of Nonlinear Estimation. In Altman, M., Gill, J., and McDonald, M. P., editors, *Numerical Issues in Statistical Computing for the Social Sciences*, pages 199–218. John Wiley & Sons, New York.

McCullough, B. D. and Renfro, C. G. (1999). Benchmarks and Software Standards: A Case Study of GARCH Procedures. *Journal of Economic and Social Measurement*, 25(2):59–71.

McCullough, B. D. and Renfro, C. G. (2000). Some Numerical Aspects of Nonlinear Estimation. *Journal of Economic and Social Measurement*, 26(1):63–77.

McCullough, B. D. and Vinod, H. D. (2003a). Comment: Econometrics and Software. *Journal of Economic Perspectives*, 17(1):223–224.

McCullough, B. D. and Vinod, H. D. (2003b). Verifying the Solution from a Nonlinear Solver: A Case Study. *American Economic Review*, 93(3):873–892.

McCullough, B. D. and Vinod, H. D. (2004). Verifying the Solution from a Nonlinear Solver: A Case Study: Reply. *American Economic Review*, 94(1):400–403.

Nash, J. C. (2014). On Best Practice Optimization Methods in R. *Journal of Statistical Software*, 60(2):1–14.

Nelson, D. B. (1991). Conditional Heteroskedasticity in Asset Returns: A New Approach. *Econometrica*, 59(2):347–370.

Soito, L. and Hwang, L. J. (2016). Citations for Software: Providing Identification, Access and Recognition for Research Software. *International Journal of Digital Curation*, 11(2):48–63.

Trapletti, A. and Hornik, K. (2018). tseries: Time Series Analysis and Computational Finance. R package version 0.10-42. https://cran.r-project.org/package=tseries.

Wuertz, D. and Chalabi, Y. (2016). fGarch: Rmetrics - Autoregressive Conditional Heteroskedastic Modelling. R package version 3010.82.1. https://cran.r-project.org/package=fGarch.

Figure 1: Google Scholar Citations Time Series

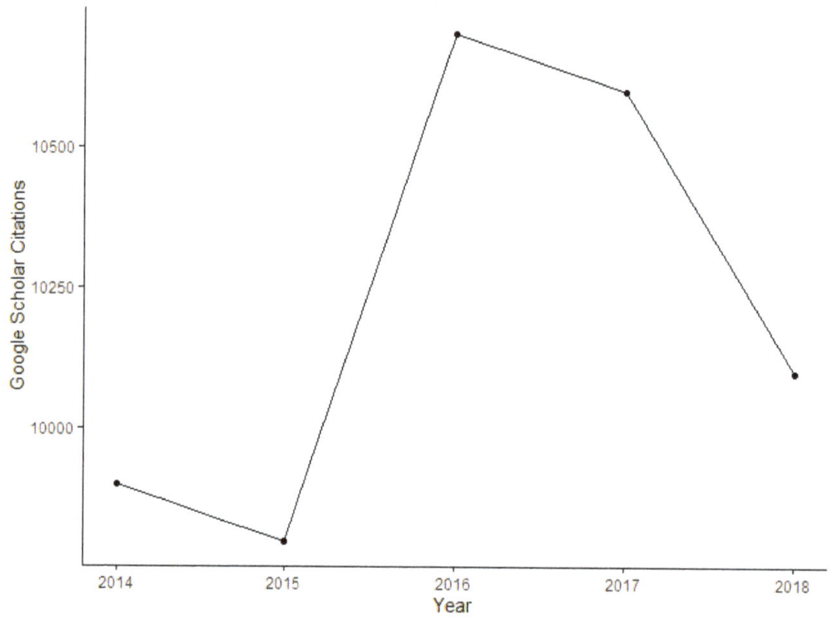

Figure 2: GARCH R Packages Google Scholar Search Result Time Series

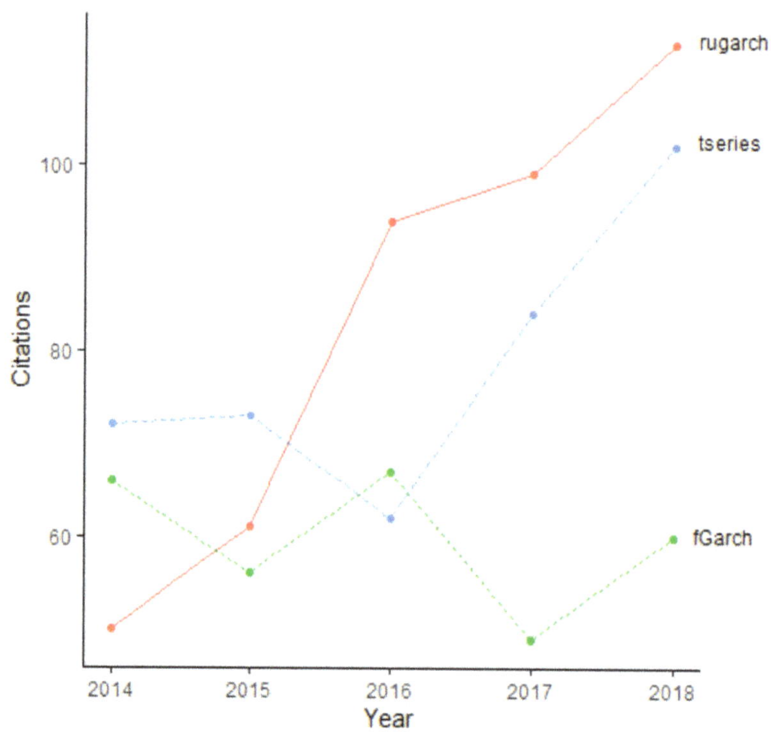

Figure 3: Package Downloads Time Series

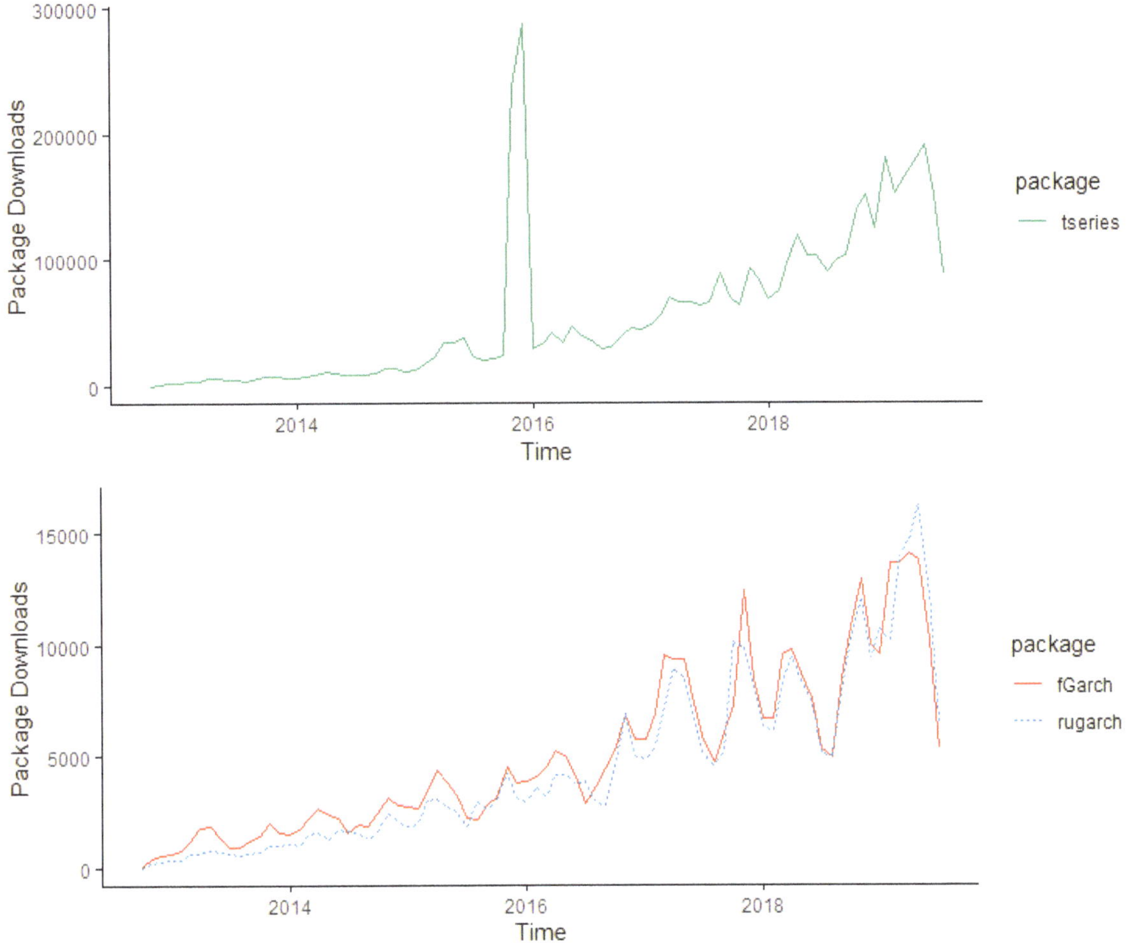

Figure 4: Reverse Dependencies, Imports and Suggestions across GARCH packages in R

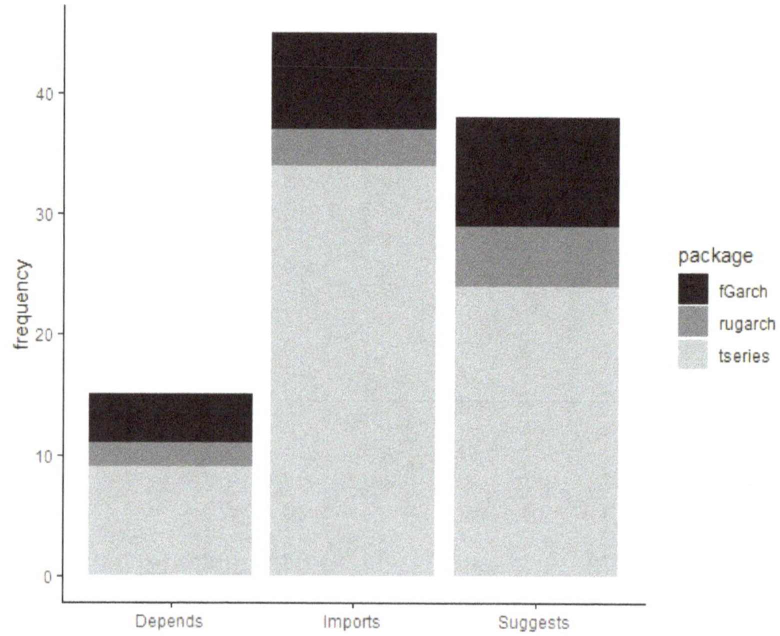

Figure 5: Benchmark data from Bollerslev and Ghysels (1996)

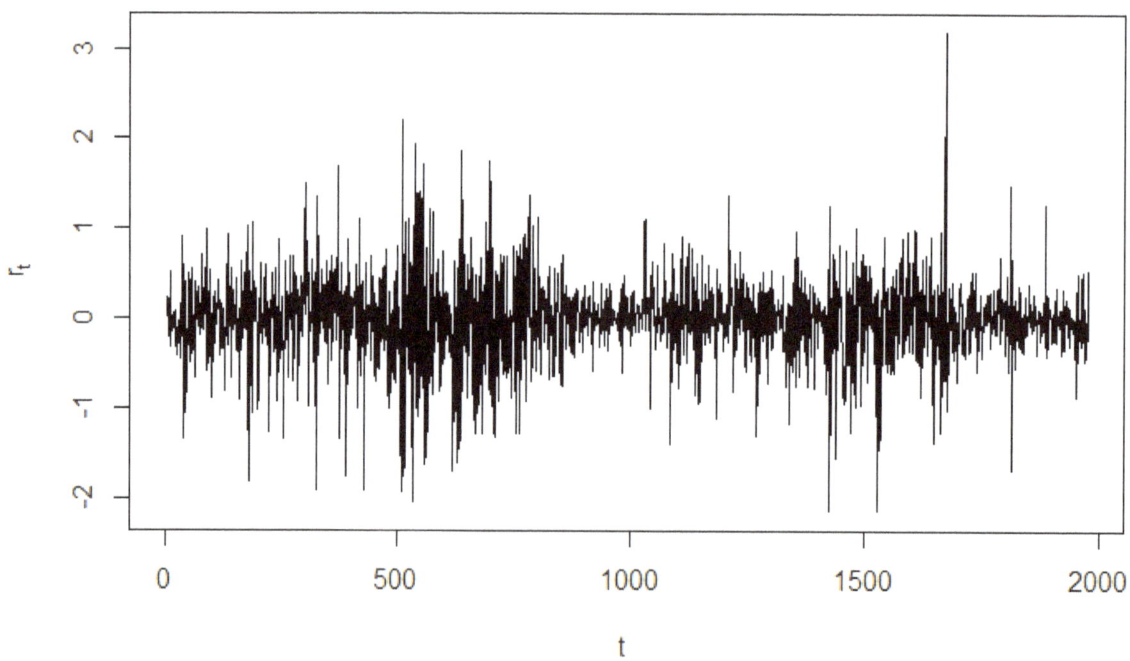

Table 1: FCP GARCH Benchmark

	coefficient	standard error				
		-H	OP	QMLE	IM	BW
μ	-.619041E-2	.846212E-2	.843359E-2	.918935E-2	.837628E-2	.873092E-2
α_0	.107613E-1	.285271E-2	.132298E-2	.649319E-2	.192881E-2	.312364E-2
α_1	.153134E-0	.265228E-1	.139737E-1	.535317E-1	.194012E-1	.273219E-1
β	.805974E-0	.335527E-1	.165604E-1	.724614E-1	.218399E-1	.301509E-1

Table 2: Coefficients for tseries

	μ	α_0	α_1	β_1
benchmark	0.00619041	0.0107613	0.153134	0.805974
default	NA	0.0107843	0.154074	0.805295
tuned	NA	0.0107825	0.154059	0.805317

Table 3: OPG standard errors for tseries

	μ	α_0	α_1	β_1
benchmark	0.00843359	0.00132298	0.0139737	0.0165604
tuned	NA	0.00128802	0.0138210	0.0159639

Table 4: Default (Hessian) standard errors for fGarch, inaccurate digits underlined

	μ	α_0	α_1	β_1
benchmark	0.00846212	0.00285271	0.0265228	0.0335527
default	0.00846200	0.00283751	0.0264217	0.0333813

Table 5: QMLE standard errors for fGarch, inaccurate digits underlined

	μ	α_0	α_1	β_1
benchmark	0.00918935	0.00649319	0.0535317	0.0724614
QMLE	0.00918577	0.00642400	0.0530562	0.0716837

Table 6: Coefficients for **rugarch**, inaccurate digits underlined

	μ	α_0	α_1	β_1
benchmark	.00619041	.0107613	.153134	.805974
default	.00618499	.0107602	.153407	.805880

Table 7: Hessian standard errors for **rugarch**, inaccurate digits underlined

	μ	α_0	α_1	β_1
benchmark	.00619041	.0107613	.153134	.805974
default	.00618499	.0107602	.153407	.805880

Table 8: Robust standard errors for **rugarch**, inaccurate digits underlined

	μ	α_0	α_1	β_1
benchmark	0.00918935	0.00649319	0.0535317	0.0724614
default robust	0.00901680	0.00649841	0.0493895	0.0691624

Table 9: Coefficients for **fGarch**

	μ	α_0	α_1	β_1
benchmark	.00619041	.0107613	.153134	.805974
default	.00619031	.0107614	.153134	.805974

Table 10: *LRE* for Coefficient Estimates

	tseries	fGarch	rugarch
μ	NA	4.8	3.1
α_0	2.7	5.0	4.0
α_1	2.2	6.0	2.7
β_1	3.1	6.0	3.9

Table 11: *LRE* for Standard Error Estimates

	H		OP	QMLE	
	fGarch	rugarch	tseries	fGarch	rugarch
μ	4.8	4.2	NA	3.4	1.7
α_0	2.3	4.0	1.6	2.0	3.1
α_1	2.4	2.7	2.0	2.1	1.1
β_1	2.3	3.4	1.4	2.0	1.3

8

Determinants of Environmental Quality in Nigeria: Assessing the Role of Financial Development

Ekundayo P. Mesagan*♣ and **Mike I. Nwachukwu**♣

♣Department of Economics, University of Lagos, Nigeria

ABSTRACT: In this study, we analyze the determinants of environmental quality in Nigeria, focusing on the role of financial development. It is a time series analysis covering the period from 1981 to 2016. The study uses the ARDL bounds testing approach to analyze data on urbanization, per capita income, environmental degradation, energy consumption, trade intensity, and capital investment. We generate the environmental degradation index using principal component analysis (PCA). Empirical results suggest that income, financial development, energy consumption, and trade are significant in explaining environmental quality, whereas investment and urbanization are insignificant in the model. Moreover, we find no causality between the capital investment, financial development, and environmental quality, although urbanization and income unidirectionally cause environmental degradation. Also, there exists a bidirectional causality between energy consumption and environmental degradation. Therefore, to ensure efficient credit allocation to low carbon emitting firms, financial sector operators should adequately screen investment proposals before committing funds to them.

Keywords: financial development, energy, income, environment, Nigeria

*Corresponding Author. Email: profdayoms@yahoo.com

Introduction

Without a doubt, the financial sector plays a significant role in mobilizing and using savings, in facilitating business transactions, and in monitoring resources for economic advancement (Nasreen et al., 2017). It plays a vital role in the growth and development of the economy because when efforts are made to develop the financial sector properly, it promotes effective mobilization and allocation of economic and financial resources (Adekunle et al., 2013). A study by Aderibigbe (2001) affirms that Nigeria's financial sector assists in facilitating the necessary business transactions for economic development. One can, therefore, agree that an efficient financial sector will increase investment activities (by issuing low-interest loans), allocate resources toward productive channels, facilitate trade activities, manage risks, effectively monitor firms' activities, and encourage firms to use environmentally friendly production techniques in their operations.

Dasgupta et al. (2001) opined that countries with more stable financial markets would, in most cases, enjoy a cleaner environment than countries with less developed financial markets. Also, the empirical literature suggests that foreign direct investment is encouraged in countries that have stable financial markets, in a quest to promote growth, and this has implications for the environment. Thus, there appears a relatively clear relationship between financial sector development and environmental quality, as there are several channels through which the financial sector impacts the environment. For instance, improvement in financial activities can spur economic growth, which has implications for environmental quality, as suggested by the environmental Kuznets curve (EKC). Again, financial sector improvement can impact the environment by encouraging the private sector to increase investments in new technologies. This investment expansion boosts the volume of industrial energy consumption, which can either increase or decrease emissions of carbon depending on the energy mix (Mesagan et al., 2018). Also, the level of a country's financial development strongly determines the allocation of credit to investments that can enhance or reduce environmental quality. The reason is that high carbon emitting firms can be denied credit facilities by financial institutions, making funds available only to firms that will emit less carbon. It is therefore apparent that financial sector development can play a crucial role, through various channels, in determining the environmental quality of a nation. Hence, the authors of a number of empirical studies have concluded that financial performance is essential in stimulating activity related to promoting or protecting environmental quality (Charfeddine and Khediri, 2016; Maji et al., 2017; Mahalik et al., 2017; Shahbaz et al., 2017; Salahuddin et al., 2018).

Regarding theoretical expositions, the EKC implies that at the early developmental stage of an economy, growth is achieved by increases in the volume of emissions. Then, as the economy becomes financially stable, it is able to achieve green growth (Andreoni and Levinson, 2001; Dasgupta et al., 2001). This is because the country can control its emissions even as growth continues to rise. The EKC implies that there is an inverted U-shaped relationship between economic growth and environmental pollution (Dasgupta et al., 2001). Interestingly, since the quality of financial services being offered in a country provides an essential stimulant to economic growth (Levine, 1996), it becomes crucial for every nation to ensure that its financial sector plays an active role in promoting green growth. Therefore, in-depth knowledge of the role of financial sector development in promoting environmental quality is critical because it enables a country to improve its financial services and attract foreign investment to boost green growth. Thus, increasing environmental efficiency through financial system improvement occupies the heart of this scientific enquiry. According to Sadorsky (2011), financial development has implications for energy demand, as well as determining energy conservation and carbon emissions policies. In such circumstances, to better understand energy demand dynamics for effective management of carbon dioxide (CO_2) emissions, Karanfil (2009) proposes augmenting the energy demand function with critical financial indicators beyond just income variables. This means that there are active links between energy use, financial resources, and quality of the environment.

For Nigeria, World Bank data suggest that between 1981 and 2014, CO_2 emissions rose by about 41.3% (i.e., from 65,958.33 kilotonnes (kt) to 96,280.75 kt). The Federal Environmental Protection Agency was established in 1992 to curtail increases in CO_2 in the country (World Development Indicators, 2017). Regarding the development of the financial sector in Nigeria, the credit available to the private sector rose from ₦8.57 billion in 1981 to ₦21,082 billion in 2016. This calls into question whether there is any linkage between the volume of investment generated by the amount of credit made available to the private sector and the size of CO_2 emissions in a country (Central Bank of Nigeria, 2017). Finally, energy consumption per capita increased from 676.38 kg of oil equivalent in 1981 to 763.39 kg in 2014 (World Development Indicators, 2017), while the real gross domestic product (GDP) also rose significantly from ₦15,258 billion in 1981 to ₦67,931 billion in 2016 (Central Bank of Nigeria, 2017). Hence, it seems evident that both energy use and the real GDP are essential drivers of CO_2 emissions in Nigeria as several empirical studies have posited (Mesagan, 2015; Shahbaz et al., 2014; Eregha and Mesagan, 2017).

Despite the number of environmental laws that have been put forward to protect the environment from degradation, oil spillage, and gas flaring in Nigeria, the degradation is still the case. For instance, the Department of Petroleum Resources noted that Nigeria recorded a total of 2,097 oil spills between 1997 and 2001 (Nwilo and Badejo, 2006). Nigeria is the focus of this study because it is the largest African economy in terms of population and output, and it depends significantly on fossil fuels for generating its electricity. The country is Africa's largest producer of crude oil and records the highest amount of gas flaring in Africa. Indeed, by the end of December 2015, Nigeria ranked 6th globally behind only Russia, Iraq, Iran, the United States, and Venezuela, with gas flaring of 8 billion cubic meters (bcm) (World Bank, 2016). It is thus pertinent to focus on Nigeria because of its size and for the fact that it can provide a template for other African countries to follow in the quest to improve environmental quality on the continent. Based on the preceding, it becomes vital to examine the determinants of environmental quality in Nigeria. Specifically, this study analyzes the impact of financial sector development on environmental degradation, investigates the causal nexus between the environment and its determinants, and tests the proposition of the EKC in Nigeria. The study is topical for Nigeria because of the need for the financial sector to play an active role in CO_2 emissions abatement efforts in order to complement the activities of other government agencies in improving environmental quality. The paper is organized in the following manner: section 1 provides the literature review; section 2 presents the research methodology; section 3 presents the empirical results; and section 4 presents the conclusion and policy recommendations.

1 Literature Review

In this section, we examine the scholarly articles in the literature to give clear direction to the purpose and understanding of the contribution of this study. To this end, we review previous country-specific and cross-country studies. A number of country-specific studies have been published that examined relevant questions in the context of a single country. Moghadam and Dehbashi (2018) analyzed the impact of financial development and trade on Iran's environmental quality and found that financial growth worsened environmental degradation, whereas trade was seen to reduce environmental damage. Similarly, Boutabba (2014) examined the nexus between financial development, income, energy use, trade, and carbon emissions and confirmed the EKC hypothesis for the Indian economy. The study also found a unidirectional causality running from income, energy consumption, and financial development to CO_2 emissions. Charfeddine et al. (2018) examined the link between economic growth and the environment in Qatar. This study, which employed the ARDL bounds testing approach, found support for the EKC hypothesis. The authors, therefore, suggested energy conservation policies to lower the adverse effects of growth on the environment. Jalil and Feridun (2011) established that financial development decreased environmental pollution in China, and also confirmed the existence of the EKC for the country. Similarly, Shahbaz et al. (2013) also proved that financial development and trade openness lowered CO_2 emissions, whereas economic growth raised CO_2 emissions in South Africa. Alam et al. (2015) analyzed Malaysia and found that carbon emissions had a positive correlation with broad money supply and domestic credit to the private sector. They also found that energy demand positively and significantly enhanced financial sector credit, but negatively affected the broad money supply. Maji et al. (2017) conducted a sectoral analysis and found that financial development intensified CO_2 emissions in both the transportation and oil and gas sectors, whereas it reduced CO_2 emissions in the manufacturing and construction sectors in Malaysia. Charfeddine and Khediri (2016) focused on the United Arab Emirates (UAE) using cointegration with structural breaks. The study found an inverted U-shaped relationship between financial development and CO_2 emissions. However, it observed that electricity consumption, trade openness, and urbanization improved environmental quality in the UAE. Javid and Sharif (2016) confirmed the EKC in Pakistan in the short and long runs, and also traced the low environmental quality in the country to the weak financial institutions and the level of energy consumption. Alege and Ogundipe (2015) focused on the Nigerian economy and found that income had a positive and linear relationship with CO_2 emissions. Also, the study established a positive correlation between foreign direct investment, trade openness, and CO_2 emissions in the country. However, the research did not support the existence of the EKC in Nigeria. Ozturk and Acaravci (2013) analyzed the Turkish economy and found a long-term relationship between CO_2 emission, energy consumption, real income, trade, and financial development. However, it found that financial development did not significantly affect the Turkish environment. Shahbaz et al. (2017) showed that, in India, no causality exists between energy consumption and financial development, whereas financial development and energy consumption negatively affected income growth.

Concerning cross-country studies, Khan et al. (2018) discussed income inequality for Asian economies and established that a significant negative relationship exists between financial development and carbon emissions. It also found that greater income inequality reduced carbon emissions, whereas increased energy use significantly worsened carbon emissions in the Asian region. Kahouli (2017) examined short-run and long-run causality between growth, energy use, and financial development in six southern Mediterranean countries. The study observed the existence of a long-run relationship between the variables, and also confirmed the presence of a short-run causal relationship in five of the countries examined. Abid (2017) established a monotonically increasing link between carbon emissions and economic growth in the Middle East, Africa, and the European Union countries between 1990 and 2011. Al-mulali et al. (2013) focused on urbanization, energy consumption, and CO_2 emissions in the Middle East and North African (MENA) countries. Their study established long-run bidirectional positive relationships between the variables investigated. Bekhet et al. (2017) focused on the Gulf Cooperation Council (GCC) countries and established a long-run causal nexus between economic growth, financial development, and CO_2 emissions. They also confirmed that financial development unidirectionally caused CO_2 emissions in the UAE, Oman, and Kuwait. Al-mulali and Sab (2012) observed that energy consumption and financial development worsened environmental pollution in 19 selected countries, subsequently calling for reduced emissions in these countries through energy protection policies. Nasreen et al. (2017) studied Asian economies and found a negative effect of increased financial stability on carbon emissions, whereas higher energy consumption and economic growth increased CO_2 emissions among the countries considered. For Omri et al. (2015), the study found a bidirectional causality between CO_2 emissions and income, as well as between trade openness and financial development. It also found a unidirectional relationship running from financial development to income and carbon emissions in MENA countries. Saidi and Mbarek (2017) observed that financial development reduced environmental degradation in emerging economies.

Based on this review of previous studies, it is evident that scholars have identified financial development as an essential determinant of environmental quality. However, most of these studies have used CO_2 emissions as the indicator of environmental quality, which might not be enough. Studies such as those by Frankel and Rose (2005) and Li et al. (2015) identified several proxies for environmental quality. The present study takes a cue from these latter studies, generating an environmental quality index from particulate emissions damage and CO_2 emissions using principal component analysis (PCA). Using this environmental quality index, we differentiate this present study from the others and check if our result is different from other country-specific results about the finance-environment nexus. Also, the shortage of studies on the Nigerian economy regarding the critical role of financial development in the environment necessitates this present study.

2 Research Methodology and Estimation Technique

2.1 Methodology

To conduct this scientific enquiry, we adopt the EKC framework which suggests that there is an inverted U-shaped relationship between income and environmental pollution. Therefore, following Andreoni and Levinson (2001), Dasgupta et al. (2002), and Stern (2004), we specify the EKC model as follows:

$$E_t = \varphi + \beta_1 Y_t + \beta_2 Y_t^2 + \varepsilon_t \tag{1}$$

In equation (1), E is the environmental quality index computed from the PCA, φ is the intercept term, β_1 and β_2 are the coefficients of income per capita of the first and second derivatives respectively, ε is the residual term, and t represents the time index. According to the EKC model formulated in equation (1), β_1 and β_2 are expected to have positive and negative signs, respectively, to confirm the EKC hypothesis in Nigeria. Notably, E is computed from CO_2 emissions and particulate emissions damage (PM) in Nigeria. To accommodate other determinants of environmental quality, we modify equation (1) as follows:

$$E_t = \varphi + \beta_1 Y_t + \beta_2 Y_t^2 + \beta_3 FD_t + \beta_4 EC_t + \beta_5 INV_t + \beta_6 TI_t + \beta_7 UBN_t + \varepsilon_t \quad (2)$$

We include all the explanatory variables to be estimated in equation (2). In equation (2), FD represents financial development and it is proxied by the available credit to the private sector. EC is the amount of energy consumed; INV represents the volume of capital investment, proxied by the gross fixed capital formation; TI is the trade intensity ratio, calculated as total trade divided by the GDP; and UBN is the rate of urbanization. The remaining variables are as explained in equation (1).

2.2 Estimation Technique

To estimate the specified model, we use the autoregressive distributed lag (ARDL) bounds testing approach. According to Pesaran and Shin (1998) and Pesaran et al. (2001), the method is built on the Wald test or F-statistic to determine the implication of the lagged values of variables in a conditional and unrestricted dynamic error correction model. Also, we use the ARDL bounds test due to the need to determine the short- and long-run effects of the explanatory variables on environmental quality, and for its superiority over other estimation techniques when the study entails a small sample. Again, in this study, we use the standard t-test and F-test to determine the strength of the lagged variables in the first difference estimation. One significant advantage of this methodology is that the F-test and t-test are applicable whether the variables are $I(0)$, $I(1)$ or integrated mutually. Hence, following Pesaran and Shin (1998), we estimate the following unrestricted error correction model:

$$\Delta E_t = \alpha_0 + \sum_{i=1}^{p} \alpha_1 \Delta E_{t-i} + \sum_{i=1}^{p} \alpha_2 \Delta V_{t-i} + \beta_1 E_{t-1} + \beta_2 V_{t-1} + \varepsilon_t \quad (3)$$

Where E is the dependent variable, V stands for independent variables, p is the lag structure, Δ is the difference operator, α_1 and α_2 are the short-run estimates, β_1 and β_2 are the long-run estimates, and ε is the white noise error term. For the models to be estimated in this study, the hypothesis to be tested is:

$H_0 : \beta_1 = \beta_2 = ... = \beta_n = 0$ (i.e., there is no long-run relationship).
$H_1 : \beta_1 \neq \beta_2 \neq ... = \beta_n \neq 0$ (i.e., there is a long-run relationship).

Hence, using the F-test suggested in Pesaran and Shin (1998) and Pesaran et al. (2001), the estimated ARDL test statistics will be compared with the two asymptotic critical values in Pesaran et al. (2001) as against the conventional critical values. Therefore, if the estimated test statistic is higher than the upper critical value, we will reject the null hypothesis of no long-run relationship, but if it is lower than the lower critical value, we will accept the null hypothesis. However, if the estimated test statistic lies between the two critical values or bounds, then the result is inconclusive.

Thus, following Pesaran and Shin (1998) and Pesaran et al. (2001), the reduced form model to be estimated in this study is specified as:

$$\begin{aligned}\Delta E_t = \alpha_0 &+ \sum_{i=1}^{p} \alpha_1 \Delta E_{t-i} + \sum_{i=1}^{p} \alpha_2 \Delta Y_{t-i} + \sum_{i=1}^{p} \alpha_3 \Delta Y_{t-i}^2 + \sum_{i=1}^{p} \alpha_4 \Delta FD_{t-i} + \\ &+ \sum_{i=1}^{p} \alpha_5 \Delta TI_{t-i} + \sum_{i=1}^{p} \alpha_6 \Delta EC_{t-i} + \sum_{i=1}^{p} \alpha_7 \Delta INV_{t-i} + \sum_{i=1}^{p} \alpha_8 \Delta UBN_{t-i} + \\ &+ \beta_1 E_{t-1} + \beta_2 Y_{t-1} + \beta_3 Y_{t-1}^2 + \beta_4 FD_{t-1} + \beta_5 TI_{t-1} + \beta_6 EC_{t-1} + \\ &+ \beta_7 INV_{t-1} + \beta_8 UBN_{t-1} + \varepsilon_t\end{aligned} \tag{4}$$

Where Δ is the first difference operator, α_0 represents the drift, α_{1-8} are the short-run dynamic coefficients of the underlying ARDL model, β_{1-8} represents the long-run multipliers, t is the time index, and ε_t is the white noise error term. Also, E is the vector of dependent variables, which represents the environmental degradation index, CO_2 emissions, and particulate emissions damage; Y is income per capita; FD is financial development; TI is trade intensity; EC is energy consumption; and UBN is the rate of urbanization.

We analyze the time series data covering a period from 1981 to 2016. We extract data for particulate emissions, CO_2 emissions, energy consumed, gross fixed capital formation, per capita income, and rate of urbanization from the World Bank's World Development Indicators (2017). We generate data on credit available to the private sector from the Central Bank of Nigeria Statistical Bulletin (Central Bank of Nigeria, 2017). In the model, variables such as CO_2 emissions and particulate emissions are used to capture environmental quality, whereas the independent variables include financial sector development proxied by commercial banks' credit to the private sector, energy consumption, and trade intensity ratio. We also include urban population as a proxy for the urbanization rate and gross fixed capital formation as a proxy for investment. The theoretical justification for the inclusion of these variables is provided next.

2.3 Theoretical Justification for the Inclusion of Variables

In this section, we analyze the choice of environmental determinants and provide theoretical justification for their inclusion in the model. For instance, *carbon dioxide emission* is the most widely used indicator of environmental degradation, as the level of environmental quality has often been related to the volume of CO_2 emissions that is prevalent in a country. According to the EKC, pollution and income growth are inseparable twins: efforts to increase income often come with increases in pollution (Andreoni and Levinson, 2001). Therefore, *income per capita* is used as an explanatory variable in this study because of its relationship with CO_2 emissions. Paul and Bhattacharya (2004) observed that income growth is the highest contributor to carbon emissions. Thus, while income per capita is used to test the rising portion of the EKC, income squared is used to test the falling part of the EKC in the model, and both are necessary to determine the inverted U-shaped curve of the EKC. We also include *particulate emissions damage*, the damage caused by exposing citizens to severe ozone pollution (World Development Indicators, 2017). We include *energy consumption* as it is an essential determinant of environmental pollution in a location. Empirical studies such as Soytas et al. (2007) and Mesagan et al. (2018) opined that energy consumption has severe implications for environmental quality because it is crucial in the production process. Again, when trade openness increases in a country, it enables the country to gain access to improved technology for pollution abatement; the country also gains access to international capital markets for the inflow of investment, which has environmental implications too (Copeland and Taylor, 1994). This informs why *trade intensity ratio* is brought into the model as a determinant of environmental quality. Assessing the critical role of financial development is germane to this study because a well-developed financial system can function to allocate credit to low-carbon emitting firms. Also, according to Solarin et al. (2017), the financial sector makes liquidity available to the real sector of the country and thereby contributes to the pollution level. Moreover, activities of an efficient financial intermediary provide the impetus for firms to obtain credit facilities to purchase automobiles used in production. Furthermore, when adequate financing is made available and new machines are acquired, energy consumption increases, and the pollution level expands as well. Other previous studies that have controlled for financial development as a determinant for environmental quality include Omri et al. (2015), Bekhet et al. (2017), Nasreen et al. (2017), Saidi and Mbarek (2017), and Shahbaz et al. (2017). This explains why *financial development* is used in this study. *Investment and urbanization rate* are used in this study because the pace of urbanization and the quality of investment are crucial indices of environmental quality. As noted by Sadorsky (2014), when urbanization increases, economic activities expand, and pollution increases too. Meanwhile, Mesagan et al. (2018) identified investment as an essential channel for improving environmental quality.

3 Empirical Results

In Table 1, we present the descriptive statistics of variables used in the study. Between 1981 and 2016, the means of per capita income, energy consumption, investment, and urban population in Nigeria are US \$1,583.22, US \$103.37, 37.26%, and 35.00% respectively. Also, the means of trade intensity ratio, particulate emissions damage, carbon emissions, and financial development in Nigeria are 50.41%, 1.96%, 0.59 kt, and ₦15.09 billion respectively.

Furthermore, regarding the maximum values, these are \$2,634.36, \$156.73, 35.22%, and 48.59% for per capita income, energy consumption, investment, and urban population respectively, whereas their minimum values are \$1,153.38, \$50.87, 5.45%, and 22.67% respectively. Also, the maximum amounts for trade intensity ratio, particulate emissions damage, carbon emissions, and financial development in Nigeria are 81.81%, 2.24%, 0.87 kt, and ₦38.39 billion respectively, whereas their minimum amounts are 21.12%, 1.30%, 0.33 kt, and ₦8.71 billion respectively during the study period.

Table 2 presents the matrix of correlations between the variables. The correlation matrix makes it possible to determine the level of association and the possibility of multicollinearity of the regressors. As presented in Table 2, the regressors used in the study are not correlated. Hence, the model formulated in this study is not affected by the multicollinearity problem.

Table 3 presents the result of the unit root test using the augmented Dickey-Fuller (ADF) test. The table shows the outcome of the stationarity test at both levels, the first difference at the trend level, and when there is no trend. In table 3, we observe that only financial development is stationary at levels while trade intensity ratio, real income, investment, particulate emissions, energy consumption, urbanization rate, and CO_2 emissions are stationary at first difference. Because we have confirmed the stationarity of the series, we can then proceed to estimate the ARDL bounds test to determine if there is cointegration among the series and also analyze the short-run and long-run effects of the estimators on environmental quality.

For the three models, the hypothesis tested include:

$H_0 : \beta_1 = \beta_2 = ... = \beta_n = 0$ (i.e., there is no long-run relationship).
$H_1 : \beta_1 \neq \beta_2 \neq ... = \beta_n \neq 0$ (i.e., there is a long-run relationship).

Table 4 presents the ARDL bounds test for determining the long-run relationship using the Akaike information criterion (AIC) to select the appropriate lag length. In selecting the critical bounds, we use the values specified in Pesaran et al. (2001) for the restricted intercept and no trend (i.e., case II). We test the hypothesis at the various significance levels with F statistics and with $k = 7$ against the specified critical bounds. The ARDL bounds test results presented in Table 4 confirms that the F-statistics computed are higher than the critical values of the upper bound tests. Hence, we reject the null hypotheses of no cointegration across the three models at the 1%, 5%, and 10% significance levels, and confirm that there is a unique and stable long-run relationship between environmental quality and financial sector development, together with other determinants in Nigeria between 1981 and 2016.

Because Table 4 has confirmed the existence of a stable and long-run relationship between the estimated regressors in the study, we present the results of the determined ARDL long-run coefficients in Table 5. In displaying the results in Table 5, we show the effect of the explanatory variables on environmental quality in model I. For the sake of conducting a sensitivity analysis, we also show the impact of the explanatory variables on CO_2 emissions and particulate emissions in model II and model III. Models II and III, therefore, serve as robustness checks in this study.

A cursory look at Table 5 suggests that income positively and significantly impacts the environmental degradation index, CO_2 emissions, and particulate emissions damage. The implication is that economic growth has often worsened environmental challenges facing the country. Therefore, the result is in line with Boutabba (2014) and Charfeddine et al. (2018), but at variance with Khan et al. (2018). The coefficient of financial sector development is positive and significant in worsening environmental degradation and CO_2 emissions, but insignificant in contributing to particulate emissions in Nigeria. It thus implies that despite the efforts to improve the Nigeran financial sector, it has neither been able to allocate credits to investments that should improve environmental quality nor significantly reduce environmental degradation in the country. This result supports earlier findings that financial development worsened environmental degradation in the UAE, Oman, Kuwait (Bekhet et al., 2017) and Iran (Moghadam and Dehbashi, 2018).

However, the result is at variance with Shahbaz et al. (2013) and Nasreen et al. (2017), who found that financial stability improved environmental quality in South Africa and South Asian economies, respectively. Regarding energy consumption, our results show support for Javid and Sharif (2016), as energy consumption positively and significantly enhanced the indicators of environmental degradation in the study. This result also conforms to a priori expectation as the country generates most of its energy from fossil fuels which intuitively means that energy consumption is a major driver of environmental degradation in Nigeria – as is indicated by the coefficient.

Moreover, empirical results in Table 5 suggest that trade intensity positively and significantly affects the environmental degradation index and carbon emissions, whereas it has a negative impact on particulate emissions. This means that the inflow and outflow of trade in Nigeria have a severe negative effect on its environmental degradation, a result in line with Alege and Ogundipe (2015), but at variance with the results of Shahbaz et al. (2013) and Charfeddine and Khediri (2016) for South Africa and the UAE, respectively. However, our results suggest that investment has a positive but insignificant impact on environmental degradation, whereas it has an adverse but significant effect on particulate emissions. This means that investment is not a significant determinant of environmental quality in Nigeria when we consider carbon emissions, but it has a substantial effect in lowering particulate emissions damage in the country. This result is at variance with Mesagan et al. (2018), who confirmed that capital investment is an essential channel for improving environmental quality in BRICS. Also, the coefficient of urbanization suggests that it positively but insignificantly affects environmental degradation and CO_2 emissions, whereas it positively and significantly increases PM emissions in the study. This study attributes PM emissions to the waste disposal from urbanization and implies that urbanization is not a significant determinant of environmental pollution in Nigeria. Lastly, this research finds support for the existence of the EKC in Nigeria as the coefficient of the income-squared is negative for all environmental indicators in the model.

In Table 6, we present both the diagnostic test and stability test for the empirical models. The error correction terms (ECT) of -1.782, -0.835, and -0.639 imply that the three models converge in the long run. It also means that the adjustment speed is fast at 178.2%, 83.5%, and 63.9% for the three models. Because the ECT terms are negative and significant at 5%, this means that the ARDL models are well specified. The results give credence to the existence of a long-run relationship between environmental quality and its determinants in Nigeria.

The diagnostic tests indicate the models are well specified as they are free from serial correlation, are homoscedastic, and are multivariate normally distributed. The cumulative sum of squared and cumulative sum statistics are within the 5% critical levels, indicating stability of the models, while the functional form tests also show that the three models are well specified.

Regarding the determinants of environmental quality, a cursory look at Table 7 shows that no causal nexus exists between financial sector development and the environment or between trade intensity and the environment in Nigeria. This implies that there is no feedback effect between the financial sector, capital investment, and environmental quality in Nigeria. The result also confirms that there is a unidirectional causal nexus running from urbanization to the environment, and from income to environmental degradation. Intuitively, it means that an increase in the pace of urban growth and per capita income causes environmental degradation to rise because waste generated from urbanization and the continuous pressure on natural resources from the rising population causes depletion of the environment. Moreover, the fact that income unilaterally causes environmental degradation in the study gives credence to the EKC proposition, which suggests that income determines the pollution level. However, both energy consumption and environmental degradation are mutually causal, implying that there is a feedback effect between energy consumed and environmental degradation in Nigeria.

4 Discussion of Results

We observe that income exerts a positive and significant impact on the environmental degradation index, CO_2 emissions, and particulate emissions damage, meaning that efforts to increase economic growth have often been made with less attention to curtailing environmental degradation. This is further supported by the continuous flaring of gas in Nigeria's Niger Delta region, in an attempt to earn foreign exchange without much consideration for the environmental effects or the effects on people's lives. As opined in Isola and Mesagan (2014), huge earnings from crude oil production without concern for the human condition is counter-productive to the nation. Though Boutabba (2014) and Charfeddine et al. (2018) found similar conclusions, the index generated for the environment in this study makes our findings different from that of Khan et al. (2018). Again, the financial sector significantly and positively worsens environmental degradation thereby negating the results of Shahbaz et al. (2013) and Nasreen et al. (2017). This means that the inability of these earlier studies to factor in particulate emissions might have resulted in their findings that financial development is associated with lower environmental pollution. Also, by factoring in PM emissions, this study confirms that although financial development increased particulate emissions, it was not significant in the particulate emissions model. This is attributable to the fact that the financial structure is not the primary determinant of particulate emissions in the country. Because the results of the analysis of energy consumption confirm the result of Javid and Sharif (2016) that higher energy consumption increases all the indicators of environmental degradation, this means that energy use continues to rise and environmental pollution also increases unabated. Because energy consumption is also significant, this implies that it is a critical determinant of environmental quality in Nigeria. Trade intensity was found to contribute significantly and positively in exacerbating the environmental degradation index and carbon emissions, but lowering particulate emissions. The implication is that trade is not only a significant determinant of environmental quality, but also an avenue to lower environmental degradation in the country through its effect on particulate emissions. Thus, using the environment index in this study has shown that the results of Shahbaz et al. (2013) and Charfeddine and Khediri (2016) for South Africa and the UAE, respectively, do not apply for Nigeria. The insignificant effect of capital investment and urbanization on environmental degradation measures in the model means these are not critical determinants of environmental changes in Nigeria. This might be attributed to the low level of industrial activity in the country. Because industrial activities in Nigeria are confined to a few states such as Lagos, Rivers, Kano, and Abuja, the rate of urbanization in this country is meagre and Nigeria has a large rural sector that is characterized by subsistence activities. This may explain why the urbanization rate is not significant in explaining environmental changes in the country.

5 Conclusion and Recommendation

In this study, we have shed light on the determinants of environmental quality in Nigeria, with a focus on the role of financial sector development. Using a time series analysis covering the period from 1981 to 2016, we analyzed several potential determinants of environmental quality, such as urbanization, per capita income, energy consumption, trade intensity, capital investment, and financial development. We also generated an environmental quality index from CO_2 emissions and particulate emissions damage, using PCA. The study applied the ARDL bounds testing approach and used the data sourced from the World Development Indicators and Nigeria's Central Bank Statistical Bulletin. The long-run result confirms that income, financial development, energy consumption, and trade are significant in explaining environmental quality, whereas investment and urbanization are insignificant in the model during the period of study. We also confirmed the EKC proposition in Nigeria. Moreover, the causality analysis revealed that there is no feedback effect between the financial sector and the environment or between capital investment and environmental quality. There is, however, unidirectional causality running from urbanization and income to the environment, and there is bidirectional causality between energy consumption and environmental degradation. We recommend that financial sector operators adequately screen investment proposals before committing funds to them to ensure efficient credit allocation to low carbon emitting firms. This will help to lower carbon emissions and make both the financial sector and capital investment drive environmental quality in the country. Also, because energy consumption significantly worsened environmental conditions, the Nigerian government should devote at least 5% of the annual budget to invest in renewable energy and increase its proportion of the energy supply mix. This will enhance the capacity of energy consumption to significantly improve environmental quality in Nigeria.

References

Abid, M. (2017). Does economic, financial and institutional developments matter for environmental quality? A comparative analysis of EU and MEA countries. *Journal of Environmental Management*, 188:183 – 194.

Adekunle, O., Salami, G., and Oluseyi, A. (2013). Impact of Financial Sector Development on the Nigerian Economic Growth. *American Journal of Business and Management*, 2(4):347–356.

Aderibigbe, J. (2001). The role of the financial sector in poverty reduction. *CBN Economic and Financial Review*, 39 (3):1 – 19.

Al-mulali, U., Fereidouni, H. G., Lee, J. Y., and Sab, C. N. B. C. (2013). Exploring the relationship between urbanization, energy consumption, and CO2 emission in MENA countries. *Renewable and Sustainable Energy Reviews*, 23:107 – 112.

Al-mulali, U. and Sab, C. N. B. C. (2012). The impact of energy consumption and CO2 emission on the economic and financial development in 19 selected countries. *Renewable and Sustainable Energy Reviews*, 16(7):4365 – 4369.

Alam, A., Azam, M., Abdullah, A. B., Malik, I. A., Khan, A., Hamzah, T. A. A. T., Faridullah, Khan, M. M., Zahoor, H., and Zaman, K. (2015). Environmental quality indicators and financial development in Malaysia: unity in diversity. *Environmental Science and Pollution Research*, 22(11):8392–8404.

Alege, P. O. and Ogundipe, A. A. (2015). Environmental quality and economic growth in Nigeria: A fractional cointegration analysis. *International Journal of Development and Sustainability*, 2(2)(2):1 – 17.

Andreoni, J. and Levinson, A. (2001). The simple analytics of the environmental Kuznets curve. *Journal of Public Economics*, 80(2):269 – 286.

Bekhet, H. A., Matar, A., and Yasmin, T. (2017). CO2 emissions, energy consumption, economic growth, and financial development in GCC countries: Dynamic simultaneous equation models. *Renewable and Sustainable Energy Reviews*, 70:117 – 132.

Boutabba, M. A. (2014). The impact of financial development, income, energy and trade on carbon emissions: Evidence from the Indian economy. *Economic Modelling*, 40:33 – 41.

Central Bank of Nigeria (2017). CBN Annual Report and Statistical Bulletin for the Year Ended 31st December. http://www.cbn.gov.ng/documents/statbulletin.asp. Accessed February 22, 2018.

Charfeddine, L., Al-Malk, A. Y., and Korbi, K. A. (2018). Is it possible to improve environmental quality without reducing economic growth: Evidence from the Qatar economy. *Renewable and Sustainable Energy Reviews*, 82:25 – 39.

Charfeddine, L. and Khediri, K. B. (2016). Financial development and environmental quality in UAE: Cointegration with structural breaks. *Renewable and Sustainable Energy Reviews*, 55:1322 – 1335.

Copeland, B. R. and Taylor, M. S. (1994). North-South Trade and the Environment*. *The Quarterly Journal of Economics*, 109(3):755–787.

Dasgupta, S., Laplante, B., and Mamingi, N. (2001). Pollution and Capital Markets in Developing Countries. *Journal of Environmental Economics and Management*, 42(3):310 – 335.

Dasgupta, S., Laplante, B., Wang, H., and Wheeler, D. (2002). Confronting the Environmental Kuznets Curve. *Journal of Economic Perspectives*, 16(1):147–168.

Eregha, P. B. and Mesagan, E. P. (2017). Energy consumption, oil price and macroeconomic performance in energy dependent African countries. *Applied Econometrics*, 46:74–89.

Frankel, J. A. and Rose, A. K. (2005). Is Trade Good or Bad for the Environment? Sorting Out the Causality. *The Review of Economics and Statistics*, 87(1):85–91.

Isola, W. and Mesagan, E. (2014). Impact of Oil Production on Human Condition in Nigeria. *West African Journal of Monetary and Economic Integration*, 14 (1):84 – 102.

Jalil, A. and Feridun, M. (2011). The impact of growth, energy and financial development on the environment in China: A cointegration analysis. *Energy Economics*, 33(2):284 – 291.

Javid, M. and Sharif, F. (2016). Environmental Kuznets curve and financial development in Pakistan. *Renewable and Sustainable Energy Reviews*, 54:406 – 414.

Kahouli, B. (2017). The short and long run causality relationship among economic growth, energy consumption and financial development: Evidence from South Mediterranean Countries (SMCs). *Energy Economics*, 68:19 – 30.

Karanfil, F. (2009). How many times again will we examine the energy-income nexus using a limited range of traditional econometric tools? *Energy Policy*, 37(4):1191 – 1194.

Khan, A., Saleem, N., and Fatima, S. (2018). Financial development, income inequality, and CO2 emissions in Asian countries using STIRPAT model. *Environmental Science and Pollution Research*, 25(7):6308–6319.

Levine, R. (1996). Foreign banks, financial development, and economic growth. *International financial markets: Harmonization versus competition*, 7:224 – 54.

Li, Z., Xu, N., and Yuan, J. (2015). New evidence on trade-environment linkage via air visibility. *Economics Letters*, 128:72 – 74.

Mahalik, M. K., Babu, M. S., Loganathan, N., and Shahbaz, M. (2017). Does financial development intensify energy consumption in Saudi Arabia? *Renewable and Sustainable Energy Reviews*, 75:1022 – 1034.

Maji, I., Habibullah, M., and Saari, M. (2017). Financial development and sectoral CO2 emissions in Malaysia. *Environmental Science and Pollution Research*, 24(8):7160–7176.

Mesagan, E., Isola, W., and Ajide, K. (2018). The capital investment channel of environmental improvement: evidence from BRICS. *Environment, Development and Sustainability*, 24:1 – 22.

Mesagan, E. P. (2015). Economic growth and carbon emission in Nigeria. *The IUP Journal of Applied Economics*, XIV(4):61–75.

Moghadam, H. E. and Dehbashi, V. (2018). The impact of financial development and trade on environmental quality in Iran. *Empirical Economics*, 54(4):1777–1799.

Nasreen, S., Anwar, S., and Ozturk, I. (2017). Financial stability, energy consumption and environmental quality: Evidence from South Asian economies. *Renewable and Sustainable Energy Reviews*, 67:1105 – 1122.

Nwilo, P. C. and Badejo, O. T. (2006). Impacts and management of oil spill pollution along the Nigerian coastal areas. *Administering Marine Spaces: International Issues*, 119:1 – 15.

Omri, A., Daly, S., Rault, C., and Chaibi, A. (2015). Financial development, environmental quality, trade and economic growth: What causes what in MENA countries. *Energy Economics*, 48:242 – 252.

Ozturk, I. and Acaravci, A. (2013). The long-run and causal analysis of energy, growth, openness and financial development on carbon emissions in Turkey. *Energy Economics*, 36:262 – 267.

Paul, S. and Bhattacharya, R. N. (2004). CO2 emission from energy use in India: a decomposition analysis. *Energy Policy*, 32(5):585 – 593.

Pesaran, M. H. and Shin, Y. (1998). An autoregressive distributed-lag modelling approach to cointegration analysis. *Econometric Society Monographs*, 31:371 – 413.

Pesaran, M. H., Shin, Y., and Smith, R. J. (2001). Bounds testing approaches to the analysis of level relationships. *Journal of Applied Econometrics*, 16(3):289–326.

Sadorsky, P. (2011). Financial development and energy consumption in Central and Eastern European frontier economies. *Energy Policy*, 39(2):999 – 1006.

Sadorsky, P. (2014). The effect of urbanization on CO2 emissions in emerging economies. *Energy Economics*, 41:147 – 153.

Saidi, K. and Mbarek, M. B. (2017). The impact of income, trade, urbanization, and financial development on CO2 emissions in 19 emerging economies. *Environmental Science and Pollution Research*, 24(14):12748 – 12757.

Salahuddin, M., Alam, K., Ozturk, I., and Sohag, K. (2018). The effects of electricity consumption, economic growth, financial development and foreign direct investment on CO2 emissions in Kuwait. *Renewable and Sustainable Energy Reviews*, 81:2002 – 2010.

Shahbaz, M., Hoang, T. H. V., Mahalik, M. K., and Roubaud, D. (2017). Energy consumption, financial development and economic growth in India: New evidence from a nonlinear and asymmetric analysis. *Energy Economics*, 63:199 – 212.

Shahbaz, M., Hye, Q. M. A., Tiwari, A. K., and Leitão, N. C. (2013). Economic growth, energy consumption, financial development, international trade and CO2 emissions in Indonesia. *Renewable and Sustainable Energy Reviews*, 25:109 – 121.

Shahbaz, M., Sbia, R., Hamdi, H., and Ozturk, I. (2014). Economic growth, electricity consumption, urbanization and environmental degradation relationship in United Arab Emirates. *Ecological Indicators*, 45:622 – 631.

Solarin, S. A., Al-Mulali, U., Musah, I., and Ozturk, I. (2017). Investigating the pollution haven hypothesis in Ghana: An empirical investigation. *Energy*, 124:706 – 719.

Soytas, U., Sari, R., and Ewing, B. T. (2007). Energy consumption, income, and carbon emissions in the United States. *Ecological Economics*, 62(3):482 – 489.

Stern, D. I. (2004). The Rise and Fall of the Environmental Kuznets Curve. *World Development*, 32(8):1419 – 1439.

World Bank (2016). New Data Reveals Uptick in Global Gas Flaring. http://www.worldbank.org/en/news/press-release/2016/12/12/new-data-reveals-uptick-in-global-gas-flaring. Accessed July 11, 2018.

World Development Indicators (2017). The World Bank Databank. http://databank.worldbank.org/data/reports.aspx?source=world-development-indicators. Accessed February 10, 2017.

Table 1: Descriptive Statistics of Variables

Variables	Descriptive	Measurement Unit	Mean	Std. Dev.	Max.	Min.
Y	Income per capita	US$ (constant 2010)	1583.22	306.12	2634.36	1153.38
EC	Energy Consumed	US$ (constant 2010)	103.37	4.64	156.73	50.87
FD	Financial Development	₦Billion	103.37	4.64	156.73	50.87
TI	Trade Intensity Ratio	% of GDP	50.41	2.82	81.81	21.12
PM	Particulate Emissions	% of GNI	1.96	1.41	2.24	1.30
CO_2	Carbon Emissions	kt of Oil Equivalent	0.59	0.03	0.87	0.33
INV	Investment	GFCF as % of GDP	37.26	42.01	35.22	5.45
UBN	Urban Population	% of Total Population	35.00	1.26	48.59	22.67

Table 2: Correlation Matrix of Regressors

	Y	CO_2	PM	INV	EC	FD	TI	UBN
Y	1							
CO_2	0.214	1						
PM	0.023	-0.492	1					
INV	-0.342	0.417	0.142	1				
EC	0.491	0.380	0.282	-0.352	1			
FD	-0.326	0.454	-0.043	0.052	-0.062	1		
TI	0.432	0.065	0.109	0.493	0.491	-0.253	1	
UBN	0.501	0.504	-0.342	0.439	0.523	0.292	0.418	1

Table 3: ADF Unit Root Tests for the Estimators

Variables	**Levels**		**First Difference**		**Stationarity**
Variables	**No Trend**	**Trend**	**No Trend**	**Trend**	**Status**
Y	-0.324	-0.403	-4.603**	-5.078**	$I(1)$
TI	-1.723**	-1.732	-5.023**	-7.347**	$I(1)$
INV	-2.887*	-2.406	-5.206**	-5.0173**	$I(1)$
PM	-0.036	-3.234	-6.267**	-6.018**	$I(1)$
EC	0.723	-1.084	-4.492**	-5.271**	$I(1)$
FD	-1.372*	-2.481*	-4.881**	-6.106**	$I(1)$
UBN	-3.204	-2.126	-5.261**	-5.528**	$I(1)$
CO_2	-0.935	-1.058	-6.923**	-7.037**	$I(1)$

Table 4: ARDL Bounds Test Result for Cointegration

Dependent variables	**Functions**	**F-statistics**
Environmental Quality Index Model	$F_E(E/Y, Y^2, FD, TI, EC, INV, UBN)$	5.7352**
Carbon Emissions Model	$F_{CO_2}/Y, Y^2, FD, TI, EC, INV, UBN)$	7.0362***
Particulate Emissions Model	$F_{PM}(PM/Y, Y^2, FD, TI, EC, INV, UBN)$	6.3032***

	1%		**5%**		**10%**	
	$I(0)$	$I(1)$	$I(0)$	$I(1)$	$I(0)$	$I(1)$
Critical bound values	2.73	3.90	2.17	3.21	1.92	2.89

Note: *** and ** denote rejection of the null hypothesis at 1% and 5% levels of significance respectively.

Table 5: Results of the Estimated ARDL Long-Run Coefficients

Explanatory Variables	Dependent Variables		
	Environmental Degradation Index	Carbon Emissions	Particulate Emissions
	I	II	III
Constant	1.734** (3.46)	-3.981 (2.80)	4.032 (2.04)
Y	0.175* (0.57)	2.631** (0.62)	0.332* (1.82)
Y^2	-1.453** (0.36)	4.39* (0.76)	-1.048** (0.29)
FD	0.397** (0.44)	0.431* (0.93)	0.621 (0.39)
EC	4.937* (0.29)	2.048** (0.43)	0.418* (0.152)
TI	0.732** (0.12)	2.912* (0.17)	-0.358* (0.34)
INV	0.037 (0.09)	0.193 (0.29)	-0.045* (0.371)
UBN	2.835 (2.21)	1.374 (0.37)	1.834** (0.72)

Note:**,*,() denote statistical significance at 1% and 5% critical levels, Stand, Error, respectively.

Table 6: Models' Diagnostic and Stability Tests

Test Statistics	Dependent Variables		
	Environmental Degradation Index	Carbon Emissions	Particulate Emissions
	I	II	III
Serial correlation	6.365 (0.056)	5.921 (0.023)	6.403 (0.058)
Functional form	2.561 (0.126)	3.052 (0.062)	1.203 (0.275)
Normality	2.831 (0.261)	1.046 (0.303)	3.925 (0.835)
Heteroskedasticity	1.336 (0.273)	2.837 (0.193)	0.289 (0.382)
CUSUM	Stable	Stable	Stable
CUSUMSQ	Stable	Stable	Stable
ECT(-1)	-1.782 (0.000)**	-0.835 (0.001)**	-0.639 (0.000)**

Note: **, () denote rejection of null hypothesis at 5% critical levels, probability values for the tests.

Table 7: Causality Analysis of the Determinants of Environmental Quality in Nigeria

No Causality			Unidirectional Causality			Bidirectional Causality		
FD	$\nleftarrow\!\!\nrightarrow$	UBN, E	FD	$\longrightarrow$	EC, INV	FD	$\longleftrightarrow$	TI
EC	$\nleftarrow\!\!\nrightarrow$	TI, UBN	UBN	$\longrightarrow$	TI, E	TI	$\longleftrightarrow$	Y
INV	$\nleftarrow\!\!\nrightarrow$	UBN, Y, E	Y	$\longrightarrow$	FD, EC, E	EC	$\longleftrightarrow$	E
TI	$\nleftarrow\!\!\nrightarrow$	INV	EC	$\longrightarrow$	INV	UBN	$\longleftrightarrow$	Y
			TI	$\longrightarrow$	E			

Note: ($\nleftarrow\!\!\nrightarrow$) denotes no causality, ($\longrightarrow$) denotes the direction of causality, ($\longleftrightarrow$) denotes bidirectional causality.

9

Testing the Validity of the Triple Deficit Hypothesis for Nigeria

Rahman Olanrewaju Raji[*♣]

[♣]Canterbury International High School, Lekki-Ajah, Lagos, Nigeria

---

ABSTRACT: This paper tests the validity of the triple deficit hypothesis in Nigeria by examining the causal relationship among current account deficit, financial account deficit, and fiscal deficit within a five-variate ARDL framework complemented with GMM framework for the period 2008-2017 using quarterly data. The paper obviates the variable omission bias that characterizes most existing studies. The ARDL-bound testing technique confirms that there is the presence of a long-run bi-causal relationship between current account and financial account deficits in Nigeria. The results based on the model and empirical outputs suggest that authorities of this economy must put in place a fully fiscal and monetary discipline policy that should ensure the drastic curtailment of fiscal deficit and create a conducive environment to attract foreign remittances and foreign investment, which would help to generate healthy external balances. In addition, exchange rate stability can promote the export sector and minimize external imbalances through creating critical surpluses in current accounts, including related comprehensive discipline policies that may be pursued, which enable the external sector, financial and fiscal sectors, and monetary sector to perform without creating adverse imbalances in this economy.

Keywords: fiscal deficit, current account deficit, financial account deficit, triple deficit hypothesis

[*]Corresponding Author. Email: rahmandole@gmail.com, rahman.raji@rocketmail.com

Introduction

Keynesian absorption theory and the Mundell-Fleming model argued that a rise in fiscal deficits would increase domestic absorption and imports. The expansion of imports would then lead to the worsening of trade deficits which, in turn, would lead to current account deficits. In addition, as fiscal deficits increase, the level of domestic investments decrease as a result of its crowd-out effects on the economy associated with upward pressure on interest rates. The upward pressure on domestic interest rates leads to an increase in capital inflows and appreciation of the currency. As domestic currency appreciates, it undermines competitiveness and widens the current account deficit. Real exchange appreciation could lead to a sudden drying up of capital flows, causing an abrupt adjustment of the current account and a negative effect on investment that could create major problems for macroeconomic management. Thus, theoretical and empirical arguments establish a strong association between fiscal deficits and current account deficits, called twin deficits.

The conventional Keynesian framework using the Mundell-Fleming model establishes the effects of fiscal balance on capital accounts of balance of payment (BoP) through interest rates and real exchange rate channels. Fiscal deficits trigger real interest rates to rise which, in turn, encourages capital inflows because the domestic financial assets have become more attractive and are associated with higher expected yields; there is a positive net capital inflow, which improves capital accounts. Fiscal deficits also have an influence on capital accounts through the real exchange rate. Tang (2014) submitted that appreciation of the real exchange rate, which is a proxy for the price of the foreign financial assets in the foreign exchange market, has resulted from twin deficits; the cheaper the foreign assets for domestic residents, the more expensive the domestic financial assets for foreign investors. If the exchange rate channel is stronger than the interest rate channel, it implies that capital account deficits in BoP show the presence of third deficits, called triple deficits (fiscal deficit, current account deficit, and capital or financial account deficit). In the balance of payment framework, there is a connection between international trade and international capital flow, meaning that there is a correspondence between net domestic outputs and short-run foreign private flows. This implies that when domestic outputs are greater than domestic absorption representing current account surplus BoP, domestic capital tends to flow out; in contrast, when domestic output is lower than domestic absorption representing current account deficit BoP, foreign capital tends to flow in. Net capital flows (inflows less outflows) respond to the saving-investment differentials between countries and they result in the flow of real resources from countries with a saving-investment surplus to ones with a saving-investment deficit, in reaction to current account imbalances (Obstfeld and Rogoff, 1995).

Empirical studies have been conducted to either validate or refute the triple deficit hypothesis, which is the extension of twin deficits. Akbas and Lebe (2016) determined the validity of the triple deficit hypothesis on the G7 countries between 1994 and 2011 and found a bi-directional causality between the saving gap proxy with capital/financial account deficit and budget deficit as well as a bi-directional causality between current account deficit and saving gap. The saving gap was discovered to have an important effect on both the current account and budget deficits. This is consistent with Tang (2014) who tested the triple deficit hypothesis on U.S. data and confirmed that there is a positive relationship between fiscal policy, current account, and capital and financial balances, and that these are cointegrated indicating the presence of a bidirectional causality between current account and fiscal balance as well as the financial position of the United States. Countering these findings, Domenech et al. (2000) tested the triple deficit hypothesis on 18 OECD economies between 1962 and 1994 and found that the cause of the fiscal deficit was not the saving deficits. This is in line with Sen and Kaya (2018) who posited that there was invalidity of the twin or triple deficit hypotheses on six post-communist countries between 1994 and 2012, which agreed with the Ricardian Equivalence Hypothesis and was contrary to conventional approaches implying an absence of the triple deficit hypothesis.

The triple deficit hypothesis debate had produced conflicting and interesting outcomes. Previous research on this debate was widely conducted for countries in developed and developing countries in Europe, Latin America, and Asia, whereas Sub-Saharan Africa and Nigeria's cases have been much less studied. In addition, causality relationships remain ambiguous because of the disparity Granger causality finding, which may be a result of omission of variable bias. This study tends to incorporate other relevant variables, such as interest rate and gross domestic product.

1 Literature Review

The persistent increase in fiscal deficits is cited as either a cause or a symptom of economic weaknesses as a result of its adverse effects on macroeconomic variables. One leading key factor receiving considerable attention is the effect of macroeconomic uncertainty on the fiscal deficit, and current and financial account deficits of balance of payment process. Studies like Kuijs (2006), Bachman (1992), Tang (2014), Sen et al. (2014), Sürekçı (2011), Akbas and Lebe (2016), Sen and Kaya (2016), and Shruti et al. (2017) are among the few empirical studies that have tested the validity of extension of the twin deficit hypothesis, called the triple deficit hypothesis. Some of these studies are time-series based, while others are both time-series and cross-section based (panel data analysis).

Regarding the validity of the triple deficit hypothesis on country-specifics, studies based on time series analysis are reviewed as follows: Bachman (1992) tested the triple deficit hypothesis using U.S. data where the findings confirmed that the twin deficits nexus was valid in the U.S. economy through the fiscal deficit impacting the economy's trade account deficit; however, the triple deficit hypothesis could not be demonstrated clearly in this study. A similar study was conducted by Tang (2014) using U.S. quarterly data between 1960 and 2013; the study discovered that the triple deficit hypothesis is valid in the United States and there is presence of a causally positive and co-integrating relationship such that the trade balance granger-caused a budget deficit along with the country's financial account position. Kuijs (2006) examined the validity of the triple deficit hypothesis on the Chinese economy in the period of 1980-2005. This study posits that rising saving rates amount to both a budget and trade surplus and that the triple deficit hypothesis applied in reverse to the Chinese economy and was tagged as "Triplet Surpluses".

Sürekçı (2011) and Sen et al. (2014) investigated separately the triple deficit hypothesis on the Turkish economy with different outcomes. Sürekçı (2011) stipulated a causality relationship between budget and trade deficits and insisted on the absence of a causal correlation for saving-investment rate and trade deficit, which shows the inexistence of the triple deficit using quarterly data spanning the years 1987-2007. Sen et al. (2014) employed annual data from 1980 to 2010 in order to find a causal relationship and effect of each on one another. Their findings indicated that the trade deficit and fiscal deficit have a causality to savings deficit, which suggests the validity of the triple deficit hypothesis. In conformity with Sen et al. (2014), Akinci and Yilmaz (2012) disclosed that current account deficits are determined by savings-investment and budget deficits. Their findings showed that both deficits have a positive effect on current account deficit for both the short and long-terms, which validates the triple deficit theory for Turkey over the period 1975-2010. Akbas and Lebe (2016) supported Akinci and Yilmaz (2012), agreeing that a bi-directional causality exists between the trade and fiscal deficit and between the trade deficit and savings gap, revealing that the triple deficit hypothesis was valid for Turkey using annual data for 1960-2012 in the study.

Winner (1993) investigated the parallel between the budget deficit, trade deficits, and savings gap by analyzing the Australian economy. The findings showed that fiscal deficits, as opposed to the savings gap, were due to diverse macroeconomic factors and validated the Ricardian Equivalence Hypothesis (REH). In addition, it was inconclusive that trade deficits were a consequence of fiscal and saving deficits, which implies that the triple deficits were not valid. This contradicts Chowdhury and Saleh (2007), who analyzed the existence of the triple deficit hypothesis using the Autoregressive Distributed Lag (ARDL) approach for Sri Lanka. The existence of triple deficits and budget and savings-investment deficits were presented as a cause of the current account deficits in Sri Lanka for the period 1970-2005.

Given that the panel data provides a time series on each cross-section unit in a group, this study further reviewed studies on panel data. Bolat et al. (2014) assessed the dynamics of the triple deficit theory in 23 European economies using quarterly data between 2002 and 2013 and with the aid of the panel Granger causality estimation. The study established evidence for the triple deficit hypothesis. In support of Şengönül et al. (2014), Bolat et al. (2014) validated that the triple deficit hypothesis was valid for Poland, Portugal, Spain, and Sweden in their study of European Union countries between 2002 and 2013 using quarterly data for analysis. Contrary to these studies, Domenech et al. (2000) found an absence of a causal relationship between fiscal deficit and saving deficit using panel VAR analysis between 1962 and 1994, establishing that the Ricardian Equivalence Hypothesis was valid in these countries contrary to conventional approaches and concluded that the triple deficit hypothesis was not valid. Furthermore, Sen and Kaya (2018) carried out a study on the validity of the triple deficit hypothesis in six post-communist countries using data between 1994 and 2012 with a bootstrap panel Granger causality estimation, and concluded the invalidity of the twin or triple deficit in their models.

Gruber and Kamin (2007) using panel data analysis attempted to establish the determinants of the trade account deficit in 61 countries for the years 1982-2003. The study concluded that in the sampled countries a growth in savings negatively affects countries that experience a savings gap, consequently resulting in a rise in the trade deficit. The findings contend that the savings-investment gap plays a role in the advent of a trade deficit. In this context, the triple deficit hypothesis was supported by the results. In support of Gruber and Kamin (2007), Özdemir et al. (2014) studied a causal relation between budget deficits, current account deficits, and savings deficits in 17 transition economies from 2003 to 2011 in order to weigh the validity of the triple deficit hypothesis. The outcomes of the study supported evidence for the Ricardian Equivalence Hypothesis, while they showed the invalidity of the triple deficit hypothesis.

Shruti et al. (2017) assessed the triple deficit hypothesis in South Asian countries using panel data analysis between 1985 and 2015. The study reiterates the presence of a long-run relationship between budget balance, current account balance, and private savings gap; that is, there is a positive impact of a budget balance and private savings gap on current account balances and, in addition, a positive causation runs from the savings gap to current account and budget deficits, thus, confirming the triple deficit theory.

In conclusion, there is no concrete consensus among the few existing studies regarding the triple deficit hypothesis because these studies observed contrary opinions in most of the few countries where they had been carried out which might be due to sample periods of their studies. In addition, most studies suffer from omission of the variable bias when testing for causality within the VAR and ARDL models. Specifically, this study incorporates relevant variables as intervening variables that influence both between budget deficit, current account deficit, and financial account deficit of balance of payment. This study tends to overcome this limitation by employing a multivariate ARDL model to examine the causal relationship between budget deficit, current account deficit, and financial account deficit of balance of payment.

2 Theoretical Framework Research

The theoretical foundation underpinning the connection between fiscal policy and current account balance of payment (BoP) is derived from national account identity through the income-output approach forwarded in the 1960s by Mundell and Fleming; that is, the goods market is in equilibrium when estimated expenditure (E) equals estimated output (Y) per period, i.e., $E = Y$.

Since

$$\text{estimated income} = C + S + T \tag{1}$$

$$\text{estimated expenditure} = C + I + G + (X - M) \tag{2}$$

where C is consumption, S is saving, T is tax, I is investment, G is government spending, X is export, M is import. Combining equations (1) and (2), equation (3) is derived as shown below:

$$C + S + T = C + I + G + X - M \tag{3}$$

Rearranging equation (3), equation (4) is thus derived as

$$(S - I) = (G - T) + (X - M) \tag{4}$$

where $(S-I)$ is saving gap (saving deficit), $(G-T)$ is fiscal deficit, and $(X-M)$ is trade deficit. Therefore, equation (4) displays the triple deficit hypothesis, which expresses imbalances as a result of negative values on both sides of equation (5), which will be even in the case of a triple deficit.

Equation (4) implies that, for a given level of saving rate, the fiscal deficit will crowd out private investment and lead to foreign capital inflows into the economy as a result of excessive government borrowing to finance its spending, which is translated into current account deficit. The crowding out of private investment establishes an increase in the domestic interest rate, which, in turn, amounts to a real exchange rate appreciation and augments capital inflow according to Sakyi and Opoku (2016).

Alternatively, BoP accounting displays the interrelationship between current account and financial account, which is known as capital account. The interrelationship between the two accounts captures responses of the financial sector and real sectors to systematic disturbances and their interaction during the adjustment process. The subsequent balance of payment identity is written as $BoP = CA + FA \equiv 0$, where an alternative interpretation of current or financial account transactions could be that $CA = -FA$ or $FA = -CA$. The BoP financial account deficit $(-FA)$ with a floating exchange rate is financed through excess net export $(X > M)$, while the BoP current account deficit is financed through net capital flow or foreign capital inflow. According to national income-expenditure relationships, it reflects that the current account balance is equivalent to the saving-investment or national saving-investment balance $(S - I)$, i.e., $CA = S - I$, and implies that in an open economy, investment can occur at home or abroad using national savings insofar as such investments can promise a good combination of safety and return. Therefore, the saving-investment relationship can be rewritten as $S = I_d + I_f$ (I_d is domestic investment and I_f is foreign investment), where the foreign investment $I_f \equiv CA = -FA$. There is an acquisition of foreign assets $(FA < 0)$ along with commensurate transfers of domestic real resources to users abroad $(CA > 0)$, so that

$$(S - I) = CA = -FA \tag{5}$$

Substituting equation (5) into equation (4), an equilibrium relation of current account can be rewritten as $CA = -FA + BB$ by rearranging this equation, making fiscal policy (BB) the subject of the formula. Thus, it becomes:

$$-BB = -CA - FA \tag{6}$$

A triple deficit is established if the three variables BB, CA, and FA are co-integrated or moving together. It indicates that a budget deficit in the long run is expected to be offset by the net deficit between current and financial accounts or a combined deficit of current and financial accounts. Therefore, equation (6) is the basis for the empirical model estimation of the study.

3 Model Estimation

This study attempts to explore the empirical relationship of the triple deficit hypothesis by applying the autoregressive distributed lag (ARDL) bounds co-integration technique to determine the long-run relationships and short-run dynamics between fiscal, current, and financial account deficits including a control variable (interest rate and gross domestic product), which was developed by Pesaran and Shin (1999) and Pesaran et al. (2001). This estimation technique has some advantages in comparison with other previous and traditional co-integration methods. First, the ARDL does not need all the variables under study to be integrated of the same order and it can be applied when the underlying variables are integrated of order one, order zero, or fractionally. Second, the ARDL test is relatively more efficient in the case of small and finite sample data sizes. Lastly, by applying the ARDL technique, we obtain unbiased estimates of the long-run model (Harris and Sollis, 2003). By adopting this technique, the study specifies the empirical ARDL model as:

$$\begin{aligned}\Delta IR_t = \phi_4 + \sum_{i=1}^{n} \beta_{40}\Delta IR_{t-1} + \sum_{i=0}^{n} \beta_{41}\Delta CA_{t-1} + \sum_{i=0}^{n} \beta_{42}\Delta BB_{t-1} + \sum_{i=0}^{n} \beta_{43}\Delta FA_{t-1} \\ + \sum_{i=0}^{n} \beta_{44}\Delta GDP_{t-1} + \beta_{45}\Delta IR_{t-1} + \beta_{46}\Delta CA_{t-1} + \beta_{47}\Delta BB_{t-1} + \beta_{48}\Delta FA_{t-1} \\ + \beta_{49}\Delta GDP_{t-1} + \mu_t\end{aligned} \tag{7}$$

$$\begin{aligned}\Delta GDP_t = \phi_5 + \sum_{i=1}^{n} \beta_{50}\Delta GDP_{t-1} + \sum_{i=0}^{n} \beta_{51}\Delta CA_{t-1} + \sum_{i=0}^{n} \beta_{52}\Delta BB_{t-1} + \sum_{i=0}^{n} \beta_{53}\Delta FA_{t-1} \\ + \sum_{i=0}^{n} \beta_{54}\Delta IR_{t-1} + \beta_{55}\Delta GDP_{t-1} + \beta_{56}\Delta CA_{t-1} + \beta_{57}\Delta BB_{t-1} + \beta_{58}\Delta FA_{t-1} \\ + \beta_{59}\Delta GDP_{t-1} + \mu_t\end{aligned} \tag{8}$$

where BB, CA, FA, IR, and GDP are fiscal deficit, current account deficit of BoP, capital account deficit of BoP, lending rate, and gross domestic product, respectively; ϕ and β are the parameters of the model; Δ is the first difference operator; t is the time period; and μ_t is the error term assumed to be identically and independently distributed.

The procedures to carry out the ARDL approach with the co-integration technique include the determination of the long-run relationships among the variables by using the Bounds F-Test and the estimation of the coefficients of the long-and short-run relationships by using the error correction model from the ARDL approach. The ARDL bounds-testing procedure for co-integrating relationships follows a non-standard asymptotic F-distribution under the null hypothesis, which maintains that there exists a minimum of one co-integrating vector. Two sets of critical values were constructed by Pesaran et al. (2001) under this null hypothesis. The first set of critical values is constructed under the assumption that variables in the ARDL model are integrated of order zero, $I(0)$.

The second set of critical values is constructed under the assumption that variables in the model are integrated of order one, $I(1)$. We do not reject the null hypothesis of no co-integrating relationships when the F-statistic falls below the lower bound. Similarly, we reject the null hypothesis of no co-integration when the calculated F-statistic is greater than the upper bound. However, the test is inconclusive when the F-statistic falls between the lower and upper bounds.

The ARDL technique is complementary with the Generalized Method of Moment (GMM) technique in order to check robustness of the estimates. In the GMM estimates, the coefficients of explanatory variables are usually taken to represent a short-term impact. One study showed that several standard estimators, including the instrumental variable method and the ordinary least squares (OLS), are special conditions of the GMM (Çamlıca, 2010). The GMM was adopted in order to avoid the problem of endogeneity in explanatory variables. Using this technique, it ensures that the estimators are extremely strong and robust. It allows formulating models and specific estimators without the need for a strong distribution assumption. The stationarity of variables and existence of the required moment conditions for estimation are sufficient using the GMM technique. In addition, it provides a unifying framework for the analysis of many familiar estimators, which include ordinary least squares (OLS) and instrumental variables (IV).

3.1 The Granger Causality Test Specification

In order to test the short- and long-run causal linkages between fiscal deficit, current, and financial account deficit, the study specifies approaches in line with previous works such as Tang (2014) and Ali and Kakar (2017). In addition, we agree with Akinlo and Egbetunde (2010) that some macro-variables could have a great impact on one another, i.e., that current account, fiscal balance, and short-term capital inflows can impact each other and that their omission could bias the direction of causality among them. In view of this, we included some control variables: gross domestic product (GDP) and interest rate. GDP is included to control the cyclical components of the current account and capital account of BoP as well as fiscal policy while lending rate is to show the transmission of the fiscal policy, current account, and capital of BoP and it is related to monetary policy actions because they have different responses to cyclical movement.

In order to examine the short- and long-run causal linkages between current account deficit, capital account deficit, interest rate, and gross domestic product, the study specifies the model below:

$$\begin{aligned}\Delta BB_t = \gamma_1 + \sum_{i=1}^{n} \alpha_{10}\Delta BB_{t-1} + \sum_{i=0}^{n} \alpha_{11}\Delta CA_{t-1} + \sum_{i=0}^{n} \alpha_{12}\Delta FA_{t-1} \\ + \sum_{i=0}^{n} \alpha_{13}\Delta IR_{t-1} + \sum_{i=0}^{n} \alpha_{14}\Delta GDP_{t-1} + \beta_{15}ECM_{t-1} + \mu_t\end{aligned} \tag{9}$$

$$\Delta CA_t = \gamma_2 + \sum_{i=1}^{n} \alpha_{20} \Delta BB_{t-1} + \sum_{i=0}^{n} \alpha_{22} \Delta FA_{t-1} + \sum_{i=0}^{n} \alpha_{23} \Delta IR_{t-1} + \sum_{i=0}^{n} \alpha_{24} \Delta GDP_{t-1} + \beta_{29} ECM_{t-1} + \mu_t \tag{10}$$

$$\Delta FA_t = \gamma_3 + \sum_{i=1}^{n} \alpha_{30} \Delta FA_{t-1} + \sum_{i=0}^{n} \alpha_{31} \Delta CA_{t-1} + \sum_{i=0}^{n} \alpha_{32} \Delta BB_{t-1} + \sum_{i=0}^{n} \alpha_{33} \Delta IR_{t-1} + \sum_{i=0}^{n} \alpha_{34} \Delta GDP_{t-1} + \beta_{39} ECM_{t-1} + \mu_t \tag{11}$$

$$\Delta IR_t = \gamma_4 + \sum_{i=1}^{n} \alpha_{40} \Delta IR_{t-1} + \sum_{i=0}^{n} \alpha_{41} \Delta CA_{t-1} + \sum_{i=0}^{n} \alpha_{42} \Delta BB_{t-1} + \sum_{i=0}^{n} \alpha_{43} \Delta FA_{t-1} + \sum_{i=0}^{n} \alpha_{44} \Delta GDP_{t-1} + \beta_{49} ECM_{t-1} + \mu_t \tag{12}$$

$$\Delta GDP_t = \gamma_5 + \sum_{i=1}^{n} \alpha_{50} \Delta GDP_{t-1} + \sum_{i=0}^{n} \alpha_{51} \Delta CA_{t-1} + \sum_{i=0}^{n} \alpha_{52} \Delta BB_{t-1} + \sum_{i=0}^{n} \alpha_{53} \Delta FA_{t-1} + \sum_{i=0}^{n} \alpha_{54} \Delta IR_{t-1} + \beta_{59} ECM_{t-1} + \mu_t \tag{13}$$

where ECM_{t-1} is the error correction term and μ_t is the mutually uncorrelated white noise residual. The coefficient of the ECM variable contains information about whether the past values of variables affect the current values of the variables under study. The size and statistical significance of the coefficient of the error correction term in each ECM model measure the tendencies of each variable to return to the equilibrium.

In order to examine the short- and long-run causal linkages between current account deficit, fiscal deficit, and financial account deficit following the previous works, evidence suggests that once there is a long-run relationship between the variables, in this case current account deficit, fiscal deficit, financial account deficit, and control variables, then there is a case for causality in one or more directions (Narayan and Smyth, 2005). Nonetheless, we could only establish the direction of the long-run causality between the variables by conducting a test of statistical significance (a z-test) on the lagged error-correction term in each equation. The direction of the short-run causal relationships between the variables could also be established by conducting a joint test of statistical significance (a P-value) of the explanatory variables in each of the equations (see Oh and Lee, 2004; Narayan and Smyth, 2005). All the variables are at the level except gross domestic product and lending rate, which were in their logarithm form to avoid measurement error and to provide reliable estimates.

3.2 Data Sources

The study is carried out using quarterly data over the 2008Q1 to 2017Q4 periods. These periods are set because, prior to 2008, some of the data were reported annually and, also, checked for how sensitive they were for a specific regime. The data used are all sourced from the Central Bank of Nigeria database, specifically, its 2018Q2 quarterly statistical bulletin compilation such as fiscal balance (defined as fiscal surplus/deficit as percentage of GDP), current account balance (defined as current account balance as percentage of GDP), financial account balance (defined as capital and financial account balance as percentage of GDP), gross domestic product, and lending. The monthly fiscal deficit/surplus and lending rate data were converted into quarterly data using an e-view package.

4 Empirical Results and Discussion of Results

4.1 Descriptive Statistics of Data Series

Table 1 presents the summary statistics of the sample data on the variables used for the analysis. The descriptive statistics show that the mean value of the fiscal deficit over the period is -1.664 with a median value of -1.714. The maximum and minimum values are 0.849 and -3.752, respectively. The mean values of the current account deficit and financial account deficit over the period are 3.877 and 0.312, respectively, with median values of 3.250 and 0.145, respectively. The maximum and minimum values for the current account are 20.870 and -5.320, respectively, whereas the financial account of maximum value and minimum value are 20.870 and -17.950, respectively. There is an indication that current account deficit, financial account deficit, and fiscal deficit over the period have been characterized by a marked disparity, implying that these variables were high in some years, whereas they were abysmally lower than the observed average in other years. With regard to dispersion, it is confirmed by the relatively high standard deviation values of 5.825 and 7.519 for current account and financial account, respectively, while fiscal balance has a low standard deviation value. Apparently, current account and financial account have been generally increasing and unstable in the country. The lending rate has a mean value of 2.822 and a median value of 2.819, with a low value of standard deviation. Its corresponding maximum and minimum values are 2.910 and 2.737, respectively. The GDP has a mean value of 31.803 and a median value of 31.970, with a low level of dispersion. Its maximum and minimum values are 32.375 and 30.837, respectively. The means and medians of all the variables lie within the maximum and minimum values, implying that the variables had a high tendency to be normally distributed.

Skewness is a measure of asymmetry of the distribution of the series around its mean. Regarding the skewness of the variable, the rule of thumb may be arbitrary; but the general threshold is 1. Since all the variables lie within 1.0 and -1.0, the skewness is not substantial and it can be said that all the distributions of the variables are symmetrical. The Kurtosis statistic measures the peakedness or flatness of the distribution of the series. A Gaussian distribution is expected to have kurtosis of 3.0 (Wooldridge, 2013); since all the variables lie within the range of 3, it implies that all the variables had a high tendency to be normally distributed. Finally, the Jarque-Bera test revealed that the variables are not normally distributed except for the financial account with a p-value of 0.424, which means that we reject H0 indicating that the hypothesis of normality in the distribution cannot be accepted. This implies that the data series may have endogeneity issues. This, therefore, necessitates the adoption of a GMM estimator to complement an ARDL which is capable of controlling the joint endogeneity effect of most of the explanatory variables with the current account deficit and fiscal deficit.

4.2 Stationarity Test

Although ARDL does not require a data pretesting, this study's author decided to determine the order of integration of all the data before estimation of the data using ARDL. The table below shows the results of the Augmented Dickey-Fuller (ADF) unit root tests for the order of integration of the variables under investigation.

The results of the Augmented Dickey-Fuller (ADF) unit root test conducted to determine the stationarity properties of selected variables by taking into account the intercept without the trend properties, the results obtained showed that, with the exception of fiscal deficit and gross domestic product, all other variables are characterized by the unit root at level, whereas all the variables revealed evidence of stationarity at first difference, mostly at a 5 percent significance level. In conclusion, all the variables revealed evidence of stationarity at first difference at a mostly 5 percent significance level in the ADF test; therefore, all the variables are integrated of order 1, which lend support to the use of ARDL.

4.3 Results of the ARDL Bounds Test for Co-Integration

Since the variables were found to be $I(1)$ processes, there is a tendency that candidate variables would move together in the long run when they drift apart in the short run. Our study employed the ARDL bounds-testing procedure to examine the potential long-run relationships between these variables. Following Pesaran et al. (2001), an F-test on equations (7) to (11) would be sufficient to examine whether or not there were co-integrating relationships between the candidate variables. The study performed an F-test on equations (7) to (11) and reported the results in Table 3.

In equation (7), the fiscal deficit equation shows that the F-statistic, 4.22, calculated for equation (1) was greater than the upper bound value at 5 percent and 10 percent levels of significance. The null hypothesis of no co-integration was rejected, which implies that there is a long-run relationship between FD, CA, FA, IR, and GDP.

In equation (8), the current account deficit equation, the F-statistic, 4.68, was also greater than the upper bound value at the 5 percent and 10 percent levels of significance. This implies that the null hypothesis of no co-integration was rejected. Therefore, CA, FA, FD, IR, and GDP were said to be co-integrated, and the co-integrating vector was explaining CA.

In equation (9), the financial account deficit equation, the F-statistic, 7.24, was also greater than the upper bound value at the 1 percent, 5 percent, and 10 percent levels of significance. This implies that the null hypothesis of no co-integration was rejected. Therefore, FA, CA, FD, IR, and GDP were said to be co-integrated, and the co-integrating vector was explaining FA. In equation (10), the lending rate equation, the F-statistic, 9.83, was also greater than the upper bound value at the 1 percent, 5 percent, and 10 percent levels of significance. This implies that the null hypothesis of no co-integration was rejected. Therefore, IR, FA, CA, FD, and GDP were said to be co-integrated, and the co-integrating vector was explaining IR.

The results show that the F-statistic, 2.28, calculated for equation (11) was less than the lower bound value at the 1 percent, 5 percent, and 10 percent levels of significance. Following Bahmani-Oskooee and Brooks (1999), the study verifies the long-run error correction model of equation (11) by estimating the long-run error correction model of equation (11). The results show that the error correction term was negative and significant at a 5 percent level of significance. So, for equation (11), the conclusion was that GDP was a co-integrating vector. Thus, the null hypothesis of level effects or co-integration was rejected in that case. In conclusion, the findings disclosed the existence of a long-run co-integrating relationship in the empirical evidence of the extension of twin deficits (so called triple deficits) in Nigeria between 2008 and 2017.

4.4 Results of the Granger Causality Test

After establishing co-integrating relationships between budget deficit, current account deficit, financial account deficit, and control variables (exchange rate and interest rate), we next tested the direction of the causal relationships between these variables, especially key variables of interests. The study conducted short-run causality tests using p-values and test for the significance of the lagged error-correction terms, ECM_{t-1}, in order to establish the long-run causality between the explanatory variables and the dependent variable, using the t-test error correction model stipulated above.

The long-run causal flow between current account deficit and fiscal deficit indicates a bi-directional causality, which was supported by the negativity and significance of the error correction terms of equations, the current account deficit, and fiscal deficit equations with a 1 percent significance level of the t-test. It implies that there is the presence of twin deficits in the case of Nigeria in the long term. In addition, a bi-directional long-run causal relationship exists between financial account deficit and fiscal deficit supported with negativity and significance of the error correction term of the equations at a 1 percent significance level of the t-test. Surprisingly, there is an absence of a causal relationship between current account deficit and fiscal deficit, and, likewise, between financial account deficit and fiscal deficit in the short run. Evidence of a bi-directional causality relationship is reported between the current account and financial account deficits in both short-term and long-term causal relationships. The current account deficit equation reveals a negative short-run causal flow from financial account deficit to current account deficit with a p-value of 0.044 associated with the joint statistical test of significance of the financial account deficit at a 1 percent significance level. In case of reverse causality, the financial account deficit equation shows evidence of a positive short-term causal flow from the current account deficit to financial account deficit with a p-value of 0.029 associated with the joint statistical test of significance of current account deficit at a 5 percent significance level. There is evidence of a bi-directional causality in the long-run causal flow between the current account deficit and financial account deficit, which is supported by the negativity and significance of the error correction terms of both equations. The current account and financial account deficit equations are under the 1 percent significance level of the t-test.

Other results show that there was a distinct unidirectional short- and long-run causal flow from fiscal deficit to gross domestic product, and from gross domestic product to lending rate, which was supported by the p-value associated with the joint statistical test of significance of fiscal deficit and gross domestic product while the coefficients of the error-correction terms were negative and statistically significant.

Furthermore, bi-directional short- and long-run causal relationships exist between fiscal deficit and lending rate, current account deficit and lending rate, gross domestic product and current account deficit, and, likewise, financial account deficit and gross domestic product. These findings were supported by the p-value associated with the joint statistical test of significance of their respective equations and the coefficient of the error-correction terms, which were negative and statistically significant.

The results of the GMM estimates are reported in Table 5 and show the estimated t-statistic and p-value of the explanatory variables, which are usually taken to represent a short-term impact. The GMM estimates lead to an almost identical conclusion with the ADRL estimates.

However, these statistics (F-statistic and t-statistic of the lagged ECM) suggest that all the five series (BB, FA, CA, IR, and GDP) are co-integrated in the long run and; hence, there is strong evidence in support of the triple deficit hypothesis in the case of Nigeria. In addition, the triple deficit hypothesis pertaining to fiscal deficit (FD), current account deficit (CA), and financial account deficit (FA) has also been validated in the long run through the Granger causality using F-statistic and t-statistic of the lagged ECM, whereas the existence of the triple deficit hypothesis is tentatively not held in the short run in the case of Nigeria.

5 Concluding Remarks

This paper studies the relationship between fiscal deficit, current account deficit, and financial account deficit and tests the extension of the twin deficit hypothesis called the "triple deficit hypothesis" in Nigeria using quarterly time-series data for the sample periods of 2008Q1 to 2017Q4 by means of ARDL co-integration and Granger causality techniques.

The findings observe a bi-directional causality relationship between the candidate variables of interest (fiscal deficit, current account deficit, and financial account deficit) in the long run. It implies that the outcome of the findings is in support of the Keynesian proposition of a long-run relationship between the twin deficits, which is valid for the Nigerian economy due to a co-integration test demonstrating the existence of a long-run equilibrium relationship between the fiscal deficit and current account deficit. This result agrees with the one earlier obtained by Egwaikhide et al. (2002) and Omoniyi et al. (2012), but it contradicts the result found in Onafowokan and Owoye (2006). In addition, the short-run causal relationship of the outcome of the study rejects an existence of a causal relationship running between fiscal deficits and current account deficits; this contradicts the Mundell-Fleming Model, which states the direction of causality running from fiscal deficit to current account deficit.

However, there are policy implications in these findings: a negative and bi-directional causal relation between current account and financial account deficits indicates that the two accounts offset each other, in such a way that they promote a balance of payment equilibrium.

More importantly, authorities of this economy must put in place a fully disciplined fiscal policy that should ensure the drastic curtailment of fiscal deficits and, at the same time, create a conducive environment to attract foreign remittances and foreign investment, which would help to generate healthy external balances. In addition, exchange rate stability can promote the exports sector, minimizing external imbalances through creating critical surpluses in current accounts and including related comprehensive discipline policies that may be pursued, which would enable the external, financial, fiscal, and monetary sectors to perform without creating adverse imbalances in this economy.

Our findings support the existence of a twin divergence relationship (twin deficit) in Nigeria. This implies that fiscal policy needs to be treated as a fully controlled policy variable (Biswas et al., 1992). Hence, budget cuts are needed, which would tend to reduce the current chronic account deficits by increasing national savings through reducing the budget/fiscal deficit and increasing private savings in these economies. With this fully controlled policy variable, there is a possibility of achieving a trimmed down current account deficit.

References

Akbas, Y. E. and Lebe, F. (2016). Current Account Deficit, Budget Deficit and Saving Gap: Is the Twin or Triplet Deficit Hypothesis Valid in G7 Countries? *Prague Economic Papers*, 2016(3):271–286.

Akinci, M. and Yilmaz, O. (2012). Validity of the Triple Deficit Hypothesis in Turkey Bounds Test Approach. *Istanbul Stock Exchange Review*, 13(50):1–28.

Akinlo, A. and Egbetunde (2010). Financial Development and Economic Growth: The Experienceof 10 Su-Saharan African Countries Revisited. *The Review of Finance and Banking*.

Ali, A. and Kakar, A. (2017). Probing the evidence of triple deficit hypothesis in Pakistan. *International Journal of Social Sciences, Humanities and Education*, 1(1).

Bachman, B. (1992). Current Account Deficit Unrelated to Budget Surplus. Technical report, National Centre for Policy Analysis.

Biswas, B., Tribedy, G., and Saunders, P. (1992). Further Analysis of the Twin Deficits. *Contemporary Policy Issues*, pages 104–107.

Bolat, S., Degirmen, S., and Sengonul, A. (2014). Does triple deficits have (Un) stable causality for the EU members? Evidence from bootstrap corrected causality tests. *Procedia Economics and Finance*, 16:603–612.

Çamlıca, F. (2010). Yeni Keynesyen Bir Bakış Açısıyla Türkiye'nin Enflasyon Dinamikleri Yönünden Yapısal Analizi. *Uzmanlık Yeterlilik Tezi, Türkiye Cumhuriyet Merkez Bankası, Ocak.*

Chowdhury, K. and Saleh, A. S. (2007). Testing the Keynesian proposition of twin deficits in the presence of trade liberalisation : evidence from Sri Lanka. *Faculty of Business Economics Working Papers*, pages 2–35.

Şengönül, A., Bolat, S., and Değirmen, S. (2014). Does Triple Deficits Have (Un)Stable Causality for the EU Members? Evidence from Bootstrap-Corrected Causality Tests. *Procedia Economics and Finance*, 16:603–6012.

Domenech, R., Taguas, D., and Varela, J. (2000). The Effects of Budget Deficit on National Saving in the OECD. *Economics Letters*, 69(3):377–383.

Egwaikhide, F. O., Ayodele, S. O., Oyeranti, O. A., and Tchokote, J. (2002). Causality between Budget Deficit and the Current Account Balance in African Countries. *West African Journal of Monetary and Economic Integration*, 2(2):10–41.

Gruber, J. W. and Kamin, S. B. (2007). Explaining the global pattern of current account imbalances. *Journal of International Money and Finance*, 26(4):500–522.

Harris, R. and Sollis, R. (2003). *Applied Time Series Modelling and Forecasting.* Wiley, Applications.

Kuijs, L. (2006). How Will China's Saving-Investment Balance Evolve? Working paper no. 3958, World Bank Policy Research.

Narayan, P. K. and Smyth, R. (2005). The Residential Demand for Electricity in Australia: An Application of the Bounds Testing Approach to Cointegration. *Energy Policy*, 33:467–474.

Obstfeld, M. and Rogoff, K. (1995). The Intertemporal Approach to the Current Account, in: Handbook of International Economics, Volume 3, Chapter 33. In Groomsman, G. and Rogoff, K., editors, *Handbook of International Economics.* North-Holland, Amsterdam.

Oh, W. and Lee, K. (2004). Energy Consumption and Economic Growth in Korea: Testing the Causality Relation. *Journal of Policy Modelling*, 26(8-9):973–981.

Omoniyi, O. S., Olasunkanmi, O. I., and Babatunde, O. A. (2012). Empirical Analysis of Twins' Deficits in Nigeria. *International Journal of Management and Business Studies*, 2(3):38–41.

Onafowokan, O. A. and Owoye, O. (2006). An Empirical Investigation of Budget and Trade Deficits: The Case of Nigeria. *Journal of Developing Areas*, 39(2):153–174.

Özdemir, D., Buzdağlı, O., Emsen, O., and Çelik, A. (2014). Causal Relationship between Budget Deficit and Current Account Deficit. In *International Conference on Eurasian Economies.*

Pesaran, M. H. and Shin, Y. (1999). An Autoregressive Distributed Lag modeling approach to Co- integration analysis. In Strom, S., editor, *Econometrics and economic theory in the 20th century: The Ranger Frisch centennial symposium.* Cambridge University Press.

Pesaran, M. H., Shin, Y., and Smith, R. C. (2001). Bounds Testing Approaches to the Analysis of Level Relationships. *Journal of Applied Economics*, 16:289–326.

Sakyi, D. and Opoku, O. (2016). The twin deficits hypothesis in developing countries: Empirical evidence for Ghana (Technical No. S-33201-GHA-1). *International Growth Centre.*

Sen, A., Senturk, M., Sancar, C., and Akbas, Y. E. (2014). Empirical Findings on Triplet Deficits Hypothesis: The Case of Turkey. *Journal of Economic Cooperation and Development*, 35:81–102.

Sen, H. and Kaya, A. (2016). Are the Twin or Triple Deficits Hypotheses Applicable to Post-Communist Countries? Technical report, BOFIT Discussion Papers, Bank of Finland.

Sen, H. and Kaya, A. (2018). Are the Twin or Triple Deficits Hypotheses Applicable to Post-Communist Countries? *Panoeconomicus*, pages 1–29.

Shruti, S., Giri, A. K., and Mohapatra, G. (2017). Assessing the Triple Deficit Hypothesis for Major South Asian Countries: A Panel Data Analysis. *International Journal of Economics and Financial Issues*, 7(4):292–299.

Sürekçı, D. (2011). Türkiye'de ÜÃ§ÃŒz Açıklar Olgusunun Analizi: Dinamik Bir Yaklaşım. *Yönetim ve Ekonomi*, 18:51 – 69.

Tang, T. C. (2014). Fiscal Deficit, Trade Deficit, and Financial Account Deficit: Triple Deficits Hypothesis with the U.S. Experience. Technical report, Monash University, Business and Economics, Discussion Paper.

Winner, L. E. (1993). The Relationship of the Current Account Balance and the Budget Balance. *The American Economist*, 37(2):78–84.

Table 1: Descriptive Statistics

	Current Account	**Financial Account**	**Fiscal Balance**	**Lending Rate**	**GDP**
Mean	3.877500	0.312000	-1.664000	2.822200	31.80304
Median	3.250000	0.145000	-1.714844	2.819815	31.97073
Maximum	20.87000	20.87000	0.849375	2.910174	32.37595
Minimum	-5.320000	-17.95000	-3.753438	2.737609	30.83782
Std. Dev.	5.825233	7.519574	0.833665	0.033627	0.527179
Skewness	1.508383	0.023932	0.265486	0.560367	-0.961089
Kurtosis	5.223504	4.012884	4.781443	4.181100	2.528093
Jarque-Bera	23.40807	1.713709	5.759115	4.418402	6.529104
Probability	0.000008	0.424495	0.056160	0.109788	0.038214
Observations	40	40	40	40	40

Table 2: Unit Root Test Results

	ADF Test	
Variables	Level	1st Difference
Current Account Deficit	-3.96*	-8.29*
Capital Account Deficit	-4.94*	-7.33*
Fiscal Deficit	-2.07	-2.93***
Lending Rate	-3.32**	-3.77**
Gross Domestic Product	-0.13	-3.05**

Note: Significance level: 1% (-3.62)(*), 5% (-2.94)(**), and 10% (-2.61)(***)

Table 3: ARDL Bounds Test for Co-Integration

Dependent variable	Function	F-statistic
BB	$BB(CA, FA, IR, GDP)$	4.22**
CA	$CA(FA, BB, IR, GDP)$	4.68**
FA	$FA(CA, BB, IR, GDP)$	7.24*
IR	$IR(CA, FA, BB, GDP)$	9.83*
GDP	$GDP(CA, FA, BB, IR)$	2.28

Critical Value Bound

1%		5%		10%	
I(L)	I(U)	I(L)	I(U)	I(L)	I(U)
3.74	5.06	2.86	4.01	2.45	3.52

Note: * and ** denotes significance at a 1% and 5% significance level.

Table 4: Granger Causality between Current Account Deficit, Capital Account Deficit, and Fiscal Deficit

Variable	t-statistics (P-value) BB	CA	FA	IR	GDP	ECM_{t-1} Coefficient (t-statistic)
BB	-	-1.09 (0.285)	-0.91 (0.369)	-2.17 (0.038)**	-0.38 (0.699)	-0.19 (-3.473)*
CA	-0.60 (0.551)	-	-2.11 (0.044)**	-3.02(0.005)*	-4.57 (0.000)*	-1.01 (-6.261)*
FA	-0.19 (0.853)	-2.29 (0.029)**	-	-0.65 (0.516)	-1.97 (0.058)**	-0.90 (-5.680)*
IR	-1.49 (0.145)***	-2.01 (0.054)**	-0.60 (0.550)	-	-3.41 (0.002)*	-0.29 (-3.181)**
GDP	-1.53 (0.136)***	-2.67 (0.012)**	-3.65 (0.001)*	-1.08 (0.289)	-	-0.20 (-2.993)**

Note: *, **, and *** imply statistical significance at the 1%, 5%, and 10% significance levels, respectively.

Table 5: GMM Results – t-statistic (p-value)

	BB	CA	FA	IR	GDP
BB	-	-0.71 (0.485)	-0.37 (0.706)	-3.93 (0.004)**	-2.31 (0.027)**
CA	-1.28 (0.211)	-	-2.83 (0.008)**	-5.87 (0.000)*	-9.61 (0.000)*
FA	-1.10 (0.279)	-5.09 (0.000)*	-	-1.49 (0.149)	-4.21 (0.000)*
IR	-2.71 (0.011)***	-4.57 (0.001)*	-0.35 (0.727)	-	-7.44 (0.000)*
GDP	-2.72 (0.011)***	-7.07 (0.000)*	-1.89 (0.068)***	-6.52 (0.000)*	-
R^2	0.27	0.61	0.18	0.54	0.75
Instrument					
Rank	10	10	10	10	10
J-statistic	6.5	1.5	2.6	3.3	6.5

Note: *, **, and *** imply a statistical significance at the 1%, 5%, and 10% significance levels, respectively.

Permissions

All chapters in this book were first published in ERF, by SGH Warsaw School of Economics, Collegium of Economic Analysis; hereby published with permission under the Creative Commons Attribution License or equivalent. Every chapter published in this book has been scrutinized by our experts. Their significance has been extensively debated. The topics covered herein carry significant findings which will fuel the growth of the discipline. They may even be implemented as practical applications or may be referred to as a beginning point for another development.

The contributors of this book come from diverse backgrounds, making this book a truly international effort. This book will bring forth new frontiers with its revolutionizing research information and detailed analysis of the nascent developments around the world.

We would like to thank all the contributing authors for lending their expertise to make the book truly unique. They have played a crucial role in the development of this book. Without their invaluable contributions this book wouldn't have been possible. They have made vital efforts to compile up to date information on the varied aspects of this subject to make this book a valuable addition to the collection of many professionals and students.

This book was conceptualized with the vision of imparting up-to-date information and advanced data in this field. To ensure the same, a matchless editorial board was set up. Every individual on the board went through rigorous rounds of assessment to prove their worth. After which they invested a large part of their time researching and compiling the most relevant data for our readers.

The editorial board has been involved in producing this book since its inception. They have spent rigorous hours researching and exploring the diverse topics which have resulted in the successful publishing of this book. They have passed on their knowledge of decades through this book. To expedite this challenging task, the publisher supported the team at every step. A small team of assistant editors was also appointed to further simplify the editing procedure and attain best results for the readers.

Apart from the editorial board, the designing team has also invested a significant amount of their time in understanding the subject and creating the most relevant covers. They scrutinized every image to scout for the most suitable representation of the subject and create an appropriate cover for the book.

The publishing team has been an ardent support to the editorial, designing and production team. Their endless efforts to recruit the best for this project, has resulted in the accomplishment of this book. They are a veteran in the field of academics and their pool of knowledge is as vast as their experience in printing. Their expertise and guidance has proved useful at every step. Their uncompromising quality standards have made this book an exceptional effort. Their encouragement from time to time has been an inspiration for everyone.

The publisher and the editorial board hope that this book will prove to be a valuable piece of knowledge for researchers, students, practitioners and scholars across the globe.

List of Contributors

Nderitu Kingori
School of Economics, University of Nairobi

Jakub Rybacki
Collegium of Economic Analysis, SGH Warsaw School of Economics

Agya Atabani Adi
Department of Economics, Faculty of Humanities, Social and Management Sciences, Federal University Wukari, Taraba State, PMB 1020, Nigeria

Joshua Sunday Riti
Department of Economics, Faculty of Social Sciences, University of Jos, Plateau State, 930001, Nigeria

Rodolfo Tomás da Fonseca Nicolay
Catholic University of Petrópolis
Candido Mendes University

Claudio Oliveira de Moraes
Candido Mendes University
Central Bank of Brazil

Bruno Pires Tiberto
Central Bank of Brazil

Tihana Škrinjarić
Faculty of Economics and Business, University of Zagreb

Thierno Thioune
Faculty of Economic and Management Sciences, Cheikh Anta Diop University of Dakar

Chelsey Hill and B. D. McCullough
Department of Decision Sciences & MIS, Drexel University

Ekundayo P. Mesagan and Mike I. Nwachukwu
Department of Economics, University of Lagos, Nigeria

Rahman Olanrewaju Raji
Canterbury International High School, Lekki-Ajah, Lagos, Nigeria

Index

www.ingramcontent.com/pod-product-compliance
Lightning Source LLC
LaVergne TN
LVHW080908210926
848485LV00004B/617